Elaine H. Pagels is Associate
Professor of Religion and
Chairman of the Department of
Religion, Barnard College. She is
the author of the article on
"gnosticism" in the new supplement of *The Interpreter's Dic-
tionary of the Bible*.

THE GNOSTIC PAUL

THE GNOSTIC PAUL

GNOSTIC EXEGESIS OF THE PAULINE LETTERS

ELAINE HIESEY PAGELS

FORTRESS PRESS   Philadelphia

Library of Congress Catalog Card Number 74-26350

ISBN 0-8006-0403-2

4581L74   Printed in the United States of America   1-403

To Heinz

CONTENTS

Preface   ix

Abbreviations   xi

Introduction   1

I.   Romans   13

II.   1 Corinthians   53

III.   2 Corinthians   95

IV.   Galatians   101

V.   Ephesians   115

VI.   Philippians   134

VII.   Colossians   .   137

VIII.   Hebrews   141

Conclusion: Gnostic Exegesis of the Pauline Letters   157

Select Bibliography   167

Indexes   171

PREFACE

When I began the present study, I intended to investigate certain patterns and themes that characteristically distinguish Valentinian exegesis of Paul from that of the antignostic fathers. Yet as the research progressed and as new evidence became available, I became aware that the problem of Valentinian exegesis is more complex than the scope of this study indicates. Codex XI, *I*, for example, soon to be published in the Nag Hammadi library edition, explicitly demonstrates what the heresiologists had suggested: that certain theological issues aroused controversy that divided different Valentinian teachers, and distinguished their schools from one another. A study of these intra-Valentinian controversies—and their hermeneutical basis— would require a more detailed and comprehensive investigation than the present one. Recognizing this, I have limited the scope here to sketch out patterns that seem to be consistent and fundamental to Valentinian exegesis in general. Investigation of exegetical and theological differences among the Valentinian schools will, I expect, become a subject of further research.

This work would not be complete, however, without grateful acknowledgment of the persons who have contributed to this work in essential ways. Helmut Koester, formerly my dissertation advisor, has continued to offer encouragement and criticism that have proven invaluable throughout the process of the research and writing. I owe special thanks as well to John Strugnell, who initially suggested the structure of this work. Morton Smith has offered generous encouragement, and has advised me on the organization of the research materials. Prof. Gilles Quispel and George Mac-Rae have provided examples of scholarly achievement as well as the opportunity for discussions for which I am deeply grateful. Cyril Richardson, Robert Kraft, and Birger Pearson kindly agreed to read sections of the work in progress, and have offered critical suggestions that have been incorporated in revision. Anne McGuire checked and, in some cases, revised the translation; she and Nancy Carlin helped prepare the manuscript for publication. Other colleagues and friends, especially Theodor Gaster and the members of the Columbia New Testament Seminar, have contributed in ways hat I deeply appreciate. To the extent that I have not measured up to the standards set by my teachers and colleagues, the fault is my own: my indebtedness to them is immeasurable.

Special thanks are due to those who have supported this work during two years of research: to the National Endowment for the Humanities, for the summer grant of 1973; to the Mellon Foundation, for the grant that enabled me to participate in the summer activities of the Aspen Institute for Humanistic Studies in 1974; to Mr. and Mrs. Joseph H. Hazen, whose keen interest in scholarly research and whose generous support for the 1975 summer work at the Aspen Institute have provided great encouragement; to the members of the Travel and Research Committee of Barnard College; and to Dean LeRoy Breunig and President Martha Peterson for their continual concern for the scholarly endeavors of the Barnard faculty.

Thanks also are owed to Mary Solazzo and Eva Pesova for their conscientious work in the preparation and typing of the manuscript.

This book is lovingly dedicated to my husband, Heinz R. Pagels, in joyful gratitude for his understanding and loving companionship throughout the process of this research, as he continues his own in theoretical physics.

E.H.P.

ABBREVIATIONS

AH   *Adversus Haereses,* Irenaeus, ed. W. W. Harvey (Cambridge, 1857); text divisions follow those of R. Massuet, in Migne, *Patrologia Graeca* 7 (1857). These are also noted in Harvey's margins.

AM   *Adversus Marcionem,* Tertullian, ed., trans., and intro. E. Evans, I-II (Oxford: Clarendon Press, 1972).

AV   *Adversus Valentinus,* Tertullian, *Opera quae supersunt omnia, Patrologia Latina* II (Paris: Migne, 1844).

CJ   *Commentarium in Johannis,* Origen, ed, E. Preuschen, GCS 4 (Leipzig: Hinrichs, 1903).

CR   *Le Commentaire d'Origène sur Rom. III. 5-V.7 d'après les Extraits du Pap. No. 88748 du Musée de Caire et les Frag. de la Philoc. et du Vat. Gr. 762,* ed. J. Scherer, in: Inst. Fr. d'Arch. Orient., Bibl. d'Étude, T. 27 (Cairo: I.F.A.O., 1957).

DC   *De Carne Christi,* Tertullian, *Tertullian's Treatise on the Incarnation,* ed., trans., and intro. E. Evans (London: S.P.C.K., 1950).

DP   *De Praescriptione Haereticorum,* Tertullian, *Opera,* II, *Patrologia Latina* 2 (Paris: Migne, 1854).

DR   *De Resurrectione Carnis,* Tertullian, *Tertullian's Treatise on the Resurrection,* ed., trans., and intro. E. Evans (London: S.P.C.K., 1960).

EF   *Epistula ad Floram,* Ptolemy, ed., trans., and intro. G. Quispel, in: Sources Chrétiennes 24 (Paris: Éditions du Cerf, 1949).

EP   *Das Evangelium nach Philippos,* Coptic text ed. and trans. W. C. Till, Patristische Texte und Studien 2 (Berlin: de Gruyter, 1963). See also English translation by R. McL. Wilson, *The Gospel of Philip* (London: Mowbray, 1962).

ER   *Epistula ad Rheginum (De Resurrectione),* Coptic text ed. and trans. M. Malinine, H. Ch. Puech, G. Quispel, W. Till, with intro. G. Quispel, H. Ch. Puech (Zürich: Rascher, 1963).

ET   *Evangelium Thomae,* Coptic text ed. and trans. A. Guillaumont, H. Ch. Puech, G. Quispel, W. Till, Yassah 'Abd al Masih (Leiden: Brill, 1959).

EV   *Evangelium Veritatis,* Coptic text ed. and trans. M. Malinine, H. Ch. Puech, G. Qùispel, W. Till (Zürich: Rascher, 1961).

Exc   *Excerpta ex Theodoto,* from *Stromata,* Clement of Alexander: ed., trans., and intro. F. Sagnard, *Les Extraits de Théodote,* Sources Chrétiennes 23 (Paris: Éditions du Cerf, 1948).

GCS   *Griechischen christlischen Schriftsteller.*

HTR   *Harvard Theological Review.*

JBL   *Journal of Biblical Literature.*

JTS   *Journal of Theological Studies.*

Ref   *Refutationis Omnium Haeresium,* Hippolytus, *Opera,* 3, ed. P. Wendland, GCS 26 (Leipzig: Hinrichs, 1916).

Strom *Stromata* I-VI, Clement of Alexandria, *Opera,* 2, ed. O. Stählin, GCS 52 (Berlin: Akademie-Verlag, 1960).

TU   *Texte und Untersuchungen.*

Vig Chr. *Vigiliae Christianae.*

ZNW   *Zeitschrift für neutestamentliche Wissenschaft.*

ZTK   *Zeitschrift für Theologie und Kirche.*

INTRODUCTION

Whoever knows contemporary New Testament scholarship knows Paul as the opponent of gnostic heresy. Paul writes his letters, especially the Corinthian and Philippian correspondence, to attack gnosticism and to refute the claims of gnostic Christians to "secret wisdom"—so Schmithals declares in his recent studies (*Gnosticism in Corinth*, 1971; *Paul and the Gnostics*, 1972).[1] Paul preaches the kerygma of "Christ crucified" (1 Cor 2:2), warns of the coming judgment, proclaims the resurrection of the body, insists on the priority of love over gnosis; in all these he demonstrates his "genuinely Christian attitude"[2] over against his gnostic opponents. Bultmann (*Theology of the New Testament*, 1947) has explained that "to Paul, the apostles who have kindled a pneumatic-gnostic movement in Corinth are interlopers . . . it is perfectly clear that to the church they have the status of Christian apostles, but to Paul they are 'ministers of Satan' disguising themselves as apostles of Christ" (2 Cor 11:13).[3] Bornkamm (*Paul*, 1969) says that Paul, much like Luther, regards the "spirit-filled people" as "fanatics," the "really dangerous element" he confronts in his churches. The apostle himself, Bornkamm adds, "utterly repudiates" the secret wisdom and gnosis they teach.[4]

Yet if this view of Paul is accurate, the Pauline exegesis of second-century gnostics is nothing less than astonishing. Gnostic writers not only fail to grasp the whole point of Paul's writings, but they dare to claim his letters as a primary source of *gnostic* theology.[5] Instead of repudiating Paul as their most obstinate opponent, the Naassenes and Valentinians revere him as the one of the apostles who — above all others — was himself a gnostic initiate.[6] The Valentinians, in particular, allege that their secret tradition offers direct access to Paul's *own* teaching of wisdom and gnosis. According to Clement,

1

"they say that Valentinus was a hearer of Theudas, and Theudas, in turn, a disciple of Paul."[7] When Valentinus' disciple Ptolemy tells Flora of "apostolic tradition" that "we too have received from succession,"[8] he refers, apparently, to this secret tradition about the savior received through Paul. Valentinus himself often alludes to Paul (in the extant fragments, and very often in the Gospel of Truth, if, as H. Ch. Puech and G. Quispel suggest, Valentinus is its author);[9] his disciples Ptolemy, Heracleon, and Theodotus — no less than Irenaeus, Tertullian, and Clement — revere Paul and quote him simply as "the apostle."[10]

Texts now becoming available from Nag Hammadi offer extraordinary new evidence for *gnostic* Pauline tradition. A sketch of several texts generally accepted as Valentinian indicates the challenge they offer.

J. Ménard states that analysis of the scriptural allusions in the Gospel of Truth demonstrate "how profound is the Pauline influence"[11] on this writing. He notes that the theological theme of the writing — the reciprocal relationship of God and the elect — "is a typically Pauline doctrine"; he finds its presentation here unparalleled in contemporary Hellenistic literature.[12] The second Valentinian text from the same codex, the Epistle to Rheginos, likewise evinces powerful Pauline influence, as Puech and Quispel note:

> The "mystical" themes of Pauline theology, and, in the first place, that of the participation of believers in the death and resurrection of Christ, as often has been observed, remained without great impact on the ecclesiastical literature of the second century. Conversely (these themes) have been taken up and developed by the gnostics . . . especially by Valentinus and his disciples. . . . It is among the Valentinians in particular that the Pauline "mysticism" has been received with the greatest favor and used in a more or less systematic fashion. . . . St. Paul is, in the treatise, the object of the highest regard . . . the work is, furthermore, permeated from beginning to end with allusions to the Pauline *corpus*. For its author, as he himself declares (45:24), Paul was really *par excellence*, and in full truth, "*the* apostle."[13]

The fourth treatise from the same codex (*Tripartite Tractate*), besides containing many allusions to the Pauline letters, concludes (according to the analysis of Quispel) with the "Prayer of the apostle Paul," in which the apostle, as one of the elect, prays to be redeemed, to receive the pleromic revelation, and to be unified with the "beloved elect."[14]

The Gospel of Philip offers another Valentinian source for examination of Pauline exegesis. R. Wilson acknowledges as "remarkable" the observation that the author's discussion on the resurrection of the flesh "reflects so accurately the Pauline doctrine."[15] Wilson notes that its author, like the Valentinian author of the texts cited above, apparently knows Romans, 1-2 Corinthians, Galatians, and Philippians; R. M. Grant suggests also allusions to Ephesians, Thessalonians, Colossians, and Hebrews.[16] Finally, The Interpretation of the Gnosis (CG 11.1) offers in its major section an interpretation of the Pauline image of the body of Christ (cf. Romans 12, 1 Corinthians 12, with references to passages in Ephesians and Colossians). The writer encourages all "members of the body," the "lesser" with the "greater," to share and to love each other in the harmonious union constituted in Christ.[17]

This brief survey, far from complete, indicates how different Valentinian authors and groups developed a wide range of Pauline themes, including the relation of God and the elect; baptism as "dying with Christ"; Paul's teaching on resurrection; his exhortation on participation in the body of Christ. This new evidence lends support to the Valentinian claim that Paul exerted a great influence on the development of their theology — apparently a far greater influence than scholars have suspected.

Previous studies of Valentinian hermeneutics, lacking these resources, have relied primarily on the heresiological accounts. G. Henrici (Die Valentinianische Gnosis und die heilige Schrift, 1871) concludes from his analysis that although the Valentinians "attempt to place gnosis on biblical soil" they fail to reckon seriously with scripture as the primary source of revelation. Gnosis itself, and not scripture, remains their primary hermeneutical presupposition.[18] C. Barth (Die Interpretation des NT in der Valentinianischen Gnosis, 1911) concludes that "the basic concepts of Valentinian teaching, as of any gnosis, clearly were older than Christianity itself. . . . The Christian element in it was only the most recent powerful element that was introduced into the synthesis. . . . Powerful conflicts and contradictions between gnosis and the NT writers were—in view of the unbiblical origin of the teaching—unavoidable."[19] N. Brox[20] and H. Jonas basically concur with Henrici that gnosis itself serves the gnostics as their hermeneutical principle.[21]

Examination of the newly available resources, however, places both the heresiological accounts and the research based upon them into a different perspective. It suggests that the scholars cited above, besides taking information from the heresiologists, also have adopted from them certain value judgments and interpretations of the gnostic material. Each of these scholars, for example, accepts Irenaeus' observation that the gnostics base their exegesis upon unwritten sources — sources not contained in the scriptures themselves.[22] Each of them also accepts, apparently, Irenaeus' judgment that these secret sources, however conceived, are alien to the NT and hence to "authentically Christian" tradition.[23] Henrici, Barth, and Brox, consequently, share the conviction of Irenaeus, Tertullian, and Hippolytus: namely, that gnostic exegesis of Paul's letters projects a pre-Christian (or non-Christian) mythological system into Paul's writings.

Yet Irenaeus himself admits that the Valentinians not only reject the charge of false exegesis, but go on to criticize their opponents on two counts. First, they accuse the "orthodox" of using source materials uncritically; second, of being ignorant of the secret traditions which alone offer the true interpretation of the scriptures. Above all, the Valentinians insist that their own unwritten sources are nothing less than Paul's own secret wisdom tradition — the key to hermeneutical understanding. Irenaeus notes that when they are refuted from the scriptures:

> They turn and accuse these same scriptures as if they were not accurate nor authoritative, and claim that they are ambiguous, and that truth cannot be derived from them by those who are ignorant of tradition. For they allege that truth was not transmitted by means of written documents, but in living speech; and that for this reason Paul declares, "we speak wisdom among the perfect (*telioi*) but not the wisdom of this cosmos" (1 Cor 2:6).[24]

Irenaeus and Tertullian consider the Valentinian view an insult to Paul. Characterizing their own struggle against the gnostics as that of true exegesis against false, they insist that the gnostic method totally distorts the apostle's meaning. Irenaeus says that he recounts their exegesis only "to demonstrate the method which they use to deceive themselves, abusing the scriptures, trying to support from them their own invention (*plasma*)"[25] Tertullian agrees with Irenaeus that the gnostics practice false exegesis, yet he acknowledges that they defend themselves with Paul's own injunction to "test all things" (1 Thes 5:21). He accuses them of "taking his words in their own way" when they cite such passages as 1 Cor 11:19 ("there must be heresies among you, so that those who are approved may be revealed among you").[26] Tertullian himself, having debated such issues with self-professed "Pauline" Christians, agrees with the author of 2 Peter that certain "unlearned and unstable" brethren have "distorted" the letters of "our beloved brother Paul" (2 Pet 3:16-17).

Tertullian and Irenaeus both attest that these controversies over Pauline exegesis extended to controversies over Pauline authorship. Both accuse the Valentinians of arbitrarily selecting certain texts and rejecting others. Noting that the heretics have dared to impugn the validity of the Pastoral Letters, Tertullian insists that the "same Paul" who wrote Galatians also wrote Titus.[27] Irenaeus, strikingly, opens his great treatise claiming "the apostle's" authority to oppose the gnostics—citing 1 Tim 1:4 and Tit 3:9 from the Pastoral Letters![28]

When we compare the heresiological accounts with the newly available evidence, we can trace how two antithetical traditions of Pauline exegesis have emerged from the late first century through the second. Each claims to be authentic, Christian, and Pauline: but one reads Paul *antignostically,* the other *gnostically.* Correspondingly, we discover two conflicting images of Paul: on the one hand, the antignostic Paul familiar from church tradition, and, on the other, the gnostic Paul, teacher of wisdom to gnostic initiates!

The Pastoral Letters take up the former tradition, interpreting Paul as the antagonist of "false teachers" who "set forth myths and endless genealogies" seducing the gullible with the lure of "falsely so-called gnosis." Irenaeus and Tertullian continue this tradition. Assuming the authenticity of the Pastorals (both in terms of authorship and of interpretation of Paul as antignostic polemicist), they claim Paul as their ally against the gnostics. Valentinian exegetes, adhering to the latter tradition, either bypass or reject the Pastorals, and cite as Pauline only the following: Romans, 1-2 Corinthians, Galatians, Ephesians, Philippians, Colossians, 1 Thessalonians, and Hebrews (a list that corresponds exactly to the earliest known Pauline collection attested from Alexandria).[29] These exegetes offer to teach the same secret wisdom that Paul taught "to the initiates": evidence of their exegesis occurs in such texts as the Epistle to Rheginos, the Prayer of the Apostle Paul, and The Interpretation of the Gnosis.

How can gnostic exegetes and theologians make this astonishing claim? Theodotus explains that Paul, having become "the apostle of the resurrection" through his experience of revelation, henceforth "taught in two ways at once." On the one hand he preached the savior "according to the flesh" as one "who was born and suffered," the kerygmatic gospel of "Christ crucified" (1 Cor 2:2) to those who were psychics, "because this they were capable of knowing, and in this way they feared him." But to the elect he proclaimed Christ "according to the spirit, as one born from the spirit and a virgin" (cf. Rom 1:3) for the apostle recognized that "each one knows the Lord in his own way: and not all know him alike."[30]

Paul communicated his pneumatic teaching to his disciple Theudas, and Theudas, in turn, to Valentinus; and Valentinus to his own initiated disciples (cf. 1 Cor 2:6).[31] In this way the Valentinians identify Paul himself as the source of their own esoteric tradition: only those who have received initiation into this secret, oral tradition are capable of understanding the true meaning of the scriptures—which include Paul's own letters.[32] Irenaeus' statement that the Valentinians derive their insights "from unwritten sources" may refer not to a generalized gnosis or gnostic myth but to an allegedly Pauline doctrine of the "mystery of Sophia" (cf. 1 Cor 2:6) which may have included the myth of Sophia's fall and redemption.[33]

The Valentinians claim that most Christians make the mistake of reading the scriptures only literally. They themselves, through their initiation into gnosis, learn to read his letters (as they read all the scriptures) on the *symbolic* level, as they say Paul intended. Only this pneumatic reading yields "the truth" instead of its mere outward "image."

The Valentinians agree with other Christians, for example, that Paul intends in Romans to contrast that salvation effected "by works," "according to the law," with the redemption that the elect receive "by grace." But most Christians read the letter only in terms of the outward image — in terms of the contrast between the revelation to the Jews and the revelation extended through Christ to the Gentiles. They fail to see what Paul himself clearly states in Rom 2:28f, that the terms ("Jew/Gentile") are not to be taken literally:

> He is not a Jew, who is one outwardly, nor is circumcision what is outward in the flesh; (but) he is a Jew who is one inwardly, and circumcision is of the heart, pneumatic, not literal.

The Valentinians take this passage as Paul's injunction to symbolic exegesis. While on the literal level he discusses the relation of Jews to Gentiles, simultaneously he intends his words to be read on a pneumatic (that is, symbolic) level. According to such exegesis, Paul's discussion of Jews and Gentiles in Romans refers allegorically to different groups of Christians — to *psychic* and *pneumatic* Christians respectively.

Practice of such exegesis enables the Valentinians to interpret Paul's letters in an entirely new way. They consider the "literal" question of the relation between Jews and Gentiles to be already (c. 140-160) a dated issue, limited to a specific historial and cultural situation. What concerns them in the present is a different issue: how they themselves, as pneumatic Christians initiated into the secret mysteries of Christ, are related to the mass of "simple-minded," "foolish" believers. They perceive that this problem (i.e., the relation of the "few" to the "many," the "chosen" to the "called") has characterized Christian communities from the first—from the time when the savior chose to initiate only a few into the secret meaning of his parables, and deliberately let them remain obscure "to those outside" (Mk 4:11). They conclude that it is this perennial problem (i.e., the relation of the "chosen few," the elect, to the "many psychics" who are "called")[34] that Paul intends to expound in his letter to the Romans.

Yet Paul, like the savior himself, chooses not to disclose his theme openly. Instead he follows Christ's example and hides his meaning in parables. In writing his letter to the Romans for example, he uses a simple, everyday situation — the relationship between Jews and Gentiles — as a parable for the relation between the called and the elect, between psychic and pneumatic Christians.

Valentinian exegetes attempt systematically to disclose to the initiate the hidden "logos" of Paul's teaching, separating it from the metaphors that serve to conceal it from uninitiated readers. For as Paul indicates in Rom 2:28, those called "Jews inwardly," "Jews in secret," the "true Israel" are (Theodotus says)[35] the pneumatic elect. They alone worship the "one God" (Rom 3:29), the Unengendered Father.[36] But because their affinity with the Father is hidden, a secret from those who are "Jews outwardly" (the psychics) and from the demiurgic god ("the god of the Jews," Rom 3:29), Paul more often calls the elect in his parable the "uncircumcised," the "Gentiles," or "the Greeks."

The initiated reader could recognize Paul's meaning when he proclaims himself "apostle to the Gentiles" (Rom 1:5). The Valentinians note how Paul contrasts his own mission to the pneumatic Gentiles with Peter's mission to the psychic Jews (Gal 2:7).[37] Paul says that he, as apostle to the Gentiles, longs to share with them his "pneumatic charisma" (Rom 1:11), but acknowledges his obligation "both to the Greeks and to the barbarians," that is, as he says, both "to the wise (*pneumatics*) and to the foolish (*psychics*)" (Rom 1:14).

This sense of dual responsibility, the Valentinians infer, impels Paul to write his letters, as he preaches, "in two ways at once."[38] As he proclaims the savior to psychics in terms they can grasp, so he addresses to them the outward, obvious message of his letters. But to the initiates, who discern "the truth" hidden there in "images," he directs his deeper communication: they alone interpret pneumatically what psychics read only literally.

What hermeneutical methods do Valentinian exegetes use to derive such exegesis from Paul's letters? This question forms the basis of the present study, as it has for those of Henrici and Barth; yet here it leads to quite different conclusions.

Methodologically, this analysis has proceeded as follows. The first step required collecting evidence of Valentinian exegesis for each passage of the writings cited in second-century sources as "Pauline." Sources considered include: (1) the extant fragments of such teachers as Valentinus, Ptolemy, Heracleon, and Theodotus; (2) passages of Valentinian exegesis cited in the accounts of Irenaeus, Hippolytus, and Tertullian, from the writings of Clement of Alexandria (especially the *Excerpta ex Theodoto*), and from Origen's anti-Valentinian commentaries on the Pauline epistles; (3) citations and allusions to "Pauline" texts available in the Nag Hammadi writings generally considered Valentinian.

Much of the work of gathering and comparing such sources, especially of certain of the Nag Hammadi texts, remains to be completed in future studies. Further investigation of these as they become available will, I trust, serve to check, modify, and extend the suggestions offered here. (Professor Quispel kindly has communicated to me, for example, that the fourth tractate of the Jung Codex contains many such Pauline references. Consideration of this text, received after the manuscript was finished, unfortunately could not be included in the present study.)

The second step has involved systematic collation of the evidence into analysis of each of the letters cited. The analysis is arranged according to the letters which (according to extant evidence) the Valentinians considered Pauline: Romans, 1-2 Corinthians, Galatians, Ephesians, Philippians, Colossians, and Hebrews. (The very few references to 1-2 Thessalonians are discussed in other sections.)

Examination of the Greek and Coptic texts is, of course, essential for scholarly evaluation of the evidence cited. For the reader's convenience, however, sections of the Greek texts of the epistles (selected according to availability of corresponding Valentinian exegesis) have been included and translated to indicate the textual basis of the gnostic reading (e.g., 1 Cor 2:14a: "the psychic does not discern pneumatic things"). Passages of Valentinian exegesis are cited below the text under discussion. Where no Valentinian citations are extant for a certain passage, the Pauline text is omitted. In some cases where parallels occur to available exegetical passages, a reconstruction of the Valentinian exegesis is suggested. (I have kept such reconstructions, necessary as they are, to a minimum: further investigation by other scholars will, I expect, confirm or correct the specific suggestions in such cases).

Finally, a note of caution. The present study focuses specifically on Paul *as he is being read in the second century*. The subject is, of course, not Paul himself but "the gnostic Paul"—that is, the figure that emerges from second-century gnostic sources. This investigation into the history of hermeneutics makes no attempt to reconstruct a historical account of the apostle himself, or of the issues he confronted in his own communities. Instead the task is to investigate how two conflicting views of Paul emerge and develop as early as the second century.

To question the assumptions of NT and historical scholars concerning the apostle Paul—as in the opening of this discussion—is essential for the purpose of this study. Only by suspending the familiar image of the "antignostic Paul" can we recognize how the Valentinians (and other gnostics), making an opposite assumption, could read and interpret the Pauline epistles. One must take care, of course, not to jump to the opposite conclusion—equally unjustified and premature in terms of historical method—and accept as "historical" the *gnostic* claim that the apostle himself was a gnostic initiate and teacher! Consideration of this issue will require far more extensive investigation of the evidence than this study permits.

Yet the evidence does indicate how the programmatic assumption of the "antignostic Paul" has directed the course of Pauline exegesis. Much of what passes for "historical" interpretation of Paul and for "objective" analysis of his letters can be traced on to the second-century heresiologists. For just as Irenaeus, Tertullian, and Origen (apparently embarrassed by the "gnostic" terminology Paul often uses) each set forth detailed—and explicitly antignostic—exegesis of his letters, so certain contemporary scholars follow their example. Bultmann, for example, describing Paul as the defender of the "genuinely Christian element"[39] in the early communities, goes on to make an exegetical case to establish Paul's claim to this role. Using form-critical methods, he attempts to show that whenever Paul uses gnostic terminology (as in 1 Corinthians 15) he turns it *against* the gnostics to construct "a great polemic against the gnosticizing party" in Corinth.[40] Similarly, U. Wilckens (*Weisheit und Torheit,* 1959), interpreting 1 Corinthians 2, characterizes Paul's teaching on wisdom and gnosis as antithetical to its gnostic counterpart.[41] Whether or not such exegesis is accurate is a question that I gladly leave to other scholars. Certainly it lies beyond the scope of this present study. Here the point is a simple one: that alternative exegeses may have been ruled out a priori, and therefore not considered as serious possibilities.

Those NT scholars who do investigate these gnostic traditions may find in them new resources for their own research. First, these traditions may suggest insights for exegeting specific controversial passages; second, by defining an alternative theological approach, they may increase awareness of one's own approach, or even challenge and extend it.

More critical for the study of gnosticism, however, is the fact that conventional exegetical and historical analysis of early Christianity often fails to account for the considerable body of evidence attesting gnostic exegesis of Paul. If the apostle were so unequivocally antignostic, how could the gnostics claim him as their great pneumatic teacher? How could they claim his writings as the source for their anthropology,[42] their Christology,[43] and their sacramental theology?[44] How could they say they are following his example when they offer secret teaching of wisdom and gnosis "to the initiates"?[45] How could they claim his resurrection theology as the source for their own, citing his words as decisive evidence *against* the ecclesiastical doctrine of bodily resurrection?[46]

The initial attempt to answer these questions directs us not toward Paul himself, nor toward his own historical situation, but toward the second-century sources that document the controversies that—by that time—surround his writings.

NOTES: INTRODUCTION

1. Translated from the German editions by J. Steely; *Gnosticism in Corinth* (Nashville: Abingdon, 1971); *Paul and the Gnostics* (Nashville: Abingdon, 1972).

2. Walter Schmithals, *Gnosticism in Corinth*, trans. J. Steely (Nashville: Abington, 1971), 301.

3. *Theology of the New Testament,* translated from the German edition by K. Grobel (London: SCM, 1965), I, 170-171.

4. Translated from the German edition by D. M. G. Stalker (New York: Harper & Row, 1971), 70, 72-77.

5. Cf.Hippolytus, *Refutationis Omnium Haeresium* (*Opera,* 3, ed. P. Wendland, GCS 26, 1916; hereafter cited as Ref) 5.7.14; Irenaeus, *Adverses Haereses* (ed. W. Harvey, Cambridge, 1857; hereafter cited as AH) 1.8.2-3.

6. Cf.AH 3.2.1-3.3.1.

7. Clement of Alexander, *Stromata* (ed. O. Stählin, GCS 12, 15, 17, 39; 1906-1939; hereafter cited as Strom) 7.17:

> ὡσαύτως δὲ καὶ Οὐαλεντῖνον Θεοδᾶ διακηκοέναι φέρουσιν· γνώριμος δ᾽ οὗτος γεγόνει Παύλου.

8. Ptolemy, *Epistola ad Floram* (*Panarion* 33.7.9, ed. G. Quispel in Sources chrétiennes 24, 1949; hereafter cited as EF) 7.9:
   ἀξιουμένη τῆς ἀποστολικῆς παραδόσεως; ἥν ἐκ διαδοχῆς και ημεῖς παρειλήφαμεν.

9. H. Ch. Puech, G. Quispel, "Les écrits gnostiques du codex Jung," *Vig Chr* VIII (1954): 30, 31, 39.

10. Cf.Clement of Alexandria, *Excerpta ex Theodoto* (ed. F. Sagnard, in Sources chrétiennes 29, 1948; hereafter cited as Exc), 22.1; 35.1; 48.2; 49.1. 67.1; 85.3; 23.3; Heracleon (in Origen's *Commentarium in Johannis*, ed. E. Preuschen, GCS 10 [Leipzig: Hinrichs, 1903]; hereafter cited as CJ) 13.25; *De Resurrectione* (*Epistula ad Rheginum*, ed. M. Malinine, H. Ch. Puech, G. Quispel, W. Till [Zürich: Rascher, 1963]; hereafter cited as ER), 45.24.

11. *L'Évangile de Vérité* (Leiden: Brill, 1972), 8, in reference to the table of biblical citations and allusions (3-8).

12. Ibid., 29.

13. ER, introduction, H. Ch. Puech, G. Quispel, xiii, xxxi.

14. *Tractatus Tripartitus*, I, ed. R. Kasser, M. Malinine, H. Ch. Puech, G. Quispel, J. Zandee (Berne: Francke Verlag, 1973).

15. *The Gospel of Philip*, ed. R. McL. Wilson (London: Mowbray, 1962), 12 hereafter cited as EP).

16. Ibid., 7; R. M. Grant, "The Mystery of Marriage in the Gospel of Philip," *Vig Chr* 15 (1961): 129-140.

17. *Interpretation of the Gnosis* (CG 11,*1*:16.24-19.37; forthcoming edition).

18. *Die valentinianische Gnosis und die heilige Schrift* (Berlin, 1871), 46 and 175:
    Eine andere Norm kennt sie [die Gnosis] nicht als sich selbst. Ihr ward keine andere Quelle der Offenbarung, kein anderes Organ, sich zu aüssern gegeben als eben ihr eigenes Wesen. Sie ist nicht Wissenschaft von der Offenbarung, sondern selbst Offenbarung.

19. *Die Interpretation des Neuen Testaments in der Valentinianischen Gnosis* (TU 37, 2: Leipzig: Hinrichs, 1911), 44.

20. N. Brox, *Offenbarung, Gnosis, und Gnostischer Mythos bei Irenäus von Lyon* (Salzburg: Anton Pustet, 1966).

21. H. Jonas, "Delimitation of the Gnostic Phenomenon" (in *Le Origini dello Gnosticismo*, ed. U. Bianchi, Leiden: Brill, 1967, 98-108), 98.

22. AH 1.8.1.

23. AH 1.9.1.

24. AH 3.2.1; cf. 3.3.1.

25. AH 1.9.1.

26. *De Praescriptione Haereticorum* 4-5 (hereafter cited as DP).

27. DP 6.

28. AH Praef:
    Ἐπὶ τὴν ἀλήθειαν παραπεμπόμενοί τινες, ἐπεισάγουσι λόγους ψευδεῖς καὶ γενεαλογίας ματαίας, αἵτινες ζητήσεις μᾶλλον παρέχουσι, καθὼς ὁ Ἀπόστολός φησιν, ἢ οἰκοδομὴν Θεοῦ τὴν ἐν πίστει· καί·· ·παράγουσι τὸν νοῦν τῶν ἀπειροτέρων · · ·ἐξηγηταὶ κακοὶ τῶν καλῶς εἰρημένων γινόμενοι· καὶ πολλοὺς ἀνατρέπουσιν, ἀπάγοντες αὐτοὺς προφάσει γνώσεως· · · ·

29. Chester Beatty Biblical Papyrus II (p. 46), 3d century; F. C. Kenyon, *The Chester Beatty Papyri*, fasc. iii (London: E. Walker, 1933-34) and fasc. iii Supplement (London: E. Walker, 1936); H. A. Sanders, *A Third Century*

Papyrus Codex of the Epistles of Paul (Ann Arbor: University of Michigan Press, 1935).

30. Exc 23.3-4:

Ἐν τύπῳ δέ Καρακλήτου ὁ Παῦλος 'ἀναστάσεως 'Απόστολος γέγονεν. Αὐτίκα μετὰ τὸ πάθος του Κυρίου καὶ αὐτός ἀπεστάλη κηρύσσειν. Διὸ καὶ καθ''εκάτερον 'εκήρυξε τὸν Σωτῆρα· γεννητὸν καὶ παθητὸν διὰ τοὺς 'αριστερούς, 'ότι τοῦτον γνῶναι δυνηθέντες κατὰ τὸν τόπον τοῦτον δεδιάσιν. καὶ κατὰ τὸ πνευματικὸν 'εξ 'αγίου Πνεύματος καὶ Παρθένου, ὡς οἱ δεξιοὶ.. .γινώσκουσιν.

31. *Strom* 7.17; see note 7.
32. AH 3.2.1.
33. AH 1.8.1; 3.2.1; see discussion of 1 Cor 2:2-6.
34. CJ 13.51.
35. Exc 58.5.
36. J. Scherer, *Le Commentaire d'Origène sur Rom 3.5-5.7.* (Cairo: I.F.A.O, 1957), 168-169, n. 15.
37. Cf. Tertullian, DP 22-24; AH 3.1-15.2; for discussion, see E. Pagels "The Valentinian Claim to Esoteric Exegesis of Romans as Basis for Anthropological Theory," *Vig Chr* 26 (1972): 241-258.
38. Exc 23.3-4.
39. Bultmann, *Theol. NT* I, 171.
40. Ibid., I, 169.
41. U. Wilckens, *Weisheit und Torheit* (Tübingen: Mohr, 1959, TWNT 7, 497-523), 77-108.
42. AH 1.8.3; Ref 6.34-35; Exc 22.1-5; 48.2; 67.1.
43. Cf. Exc 35.1.
44. Exc 22.1-5; 80.3; ER 45.14-46.2.
45. AH 3.3.1-2; 3.15.2.
46. Cf. AH 5.9.1; for further citations, see discussion of 1 Corinthians 15.

I
ROMANS

Rom 1:1: Paul, slave of Jesus Christ, called apostle, separated for the gospel of God. . . .

Paul opens his letter indicating his dual responsibility—indeed, his dual identity—so Valentinian exegetes might claim. For the apostle first identifies himself as "slave of Jesus Christ" (1:1), that is, as a psychic, standing "as a slave" in relation to the pneumatic revelation.[1] Paul identifies himself psychically a second time when he says he is "called" (by contrast with the pneumatics, who are "chosen").[2]

Yet paradoxically he goes on to identify himself as one "separated for the gospel of God" (1:1). Valentinian exegetes correlate this passage with his praise for "the one who separated me from my mother's womb" (Gal 1:15), "seizing upon these passages," Origen says, to prove that Paul is of the pneumatic elect.[3] The apostle, they explain, uses this symbolic language to reveal that he has been born from God, the Father above, through the Mother, who is Wisdom (*sophia*) or Grace.[4]

Why does Paul, the great pneumatic teacher, identify himself first as a mere psychic slave? Theodotus, citing Phil 2:7-9, recalls how the pneumatic Christ "emptied himself" to take on the psychic "form of a slave," Jesus, so that "being found in human likeness" he might become accessible to psychics.[5] As "slave," Paul imitates Christ; he, although "chosen," identifies himself voluntarily with the psychics who are "called."

Rom 1:3-4: . . . (the gospel of God) concerning his son, who came into existence of the seed of David according to the flesh, the one designated son of God in power according to the spirit. . . .

Paul now demonstrates how he preaches the "gospel of God" in two different forms: first he proclaims the one who "came into existence of the seed of David according to the flesh," and second, the one "designated son of God . . . according to the spirit." What does Paul mean? Does he refer first to the savior's human lineage, and second to his relation to Yahweh, the creator? So the psychics understand Paul's message; but the Valentinians reject such "literal" exegesis.

The initiated reader learns from secret tradition that here again Paul is speaking symbolically. "David" signifies the demiurge himself—an appropriate metaphor, first, in that he dominates his creatures like any petty king;[6] and second, in that, as demiurge, he has formed and "fathered" mankind "according to the flesh."[7] Paul characterizes in 1:3, then, the psychic preaching of the savior "according to the flesh," as son of the demiurge ("David"); but in 1:4 the pneumatic proclamation of Christ "according to the spirit" as "one designated son of God"—of the Father.

The initiate, trained to read the deeper structure of the text, then, could see from 1:1 how Paul identifies himself both as a psychic and as a member of the pneumatic elect, and from 1:3-4 how he demonstrates two different modes of his preaching. Theodotus explains that Paul "became the apostle of the resurrection in the image of the Paraclete. Immediately after the passion of the Lord he began to preach. Therefore he preached the savior in each of two ways." For the sake of the psychics ("those on the left") he preached the savior "according to the flesh" (cf. Rom 1:3) as one humanly born, humanly suffering, "because this they can grasp, and in this way they fear him." But he also preached the savior "according to the spirit" (cf. 1:4) as one generated from "the holy spirit and a virgin," as those who are pneumatic ("on the right") recognize him. For, Theodotus explains, the apostle knows that "each one knows the Lord in his own way; all do not know him alike."[8]

Rom 1:5-7: . . . through whom we received grace (*charis*) and apostleship . . . among all the nations for the sake of his name, in which you also are called of Jesus Christ, to all those who are . . . beloved of God, (and) to those called holy. Grace to you and peace from God our Father and from the Lord (of) Jesus Christ.

Paul, having "received grace," sees his primary role as apostle to "all the nations" (1:5), to the Gentiles, who signify the pneumatic elect. The Valentinians note how Paul contrasts his own mission to the Gentiles (to pneumatics) with Peter's mission to the Jews (that is, to psychic Christians, who regard Peter as the founder of their church).[9] As apostle to the "Gentiles," Paul says in 1:11 that he longs to share with them his "pneumatic charisma." Yet he admits in 1:14 that he is obligated both "to the Greeks and to the barbarians," that is, both "to the wise" pneumatics and "to the foolish" psychics. The Valentinian might infer that for this reason the apostle balances his phrases, blessing first the pneumatics (those "beloved of God") with "grace" from "God our Father" and then the psychics (those "called holy") with "peace" from "the Lord." (This passage illustrates a basic principle of Valentinian exegesis: that Paul uses the term "Lord" to designate Yahweh, as "God" designates the Father.)[10]

Valentinian exegetes admire Paul's skill as he interweaves these phrases so subtly that simple-minded readers never discern the deeper meaning. They claim that when they ask such persons pointed questions, trying to direct them to the deeper meaning, psychics reject it as "foolishness."[11] The Valentinians take such response as evidence that (as the apostle says) "the psychic does not receive the things of the spirit of God; they are foolishness to him; he cannot recognize them, because they are pneumatically discerned, but the pneumatic discerns all things" (1 Cor 2:14-15).[12]

Rom 1:9-14: God is my witness, whom I worship in my spirit in the gospel of his son, that continually I make mention of you in my prayers . . . I long to see you, so that I may share with you a certain pneumatic charisma to establish you. . . . I do not want you to remain ignorant, brothers. For many times I intended to come to you, but I have been prevented from doing so up to the present. . . . I am obligated both to Greeks and to barbarians, to the wise and to the foolish.

If Paul wants to share something with his correspondents, why doesn't he write it in his letter? Why would he refrain from writing it, and insist that he must see them in person for this purpose? So the simple-minded reader might ask; but the initiated claims to discern a deeper meaning hidden in Paul's words. When Paul says "I thank my God" (1:8) for their faith he refers not to the demiurge as "his God," but to the God "whom I worship in my spirit" (1:9) as pneumatics worship the Father.[13]

What he wants to share is *pneumatic charisma* (1:11); of this, he says, "I would not have you remain ignorant" (1:13). As any initiate would know from his own initiation into gnosis, such pneumatic truth cannot be communicated by means of written documents but only through oral communication.[14] For this reason the apostle says "we *speak* wisdom among the initiates" (*teleioi,* 1 Cor 2:6) and to them only "in secret," since most people remain incapable of receiving it.[15] Paul is willing to share his charisma with them, but reveals in 1:14 what restrains him: at present he is obligated not only to Greeks (to pneumatics) but also to the barbarians (psychics); not only to "the wise," but also to "the foolish" (1:14).

Who are those whom Paul calls "foolish"? Heracleon and Ptolemy agree that those who persist ın worshiping the demiurge, who himself is "foolish" (ignorant of the Father) can only be called "fools" themselves. The story of Moses veiling his face, symbolically interpreted, teaches that the demiurge "wears a veil" that prevents him from seeing the truth of God. Those who worship him, the psychics, wear the veil of ignorance over their hearts, and so remain blind to the truth of the Father.[16]

How has this come to be so? How can men be blind to the very truth of all things—to the Father of truth?

Rom 1:19-20: What is known of God is manifest in them, for God has revealed it to them. For the invisible things of him, from the creation of the cosmos, are clearly perceived in the things that have been made, namely, his eternal power and divinity. . . .

The teacher Valentinus, alluding to this passage, explains that those who see "in faith" perceive in the visible cosmos an image of the invisible God. He gives an example: a painted portrait conveys less than the living presence of the person who models for it; but the name makes up what the form lacks, so that the person can be recognized from the portrait. So whoever knows the divine name perceives that "the invisible things" of God (cf. 1:20) energize the visible creation.[17]

Theodotus says that Wisdom (*sophia*) created the demiurge in the "image of the Father" manifested in creation.[18] The Marcosians explain how the demiurge, in turn, created the visible cosmos "in the image of the invisible things" above.[19]

Rom 1:21-25: Although they knew God, they did not glorify him as God, or thank him, but became vain ın their imagination, and their foolish heart was darkened. Claiming to be wise, they became fools, and exchanged the glory of the incorruptible God for the image of the corruptible man (*anthrōpos*) . . . and exchanged the truth of God for a lie, and they revered and worshiped the creation and not the one who created, who is blessed among the aions.

Paul explains that some refused to worship "the one who is blessed among the aions" (1:25); for in such passages, Ptolemy claims, the apostle follows his frequent practice of mentioning the divine aions above.[20] Such persons "became futile in their minds, and their foolish hearts were darkened," until finally they "became fools," worshiping "the creation instead of the creator" (1:21-22, 25).

What is the meaning of this mysterious passage? Taken literally, it warns against pagan idolatry; but interpreted symbolically it warns against a far subtler and more pervasive kind of idolatry: namely, worship of the demiurge, who himself is only "the creation" of the higher powers.[21]

Heracleon explains from 1:21 that the majority of Christians—the psychic Christians—now worship this demiurge, the "creation instead of the true creator," who is "Christ the Logos" (cf. Jn 1:3).[22] The demiurge, created to serve as an image and instrument of divine revelation, now has been mistaken as a substitute for God, and is worshiped as a god himself!

This means that many have "exchanged the truth of God"—the knowledge of his primal being[23]—for a "lie," that is, for the false principle of materiality, the devil.[24] The "many" psychics have fallen into "flesh and error"[25]—which results in the situation Paul describes in 1:26-27.

Rom 1:26-27: Therefore God gave them up into the sufferings (*pathē*) of dishonor, for their females exchanged natural relation for that contrary to nature, and likewise the males, having abandoned the natural relation with the females were consumed in their lust toward one another, males with males, effecting what is inappropriate (*aschēmosunēn*) and receiving in themselves the due penalty for their error (*planē*).

What can this passage mean? Read literally, the meaning is simple enough: man's distorted relationship to God has resulted in "unnatural" human relationships, above all, in homosexuality. The psychic reader, grasping only this, may learn from it a useful moral warning.[26] But the pneumatic, knowing that in Christ "all things are permitted," need not concern himself with conventional morality.[27] How is he to understand this passage?

By examining the technical terms of this passage[28] and comparing these with a Naassene exegesis,[29] we may suggest reconstructing a Valentinian exegesis as follows: in this passage the apostle reveals that the Father has yielded his creation into "sufferings" (*pathē*) which form the elements of cosmic existence. In the process those who became psychic, having fallen victim to "error" (*planē*) were separated from the pneumatics, who, being divinely chosen, remained secretly related to the Father. Originally, these two were part of the same being: they belong together; but now they have been separated, their natural relationship disrupted, and both suffer from this alienation. According to Theodotus, this is the mystery hidden in the story of Adam and Eve. Although originally they were one being (cf. Gen 1:26), Eve's separation from Adam typifies the psychics' separation from the pneumatic elect (as "females" separated from the "males"). Now (as Paul explains through the metaphor of homosexuality in 1:21-25) the "males" and the "females" group themselves separately, instead of uniting with each other in loving relationship.[30]

Reading Romans 1 as Paul's symbolic description of the present situation of the Christian community, the Valentinians could account for their own relationship—as allegedly pneumatic Christians—to those they consider the psychic majority. Irenaeus describes their dilemma: why, they ask, do psychic Christians accuse us of malice, lies, arrogance, and heresy? Why do they attempt to exclude us from common worship, and their bishops urge others to shun us as "offspring of Satan"—when we ourselves confess the same creed and hold the same doctrines that they do?[31]

Paul's letters—pneumatically interpreted—could offer them great insight onto the situation. By means of allegorical exegesis, they read in Romans 1 how the psychics, misled by error (*plane*, 1:27), having rejected the truth of God (1:25-26), have become blinded to the truth (1:20-25), and now worship the demiurge instead of the Father (1:25). In the process they have forced an unnatural separation between psychics and pneumatics (females/ males; 1:26-27) within the community.

The Valentinian, asking how he, as one of the pneumatics, should respond to the situation, could see the apostle—himself pneumatic—offering himself as an example to others. According to Valentinian exegesis, Paul willingly identifies himself with psychics as well as with pneumatics, acknowledging his responsibility to both Jews and to Greeks (1:14). Accommodating himself to the different capacities of each group, he preaches the gospel "in each of two ways."[32] Paul also intends his own letter to be read "in each of two ways." He addresses the literal level to psychics, who may read in Romans 1 only of his concern to visit Christians in Rome, his responsibility to Jews and to Greeks, and his account of the origin of idolatry and homosexuality. But he addresses the symbolic level to those who, like himself, are pneumatic.[33] They alone, having received initiation into the technique of pneumatic exegesis could discover here his teaching, veiled in symbols, of the relationship between themselves and the psychic Christians.

The initiated reader could learn from such reading of Romans that psychics, on the one hand, and pneumatics, on the other, hear the message of Christ and experience redemption in qualitively different ways.

How, specifically, does their experience differ? The exegete could infer that this is the question that Paul takes up in Romans 2: how the psychic "Jews" differ from the pneumatic "Gentiles."

Rom 2:1-10: Therefore you are inexcusable, oh man, whoever you are who judge; for in that you judge another, you condemn yourself. . . . We know that the judgment of God is according to truth upon those who do such things. . . . Do you not know that the kindness of God is meant to lead you into repentance? But by your hard and unrepentant heart you store up wrath for yourself on the day of wrath and of the revelation of God's ordinances, who will requite each one according to his works. . . . there shall be tribulation and distress upon every soul of man who does evil, to the Jew first . . . but there will be glory and honor and peace to everyone who does good, to the Jew first, then to the Greek.

Paul speaks here "to the Jew first" (2:9-10), to those "under the law" (2:12)—that is, to the psychic. He warns that "every soul" (*pasan psychēn,* 2:9: that is, every *psychic*) will be requited "according to his works." Heracleon offers a parallel exegesis of Rom 13:1 where Paul warns "every soul" that he is "subject to the higher powers," above all to "him who bears the sword" in judgment to punish evildoers and to reward those who do good (13:3-5). Heracleon explains that "the one who judges and avenges" is "Moses, that is, the lawgiver himself," the demiurge: he is "the servant of God who executes his wrath" (13:4).[34] By contrast, God (the Father) judges "according to truth" (2:2), intending in his "kindness" to lead the psychics "into repentance"(2:4).

Rom 2:12-16: All who have sinned without the law also perish without the law: and all who sin in the law shall be judged through the law. . . . When the Gentiles who do not have the law do by nature (*physei*) the things of the law, they themselves, not having the law, are law for themselves. They show that the effect of the law (*to ergon tou nomou*) is written on their hearts, their conscience bearing witness . . . accusing or defending them, on the day when God judges the secrets of men according to my gospel through Jesus Christ.

While he warns the psychic "Jews" who remain "in the law" that they face its judgment, Paul reveals that the pneumatic "Gentiles" do not stand under the demiurge's law. Although they seem to be "perishing in materiality,"[35] as Heracleon admits, they actually are exempt from the demiurge's law and from his jurisdiction.[36] Basilides, offering a similar exegesis, explains that the pneumatics "delight in the law of God"—of the Father—"according to the inner *anthrōpos*" (cf. Rom 7:23).[37] Being of pneumatic nature (*pneumatikē physis*), they "do by nature (*physei*) the things in the law" (2:14). Yet their natural affinity with the Father is a secret, hidden from psychics and from the demiurge;[38] only "their own conscience" testifies to it (2:15). This secret shall be revealed only when "God (the Father) judges the secrets of mankind." Paul declares, however, that God shall not judge, as the demiurge does, through the law (cf. 2:12) but "according to my gospel" (2:16).

Rom 2:26-29: If then the uncircumcised keeps the precepts of the law, shall not his uncircumcision be accounted as circumcision? And the one by nature uncircumcised who keeps the law shall judge you, who through literalism and circumcision transgress it. For he is not a real Jew who is one outwardly, nor is true circumcision something external in the flesh: but he is truly a Jew who is one in secret; his circumcision is of the heart, pneumatic, not literal; and his praise is not from men but from God.

Paul explains here the deeper meaning of his symbolism. As the "Jews," the "circumcised," signify the psychics, circumcised "in the flesh" (2:28), so the "Gentiles" who are "by nature uncircumcised" (2:27) signify the pneumatic elect. The pneumatics "keep the precepts of the law" far better than psychics, who are bound to obey the demiurgic law. The inner, natural law of the pneumatic nature, the "law of God," is "written on their heart":[39] this is the "circumcision of the heart, pneumatic, not literal" (2:29) that relates them to God the Father.[40] In a deeper sense, then, the pneumatic is the one who is "truly a Jew," a "Jew in secret" (2:28-29), as Theodotus says: "Israel is an allegory of the pneumatic who sees God."[41]

How can Paul, having censured the psychic "Jew" for judging the "Gentiles" (2:17-25) go on to approve the pneumatic "Gentile" ("the one by nature uncircumcised who keeps the law" 2:26) who judges the psychic "Jew" (2:27)? The initiated reader could follow Paul's argument. For the psychic to judge the pneumatic is impossible, since "the psychic does not receive pneumatic things" (1 Cor 2:14).[42] But Paul teaches, on the other hand, that "the pneumatic judges all things" (1 Cor 2:15), not only the psychics themselves, but even angels who belong to the psychic creation.

According to a symbolic reading of the passage, then, Paul contradicts the psychics' whole self-understanding. Although they boast of their reliance on the law, of their relation to their god (the demiurge), and of their superiority to the Gentiles (2:17-20), now they are shown to be far inferior to the despised "Gentiles" — those secretly related to the God who transcends their demiurgic god!

Rom 3:1-2: What advantage, then, has the Jew? What is the value of circumcision? Much in every way. First, that they were entrusted with the pronouncements of God (*ta logia toū theoū*).

What advantage, then, is there in "circumcision" — in the psychics' relation to the demiurge through the law? The writer of the Gospel of Thomas implies that there is none: he insists that it is the "true circumcision in spirit" that is beneficial "in every way."[43] Yet certain Valentinian exegetes note the advantage of the psychics' relation to the demiurge that Paul cites in 3:2: through them the "words of God" (the Father) were transmitted to the elect.[44] Although the psychics who received these "words" from the demiurge themselves understood them only literally, they conveyed them to the elect, who could perceive their spiritual (that is, symbolic) meaning.

Rom 3:5-6: Is God unjust to bear wrath against mankind (*hoi anthrōpoi*)? I say: may it not be. How then could God judge the cosmos?

Paul asks, then, whether God will "bear wrath against the *anthrōpoi*"—that is, against the elect. Will he judge legalistically those who interpret the law symbolically? Paul answers that this is impossible: if God were so unjust, how could he judge "the cosmos" (3:6)? Origen's Valentinian opponents apparently punctuate this passage so as to conclude that only the psychic *cosmos* shall be judged according to the law: the pneumatic *anthrōpoi*, the "Gentiles," are exempted from such judgement.[45]

Rom 3:9b-20: We have already accused both Jews and Greeks alike of being under sin, as it is written: "he is not just, not one; he does not understand; he is not seeking God; all have fallen, together they have fallen short: no one does kindness; there is not one. . . ." For we know that whatever the law says, it addresses to those in the law, so that every mouth may be silenced, and the whole cosmos may become liable before God. Therefore, all flesh will not be justified before him from works of the law. For through the law comes awareness of sin.

Now Paul deals with an obvious objection. How can pneumatics be exempted from judgment if "both Jews and Greeks," that is, psychics and pneumatics alike, are "accused . . . of being under sin" (3:9)? Are not "all alike" subject to sin—to the power of materiality,[46] as 3:12-18 seems to confirm? Valentinian exegetes insist, on the contrary, that this passage applies *only* to psychics. It is the demiurge, they claim, who is "not one" (3:10), as God the Father alone "is one."[47] It is the demiurge—and the psychic nature he generates—that "lacks understanding" and "is not seeking God." Valentinian exegetes conclude that Paul is describing the psychics in 3:12-18 as those who are ignorant of "the invisible depth (*Bythos*)," having "fallen away" from God.[48] The apostle censures them for their deceit, perversity, and violence, and above all for not "fearing God" (3:18), since they alone are called to fear him[49] (and not, as are the elect, to know and to love him). The gnostic might well ask how, indeed, this passage could refer to the elect, whose nature is one and harmonious, who do have understanding, and who, by their very nature, "seek God"?[50]

So Paul explains in 3:19 that "whatever the law says, it says to those in the law (to the psychic "Jews") so that the whole cosmos (the *psychic* cosmos) may become liable before God." Origen's Valentinian opponents explain from 3:20 that since the law evokes "awareness of sin" the ideas of *sin, liability,* and *judgment,* emerge dialectically with the idea of law.[51] The author of the Gospel of Philip expresses a similar conception in metaphor; he describes the law as the "tree" which "has power to give knowledge of good and evil," but cannot help man to implement this knowledge (see n. 51).

Rom 3:21-24: But now the righteousness of God has been revealed apart from the law, the law and the prophets witnessing to it, the righteousness of God, through faith in Jesus Christ for all who believe. For there is no difference: all have sinned, and they lack the glory of God, being justified as a gift by his grace through the redemption (*apolytrōsis*) is Christ Jesus.

Here Paul declares, conversely, that where there is no law, there can be no idea of *sin, liability* or *judgment.* Therefore the pneumatics, who are not "in the law" (cf. 3:19) are exempt from this whole paradigm. Valentinian exegetes cite Rom 4:15 ("where there is no law, there is no transgression") and 5:13 ("sin is not accounted where there is no law") to show that even if the pneumatic is immersed in materiality, he is not "in sin,"[52] nor is he liable to "judgment" on the basis of his works. On the contrary, to him "the righteousness of God has been revealed," attested through pneumatic interpretation of the law and the prophets. Those who "all sinned" (3:23) are the psychics, who, standing "in the law," are held "under sin" (3:9, 3:19). But the pneumatics, although exempt from sin, have "lacked the glory" of the Father (3:23), and now are "justified as a gift of his grace through the redemption that is in Christ." Valentinian exegetes apparently conclude that Paul intends here to distinguish the pneumatic redemption (*apolytrōsis*) from the salvation (*sōtēria*) that psychics must strive to attain through the law.[53]

Rom 3:25-28: What God foreordained as a reconciliation through faith in his blood to demonstrate righteousness (lit.: for a demonstration of his righteousness, *eis endeixin tēs dikaiosunēs autou*) through his forgiveness of previous sins in the forbearance of God, was done to demonstrate his righteousness in the present time (for he himself is just, and justifies the one from faith in Jesus). Where then is boasting? It is excluded. By what law? The law of works? No—but through the law of faith. For we reason that a person (*anthrōpos*) is justified by faith apart from works of the law.

Paul reveals the basis for this distinction in 3:25. Many Christians—psychic Christians, the Valentinians would say—assume that this passage refers to the passion and crucifixion of Jesus. Gnostic Christians, however, say that "what God foreordained as reconciliation through faith" is the *pneumatic elect,* foreordained "to demonstrate his righteousness." What psychics refer to the passion of Jesus, pneumatics refer to "what the passion of Jesus signifies in the cosmos."[54] "They claim that the Lord came in the last times of the cosmos for this purpose, for the passion, so that he might demonstrate the passion that had occurred to the last of the aions."[55] Sophia's passion and restoration, in turn, prefigure that of the "fore-ordained" elect.

These two interpretations of the passion (psychic and pneumatic) lead to two different types of eucharistic theology. When the psychics celebrate the eucharist, they "recall the Lord's death" and his passion, drinking the wine as Jesus' blood. But when the pneumatics celebrate the eucharist, they recall the Mother's passion, and drink the eucharistic wine as a symbol of *her* suffering. In their eucharistic invocation, the Marcosians pray that as the wine symbolizes the "blood of charis," so as they partake of the wine "grace may flow into them."[56] The gnostic reader could assume, then, that Paul speaks of the pneumatic redemption effected through grace when he concludes, "where is boasting?" and answers that it is excluded—but "through the law of faith" that operates "through grace" (*charis*).

From such passages as these, Valentinian exegetes infer that Paul intends his allegory of "Jews" and "Greeks" to characterize two distinct processes. The psychics, being "under sin" (3:19) are bound to the "law of works" (3:27). To escape the penalty of death for sins, they do need faith, but theirs is specifically faith "in Jesus" (3:26), in the psychic son of the demiurge. Those who repent and believe in him receive forgiveness, and are required to do "good works." The process of their salvation depends upon their choice and their own activity; it operates according to what Paul calls the "law of works" (3:27).

The pneumatics, on the other hand, are of the elect: they receive redemption according to the "law of faith"—faith not in the psychic Jesus but in the pneumatic Christ. Unlike the works-salvation of the psychics, the pneumatic redemption excludes all human effort (and hence all "boasting"): it depends entirely upon "what God foreordained" (3:25) in election. Paul says of this in 3:28, "we reason that the *anthrōpos* (the pneumatic) is justified by faith apart from works of the law."

Rom 3:29-31: Is God only the God of the Jews? Is he not also the God of the Gentiles? Yes, of the Gentiles, if, indeed, God is one, who will justify the circumcised from faith, and the uncircumcised through faith. Do we then abolish the law through faith? No—instead we establish the law.

Here Paul sets the essential question: is God only the "God of the Jews"—that is, only the demiurge? Is he not also the "God of the Gentiles"—the Uningendered Father, who alone can be called "one God" (3:30)?[57] Origen's Valentinian opponents explain from 3:29-30 that the "one God"—the Father—justifies "the circumcised" ("the Jews," 3:29; i.e., the psychics) *from* faith (*ek pisteōs*) and the "uncircumcised" (the "Gentiles" of 3:29, the pneumatics) *through* faith (*dia pisteōs*, 3:30). For the psychics' faith, being limited, comes "from works" (4:2) as well as "from faith"; but the pneumatic is redeemed entirely "through faith" (3:30b) as Paul says, "apart from works of the law" (3:28).

Paul concludes in 3:31 that the pneumatics "abolish the law through faith." How then can he claim simultaneously to "establish the law"? Valentinian exegetes explain that although the law is abolished in relation to the elect, it is sustained and even affirmed in relation to the psychics.[58] Through this discussion, they claim, Paul has answered the question he asked rhetorically in 3:1: the "advantage of circumcision" is that it offers the possibility of salvation to those psychics who are not included among the elect.

Rom 4:1-3: What then shall we say of Abraham, our forefather according to the flesh? If Abraham was justified from works, he has reason to boast, but not before God. For what does the scripture say? Abraham believed God, and it was accounted to him for righteousness.

What concerns Paul here? Is he asking about Abraham, the progenitor of the people of Israel? The initiated reader would recognize that here again Paul speaks symbolically: he is asking about the demiurge, who, typified by Abraham, "fathers" mankind "according to the flesh."[59] Is the demiurge justified by the "law of works" like the psychics, or through the "law of faith" like the elect? Valentinian exegetes interpret 4:3 to mean that since the demiurge ("Abraham") "believed God"—the Father—"his faith was accounted for righteousness." Yet, they add, those who worship the demiurge himself as God, who do *not* believe "on the God in whom Abraham believed"—on the Father—are *not* justified, as he himself is, "through faith."[60]

Rom 4:4-8: For the one who works, the reward is not accounted according to grace but according to obligation. And to the one who does not work, but believes on him who justifies the unholy, his faith is accounted for righteousness. So also David speaks of the blessedness of the one whom God accounts righteous apart from works: "blessed are those whose transgressions are forgiven, whose sins are covered; blessed is the man (*anēr*) to whom the Lord does not impute sin."

Paul draws the consequence of this in 4:5: "to the one who works" (that is, to the *psychic*) "the reward is accounted not according to grace, but according to obligation." But "to the one who does not work" (to the *pneumatic*) who "believes on him who justifies the unholy (on the Father) his faith is accounted for righteousness." Paul cites the testimony of "David" (that is, of the demiurge) in 4:7-8.

To whom do these phrases apply? Since Paul himself says in 4:15 that "where there is no law, there is no transgression," and in 5:13 that "sin is not accounted where there is no law," Valentinian exegetes infer that those described in 4:7 cannot be pneumatic "Gentiles." It must refer to the psychics, and specifically to those who have received forgiveness, whose "sins are covered." But the second phrase, describing the one "to whom the Lord (the demiurge) does not impute sin," can only refer to the pneumatic. So Paul introduces this verse in 4:6 in praise of the "blessedness of the man whom God accounts righteous apart from works." The passage offers a third textual clue that could serve to confirm this exegesis for the initiated reader: while the first phrase is plural, denoting the plurality of psychics, the second is singular, designating the "unique, unified, single-formed nature"[61] of the elect. Paul concludes in 4:9-12 that the demiurge ("Abraham") having received justification "through faith," like the elect, becomes not only the father of the "circumcised," the psychics, but also of the "uncircumcised," the pneumatics.

Rom 4:13-15: For it was not through law that the promise came to Abraham or to his seed—to be the heirs of the cosmos—but through the righteousness of faith. For if those who are from the law are heirs, faith is empty, and the promise is void. For the law effects wrath. But where there is no law, there is no transgression.

"Those who are from the law" are excluded from the pneumatic inheritance.[62] For the demiurge's law, being correlated with sin and death,[63] "effects wrath" (4:15). Only those who stand apart from law—the pneumatic "Gentiles"—escape the demiurge's wrath, for "where there is no law there is no transgression."[64]

Rom 4:16-17: Therefore it is from faith, so that, according to grace, the promise may be certain to the entire seed; not only to the seed from the law, but also to that from Abraham's faith. He is the father of all of us . . . in the presence of the God in whom he believed, who gives life to the dead, and calls into being those who are not (*kalountos ta mē onta hōs onta*).

The Valentinian exegete, noting that the promise is given "to the entire seed" (4:16), sees in this phrase the contrast between two different elements of the "seed": the first ("that which is of the law") is the seed sown into the psychic creation;[65] the second ("that which is of Abraham's faith") is that sown into the pneumatic elect, who believe in the Father ("the God in whom Abraham believed"). Paul has shown that the elect seed receive the promise "through faith" since they come forth from God as "the living"; but how can the psychics, who are "nonexistent" (*ta mē onta*)[66] receive the promise given only "through faith"? The Valentinians claim that Paul answers this question through the allegory of Abraham and Sarah (4:18-22).

Rom 4:18-24: In hope he believed against hope, that he should become the father of many nations . . . he did not weaken in faith when he considered his own body already deadened, nearly one hundred years old, and the deadness of Sarah's womb . . . he grew strong in faith, giving glory to God, fully convinced that what God had promised he also was able to do. For this his faith was accounted for righteousness. But is is not written of him alone . . . but also for our sake, to whom it was to be accounted, to those believing in the one who raised Jesus our Lord from the dead. . . .

Here again Paul indicates that he speaks allegorically (cf. 4:23): he reveals how the demiurge ("Abraham") came to recognize his own "deadness" and the "deadness of the womb of Sarah" (4:19), that is, of Sophia, the Mother who brings forth "unformed, female seed" as "abortions" generated "into death."[67] Even realizing this, the demiurge held to his faith in the Father, "in the God who makes the dead live, and calls into being those who are not" (4:17).[68]

Paul concludes this passage saying that this account of justification "through faith" was not written "for his sake only," that is, not only for the demiurge, but for all who believe in the Father, "in him who raised Jesus our Lord from the dead" (4:24). In this he directs the initiated reader not only to discriminate clearly between the *demiurge* and the *Father,* but also to believe (as the demiurge does) in the transcendent God.

Rom 5:6-9: For while we were still weak, at the right time Christ died for the unholy. One will hardly die for the sake of the just (*dikaios*); for the good (*agathos*) perhaps one might even dare to die. But God extends his own love toward us, in that while we were still sinners, Christ died for us. Much more, then, being justified in his blood, we shall be saved by him from wrath.

Paul explains here how the savior came to destroy the power that hostile archons held over mankind.[69] For that "we were still weak" recalls that mankind was generated in "flesh, that weakness that issued from the woman above," from the passion of Sophia.[70] Subjected to the cosmic powers, helpless to resist the evil powers "who attack the soul through the body," mankind is "weak," easily prey to their influence and tyranny.[71] The savior responded with compassion to human helplessness and "came down to draw us from the passion," to overcome the evil powers, and to "adopt us to himself."[72] For, as Paul goes on to say, "one would hardly die for the sake of the just (*dikaios*; that is, the psychic),[73] but for the good (*agathos*, the pneumatic) one might dare even to die" (5:7). Valentinian exegetes claim that the elect alone recognize "what the passion of the savior symbolized in the cosmos,"[74] that he came and suffered in order to reveal through his own passion the passion of Sophia, and to reveal her restoration into the divine being.[75]

But, one may ask, what about the psychics, who remain ignorant of the mystery symbolically revealed in the savior's passion? Does their ignorance mean that they receive no benefit from the savior? The Valentinians claim that, on the contrary, since the savior came into the cosmos "to save the psychic,"[76] he chose to reveal himself to psychics in terms they were able to grasp.[77] Paul follows his example in 5:8-9 where he too speaks in terms the psychics can understand, giving a second interpretation of the savior's passion — this time a psychic interpretation: that while they were "sinners," Christ died to save them "from wrath," that is, from the demiurge's judgment.[78]

Rom 5:12-14: Therefore as through one man (*anthrōpos*) sin came into the world, and through sin, death, so that death came upon all men, in that all sinned before the law; sin was in the cosmos, but sin is not accounted where there is no law. But death reigned from Adam to Moses, even upon those who had not sinned in the likeness of the transgression of Adam, who is the type of what is to come.

Here Paul reveals the secret of the cosmic creation: how sin brought death into the cosmos along with the law, so that "death reigned from Adam to Moses, even over those who had not sinned" (5:14).

How has death gained such power, and what is its power? To what — or to whom — does this mysterious phrase refer? Basilides says that the demiurge himself is the power called "death" or "sin." In his exegesis of this passage, he quotes a variant reading: " 'sin reigned from Adam to Moses,' as it has been written, for the Great Archon reigned, having an empire that extends to the heavens, and imagining himself alone to be God."[79]

The Valentinians agree that here Paul describes the demiurge's reign, but they apparently hesitate to identify the demiurge himself (as Basilides does) as sin or as death. Instead Valentinus describes the demiurge as the cause of death: he explains that "the origin of death is the work of the cosmic demiurge."[80] Yet the demiurge himself did not intend this; initially his reign, instituted by Christ and his Wisdom (*sophia*)[81] bore "a great and fair promise."[82]

How, then, was that promise broken, so that now in the present situation, death has gained power to reign over mankind? Apparently the demiurge was helpless to avert the corruption that plagued his creation from its beginning,[83] so that sin and death became inevitable correlates of his reign. His reign, became, in effect, the "reign of death," which enslaved mankind to the "service of death,"[84] and tyrannized even "those who had not sinned in the likeness of Adam's transgression" that is, even the elect.

Rom 5:15-21: But the gift of grace (*charisma*) is not like the transgression. For if, through the transgression of one, the many died, much more the grace of God and the gift in the grace of the one man (*anthrōpos*) Jesus Christ abounds to the many. . . . For the law came in to increase the transgression; but where sin increased, grace abounded, so that as sin reigned in death, so also grace may reign through righteousness in eternal life through Jesus Christ our Lord.

Paul explains that "the charisma is not like the transgression" (4:15). Here he discloses the secret of the difference between those he calls "the many" (the psychics)[85] and "the one" (Christ and the elect).[86] "Through the transgression of one (not of Adam, but of Eve, or Sophia whom she typifies)[87] many died"—that is, the "many" psychics have been generated "into death," into cosmic existence.[88] Yet "through the one *anthrōpos*, Jesus Christ, the gift of grace (of *charis*, the divine aion) abounded to the many" (5:15). Who is the "one *anthrōpos*" through whom "the many" receive the gift of divine grace? Theodotus says it is Jesus, the "one" who willingly allowed himself to be "divided" in order to restore "the many" into unity.[89]

Do Valentinus and Heracleon contradict Theodotus when they interpret the "one *anthrōpos*" not as Jesus but as synonymous with the *pneumatic elect*? The Valentinians, perhaps, would see no contradiction here, since they identify the savior and the elect as being essentially identical, as one being.[90] Valentinus explains that "together with Christ (the elect) battle against death" for the sake of redeeming the demiurge's lost, corrupted creation; together they "attempt to save the psychic image which he was not able to rescue from corruption."[91] The savior and the elect simultaneously constitute the pneumatic nature (*to pneumatikon*) which has come into the cosmos "to save the psychic."[92] Together they deliver it from death, and "will reign over creation and over all destruction."

Through this entire chapter, then, Paul discloses that the demiurge's creation, lost to sin and death, is to be released by Christ and the elect. Although the demiurgic law came "to increase transgression," even where "death has reigned" through the demiurge (cf. 5:14) "the power of grace" finally will reign "into eternal life" (5:21).

Rom 6:3-11: Do you not know that those of us who were baptized into Christ Jesus were baptized into his death? For we were buried with him through baptism into death, so that as Christ was raised from the dead through the glory of the Father, we too might walk in newness of life. For if we have become identified in the likeness of his death, so shall we be identified in the likeness of his resurrection. We know that our old man (*ho palaios hēmōn anthrōpos*) has been crucified, that the body of sin (*to sōma tēs hamartias*) may be destroyed, and we are no longer enslaved to sin . . . but if we have died with Christ, we know that we also shall live with him . . . the death he died he died to sin . . . but the life he lives he lives to God. So also you must consider yourselves dead to sin, but alive to God.

Previously Paul has described in universal scope the cosmic battle Christ wages against the rulers and archons who have held creation captive. Now he changes his focus to show how Christ's victory over these powers becomes effective in the believer's inner experience. He explains that it is in baptism that the believer dies, is buried, and is raised from the dead. What does this mean?

Most Christians—psychic Christians, the Valentinians call them—interpret this literally, believing that whoever is baptized in the church receives hope that after his actual death, he will be restored—body and soul—and raised back to life. Gnostic theologians reject this belief as simple-minded, the "faith of fools."[93] They claim that psychic believers fail to see that Paul is not speaking here literally of a future bodily resurrection: instead he is speaking symbolically of the process of receiving gnosis. Irenaeus says that "they maintain that 'the resurrection from the dead' is knowing the truth that they proclaim."[94] The teacher of Rheginos alludes to such passages as Rom 6:3-11 and Col 3:4 as he explains the meaning of resurrection:

> The savior has swallowed up death, so you should not remain in ignorance [i.e., "death"] . . . having swallowed up the visible through the invisible; and he has offered us the way of our immortality. Therefore, as the apostle says, we suffered with him, and we arose with him, and we went to heaven with him.[95]

For, he continues, the resurrection is "the revelation of that which is the change of things, and transformation into newness" (cf. 6:4).[96]

Paul indicates in 6:3-4 (as Tertullian's account confirms) that this process occurs in the experience of baptism. Theodotus cites this passage as he explains that "baptism is called 'death,' and an 'end of the old life,' when we depart from the evil archons (*sin*, 6:7, and *death*, 6:9) but it is called 'life according to Christ' which he alone rules."[97] What is transformed in baptism, he continues, is not the body but the soul. Although the initiate physically remains unchanged, spiritually he "dies to the cosmos, but 'lives to God' (cf. 6:10), that death may be released by death, and corruption by resurrection."[98] Whoever receives this pneumatic baptism receives gnosis of "who we were, what we have become . . . whence we came, from what we have been redeemed; what birth is, and what rebirth."[99] To receive this enlightenment is to be "raised from the dead": this *is* the resurrection![100]

In the process, as Paul says (6:6), the "old man" is "crucified with Christ." Since crucifixion signifies separation from the passions,[101] this means that the "body of sin" (6:6), the "mortal bodies" in which "sin reigns" (6:12) are separated from the inner pneumatic "new man."[102] Those who "strip off the flesh" thereby are freed from "the power of sin," the devil; those who undergo "death" are released from the demiurge. Rheginos' teacher enjoins his disciple to realize that "already you have the resurrection . . . consider yourself as risen already."[103] These Valentinian sources accord with Tertullian's account: the heretics, "claiming that death itself must be understood in a pneumatic way," say that

> death . . . is ignorance of God, by reason of which one is dead to God [cf. Rom. 6:10] . . . Therefore, that must be held to be resurrection, when one is reanimated by access to the truth, and having dispersed the death of ignorance, and being endowed with new life by God, has burst forth from the sepulchre of the "old man" [cf. Rom. 6:6]. From this it follows that those who by faith have attained to the resurrection are with the Lord once they have "put him on" in baptism [cf. Rom 6:4-5]. [104]

Rom 6:12-19: Do not let sin reign in your mortal bodies so that you obey its desires, or lend your members as weapons of injustice to sin, but establish yourselves to God as if alive from the dead and your members as weapons of righteousness to God, for sin shall not reign over you: for you are not under law, but under grace. . . . Do you not know that you are the slaves of the one you obey, either sin, which leads to death, or obedience, which leds to righteousness? But thanks be to God, that you who once were slaves of sin have become obedient . . . to the type of the teaching (*ton typon tēs didachēs*); having been freed from sin, you became slaves of righteousness. I speak humanly, because of the weakness of your flesh.

If the pneumatic has already been released from sin and death and has been resurrected, why does Paul now warn against the power of sin and death? The gnostic reader would recognize that Paul here no longer speaks of the elect themselves; from 6:12 he speaks of the psychics. The elect themselves have "died to sin," in separation from the "body of sin" (6:6); but their "mortal bodies," the psychics (see discussion on Rom 8:11), still may be ruled by sin (the devil) and compelled to obey the passions.[105] So, according to the Gospel of Philip, "whoever has gnosis of the truth is a free man, but the free man does not sin, for 'he who sins is the slave of sin.'"[106] But "whoever has become a slave (to sin) against his will will be able to become free."[107] This suggests that the psychics, although enslaved to sin, have the possibility of attaining their freedom. For the psychics stand "in the middle" between flesh and spirit; they must choose to identify with one or the other — with the devil or with the spirit of God.[108] Heracleon explains that the psychics either must obey the will of the devil, fulfilling the desires of the flesh, or they obey "righteousness," the demiurge's law.[109] In the latter case, they become obedient to "the *type* of the teaching" (6:17-18) which they received (since psychics receive only "types and images" of the truth).[110] Nevertheless, although now they receive only "types and images," the writer of the Gospel of Philip says that when the "hidden things of the truth" are revealed to them, "then the perfect light will pour out upon everyone; then the slaves will be free, and the captives delivered."[111] For the present, however, Paul says he must speak to them "in human terms, because of the weakness of your flesh" (6:19).[112]

Rom 7:4-14: So, my brethren, you have died to the law through the body of Christ, that you may belong to another, the one who has raised him from the dead, that we might bear fruit to God. While we were living in flesh, the passions of sin through the law were energized in our members to bear fruit for death. Now, however, we have been released from the law, we have died in him by whom we were being held captive, so that we might serve in newness of the spirit, not in the old written letter.

What shall we say? Is the law sin? No—but I would not have known sin except through the law . . . sin, taking advantage of the commandment, energized in me every desire. I once lived apart from the law. Apart from the law, sin is dead. But when the commandment came, sin came to life and I died . . . the commandment . . . proved to be death to me. Sin, finding opportunity in the commandment, deceived me and, through it, killed me. So the law is holy, and the commandment is holy and just and good. Did the good, then, bring death to me? By no means! It was sin, effecting death in me . . . we know that the law is pneumatic. . . . .

Valentinian theologians understand Paul's discussion of sin and law in terms of mankind's subjection to the devil and the demiurgic "lawgiver." Those who have "died to *sin*" (to the devil) also have "died to the *law*," that is, to the demiurge who imposed it; "to him who held us captive" (7:6). Now they "belong to another" (7:4), "to God" the Father (7:4b). Theodotus explains from 7:5 ("while we were living in the flesh") that even the elect prior to redemption were oppressed by "the passions" (*ta pathēmata,* 7:5), that is, the elements of Sophia's passions, which were formed into the cosmic elements.[113]

Is the law which energizes the passions itself "sin"? Paul answers that it is not, but adds that "I would not have known sin apart from the law" (7:7). According to the Gospel of Philip, the law evoked the awareness that destroyed Adam's innocence: "the law was the tree: it has power to give knowledge (*gnōsis*) of good and evil." But the law could not keep man from evil or "place him in the good"; the knowledge it conveys to man only destroys him.[114] Effectively, "the law of nature" is only "death."[115] The pneumatic, then, so long as he lives "apart from the law" (7:9) lives without sin. Basilides takes this to mean that the pneumatic "lives" spiritually prior to his bodily incarnation.[116] But when he is generated into bodily existence, even the pneumatic experiences sin as an active power (7:9).

Yet, while Paul says in 7:11 that the commandment "deceives and kills" mankind, he acknowledges in 7:12 that "the law is holy, and the commandment is just and good." How can this contradiction be resolved? Ptolemy explains that in these two phrases Paul refers to two different types of law. The first is the law of the demiurge, which, although "just," deceives and destroys mankind; but the second is the "good and holy" law of the pneumatic nature, as Paul reveals in 7:14 ("*we know* that the law is pneumatic").[117]

Rom 7:14b-25: . . . but I am sarkic . . . I do not understand what I do. For what I do not will, I do; but I do the very thing I hate. Now if I do what I do not will, I agree that the law is good: so it is no longer I that do it, but sin which dwells in me. For I know that there is nothing in me, that is, in my flesh, that is good. I can will what is good, but I cannot do it. . . . if I do what I do not will, it is no longer I that do it, but sin dwelling in me. . . . For I delight in the law of God according to the inner man (*ton esō anthrōpon*) but I see another law in my members at war (*heteron nomon en tois melesin mou*) with the law of my mind (*tō nomō tou noos*) enslaving me to the law of sin that dwells in my members. Wretched man that I am! Who shall deliver me from this body of death? Thanks be to God through Jesus Christ our Lord! For I myself serve the law of God in my mind, but in my flesh the law of sin.

Valentinian theologians give great attention to this passage: each of the major writers whose work remains has described the experience of the conflict that makes Paul cry out in despair that "it is no longer I who act, but sin that dwells in me" (7:20). In their view Paul here expresses the conflict inherent in the pneumatic's experience. For the pneumatic perceives intuitively the "pneumatic law" within himself, but finds himself bound in materiality; he finds his actual condition hopelessly "sarkic." Valentinus describes how evil spirits dwell in the heart, effecting evil actions: "each of these (demons) effects its own acts, insulting the heart many times with inappropriate desires." The tormented heart, having become the "dwelling-place of many demons" cannot cleanse itself; the Good Father must intervene to cleanse and to illuminate it.[118] The writer of the Gospel of Philip refers to Rom 7:19 to describe how evil "masters us, and we are its slaves. It takes us captive, so that we do what we do not want, and what we want we do not do."[119] Heracleon shows how the pneumatic nature is tormented, overrun, and abused by sinful desires until the savior comes to purify it throught the holy spirit.[120] Theodotus expresses the same empathy with human helplessness before the powers of evil. He explains that the indwelling evil, located in the flesh ("in the members," 7:23), contradicts what Paul calls the "law of the mind." The lower element of the psyche, susceptible to passions, "wars" against "the law of the mind."[121]

For the pneumatic "delights in the law of God"—of the Father— "according to the inner anthropos" (7:22), that is, innately in the pneumatic nature. But he perceives "another law" opposing him, the "law of sin that dwells in my members." This is the law of the demiurge, which first arouses physical passions (7:8-11) and then punishes the person who responds to them with death.[122] The pneumatic, seeing himself powerless to liberate himself by freely chosen moral action, cries out with Paul to be delivered from "this body of death" (7:24) which involves him in such an irreconcilable contradiction. So Rheginos learns from his gnostic teacher that the body, irrevocably bound to the processes of aging, is "corruption."[123] Valentinus, Heracleon, and Theodotus agree that only God the Father, through the savior, can deliver the suppliant from the demiurge and from the "law of sin in the flesh" to follow the pneumatic "law of God."

Rom 8:1-4: There is therefore now no condemnation for those who are in Christ Jesus. For the law of the spirit of life in Christ Jesus has liberated me from the law of sin and death. For what the law could not do, in that it was weak through the flesh, God sending his son in the likeness of sinful flesh, and for sin, condemned sin in the flesh, so that the requirement of the law might be fulfilled in us, who walk not according to the flesh but according to the spirit.

In Romans 8 Paul celebrates the pneumatic redemption. To those who are "in Christ Jesus" (8:1),[124] in whom "the spirit of God" dwells,[125] he proclaims that "there is therefore now no condemnation" to fear from the demiurge.[126] While psychics still fear condemnation,[127] since they remain under "the law of sin and death,"[128] the pneumatic may rejoice with Paul that "the law of the spirit of life in Christ Jesus has delivered me!" (8:2).

What proved to be impossible for the law (and for the demiurge) "in that it was weak through the flesh" now has been accomplished by the Father in sending his own son, the Monogenes. The exegete Alexander, apparently a Valentinian, claims Rom. 8:3 as evidence that the Savior took on only the appearance of a human body, being sent "in the likeness of sinful flesh," to abolish this sinful flesh (he "condemned the sin in the flesh," 8:36).[129]

Through the redemption he offers, then, "the just requirement of the law might be fulfilled" by those who walk "according to the spirit," fulfilling the requirements of the law pneumatically.[130] So Rheginos' teacher urges him, "do not conduct yourself according to the flesh" but to apprehend the unity of the spirit, in which "you already have the resurrection!"[131]

Rom 8:10-11: If Christ is in you, the body, indeed, is dead because of sin, but the spirit is alive because of the righteousness. If the spirit of him who raised Christ Jesus from the dead dwells in you, he who raised Christ Jesus from the dead will give life to your mortal bodies also through his spirit which dwells in you.

Those who receive the "spirit of God" dwelling "in them," according to Valentinian exegesis, must be the elect, who share in the divine nature which is spirit.[132] For them "the body is dead because of sin" but the "spirit is alive"—through the Father, "him who raised Christ from the dead" (8:11).[133] The elect are promised even more: that "God will also raise your mortal bodies." What does this mean? Does Paul anticipate bodily resurrection, as ecclesiastical writers insist?[134] Ptolemy and Heracleon reject such exegesis, claiming instead that the phrase "mortal bodies" must be taken symbolically: it describes those who are "dead," namely, the psychics.[135] Tertullian admits that the heretics question the literal interpretation of the term "body" in such passages; some, he says, interpret the "mortal body" of Rom 8:11 to mean the *soul* of the person who is "spiritually dead."[136] When the elect interpret pneumatically the promise that "your mortal bodies" shall be "raised," they understand that the psychics, related to the elect as body to spirit, shall be "raised" to pneumatic life![137]

Rom 8:12-15: So, brothers . . . if you live according to the flesh you will die, but if by the spirit you put to death the deeds of the body you will live. For all who are led by the spirit of God are children of God. For you did not receive the spirit of slavery to fall back into fear, but you have received the spirit of adoption, in which we cry: "Abba, Father!"

A Valentinian reader could see here Paul's warning that whether each psychic will share in this resurrection depends upon his own choice. For as Heracleon explains, their situation differs entirely from that of the elect. Those who are elected are what they are, so to speak, "by nature": their situation has nothing to do with their own will, but depends entirely upon the will of the Father.[138] The pneumatic cannot choose to love God; he remains totally dependent on God's will in choosing and loving him as the natural "child of God." Similarly, in the opposite case, the reprobate are "children of the devil" by nature, according to the Father's will: they too are incapable of choice in the matter of their eternal destiny. The psychics alone apparently are not elected: they stand "in the middle" between two alternative elections. They alone have choice; they can will to serve either the devil or the Father. According to their own choice they become children of God or of the devil—whichever they choose—not "by nature" but, as Heracleon says, "by adoption."[139]

This passage (8:12-15) may have served as the basis for Heracleon's theory of adoption. Heracleon could read in this passage how Paul shows psychics the choice that confronts them. They must choose either to live "according to the flesh" and to die, or to live "according to the spirit" and to live, becoming "the sons of God." Contrasting this promise of adoptive sonship with their previous servitude to the demiurge, their "father according to the flesh" (cf. discussion of Rom 4:1) whom they served "in fear," he says, "you have not received the spirit of slavery again to fear, but you have received the spirit of adoption, in which we (the pneumatic elect) cry, 'Father!'" For if the psychics' relationship to God remains contingent upon their own choice "in adoption," the pneumatics' relationship to God as "sons of God" is utterly unconditional: the elect are "sons of God by nature." Paul rejoices in that certainty in 8:16: "the spirit itself witnesses together with *our spirit* that we *are* children of God!"

Rom 8:18-23: I consider that the sufferings (*ta pathēmata*) of the present time are not worthy to be compared with the glory that shall be revealed in us. For the creation waits with eager longing for the revelation of the sons of God; for the creation was subjected to futility, not willingly, but through him who subjected him in hope; therefore the creation shall be set free from slavery to corruption and gain the glorious liberty of the children of God. We know that the whole creation has been groaning in labor even to the present time; and not only the creation, but we ourselves, who have the first fruits of the spirit, groan inwardly awaiting the adoption, the redemption of our bodies.

During the present time, the pneumatics too share in the conditions of creation (*ta pathēmata*, 8:18) while they anticipate "the glory that shall be revealed in us." Yet Valentinian exegetes note from this passage that the pneumatics are not alone in their hope: "the expectation of the *creation* awaits the revelation of the sons of God" (8:19). To what—or to whom—does Paul refer? Valentinians interpret this term (creation, *ktisis*) as a hidden reference to the demiurge.[140] So Theodotus interprets this passage:

Since he (the demiurge) did not know her (Sophia) who acted through him, and thought he created by his own power . . . therefore the apostle said, "he was subjected to the futility of the cosmos, not willingly, but by reason of him who subjected him, in hope that he also shall be set free" (8:20) when the seeds of God are gathered together.[141]

Having come to recognize Sophia as the one "who acted through him," the demiurge recognizes also the Father as "him who subjected him" (8:20) against his own will.[142] Now, having given up the illusion of his own autonomy, the demiurge awaits "in hope" his own deliverance along with the rest of "the cosmos," the psychics who are to be saved.

Basilides similarly explains that the Great Archon ("the creation," 8:20) therefore "groans and labors until now" (8:22) as he awaits "the revelation of the sons of God," that is, the revelation of "us who are pneumatic."[143] He says that this revelation has been delayed and the elect subjected to the conditions of cosmic existence so that they may "correct, teach, and form" the psychic cosmos.[144]

Paul reveals in 8:23 that the elect (who, according to Valentinian exegesis, are the "first fruits of the spirit")[145] share both in the suffering (pathēmata)[146] and in the anticipation of the adoption of the psychics "as sons." Their adoption means for the elect the "redemption of our bodies," for the psychics are related to the pneumatics as the body to the spirit.[147] Theodotus teaches that the elect cannot enter into the pleroma until their psychic counterparts are "raised" to join in union with them so that all may receive access to God together. Until that time, he says, the elect themselves are constrained to "wait" for the sake of the psychics.[148]

Rom 8:28-39: We know that to those who love God all things work for good, to those called according to his purpose. For those whom he foreknew, he also predestined to be conformed to the image of his son, that he might be the first born among many brethren. . . . if God is for us, who can be against us? . . . who shall make any accusation against the elect of God? God justifies—who condemns? . . . I am convinced that neither death, nor life, nor angels, nor principalities, nor things present, nor things to come, nor powers, nor height, nor depth, nor any other creature will be able to separate us from the love of God in Christ Jesus.

Paul assures the elect that the spirit joins with them in longing and in prayer, effecting "all things together for good" both for the psychics who are those "called" (8:28) and for the pneumatics, who are "foreknown, preordained to be conformed to the image of God's son" (8:29). The teacher of Rheginos explains that "this is the reason that we are elected to salvation and redemption — that we have been predestined from the beginning not to fall into the foolishness of those who are ignorant, but that we should enter into the wisdom of those who have known the truth."[149]

Finally Paul praises the election: "If God be for us, who can be against us? Who can make accusations against the elect of God?" (8:33). Certainly, the demiurge,[150] "he who condemns," cannot accuse those for whom Christ intercedes, and surpass his authority.[151] The apostle concludes that there is no power, authority, or archon of the demiurge that has the power to separate "his own" (apparently the Father's own)[152] from "the love of God" (8:39).

Rom 9:1-5: . . . my conscience bears witness in the holy spirit that I have great pain and continual sorrow in my heart . . . for the sake of my kinsmen according to the flesh. They are Israelites; theirs is the adoption and the glory, the covenants, the giving of the law, the worship, and the promises; theirs are the fathers, from whom is Christ according to the flesh: God, who is over all things, be blessed among the aions.

Paul's ecstatic praise of the pneumatic election (8:28-39) changes to concern as he considers the situation of those *not* included among the elect. He claims that his conscience (clearly pneumatic; cf. 8:16) "witnesses with the holy spirit" to the "continual pain" he suffers for their sake. From the opening of his letter he has identified himself with them: here again he calls them "my brothers, my kinsmen according to the flesh" (9:3). The Valentinian could read in this Paul's acknowledgment that he himself, although pneumatic, has been generated, like the psychics, from the demiurge. For these are, as he says, "Israelites, to whom belongs the adoption as sons"; from among them came "Christ according to the flesh." Ptolemy and Heracleon apparently have in mind such passages when they recount how the psychic Christ was generated "from the Jews," that is, from among the psychics,[153] and "from Judea," that is, from the psychic region.[154]

Rom 9:6-8: But it is not as though the word of God (*logos tou theou*) had failed. For not all who are from Israel are themselves Israel. Not all who are seed of Abraham are his children, but "in Isaac shall your seed be named." That is, it is not the children of the flesh that are children of God, but the children of the promise are counted as seed.

Paul goes on to say (according to Valentinian exegesis) that the psychics' present situation does not mean that the "logos of God" has failed in his soteriological mission. He shows in 9:7 that of those who seem to be psychic ("from Israel") not all actually are psychic ("Israel"); nor are all who are generated from the demiurge ("seed of Abraham")[155] actually "his children." The Valentinian exegete could argue that although the psychic "children of the flesh" (of "Abraham," the demiurge) are not really children of God (the Father) the converse is *not* true. The "children of the promise" (pneumatics) *are* accounted as "seed of Abraham" (the demiurge), just as the savior himself, although pneumatic, appeared as a psychic. To account for the difference between the two types of offspring "Abraham" has generated, Paul offers the allegory of the twins, Jacob and Esau.

Rom 9:10-18: . . . so when Rebecca had conceived children by one . . . though they were not yet born, and had not done anything, good or bad, so that God's purpose in election might remain, not from works, but from him who calls, she was told "the elder shall serve the younger." As it is written, "Jacob I loved, but Esau I hated." . . . therefore it does not depend upon human will or effort, but upon God who shows mercy. . . . he has mercy on whom he wills, and he hardens the heart of whomever he wills.

Origen indicates that this passage had become a *locus classicus* of controversy between "herterodox" and "orthodox" exegetes. He considers the basic issue to be the question of free will. Origen says that his Valentinian opponents "claim that if it depends 'on God who shows mercy' (9:16) that a person is saved, our salvation is not in our power . . . but rests solely on the will of Him who, if he wills, 'shows mercy' and confers salvation."[156] He continues, "it is on these passages primarily that the heretics rely for their claim that salvation is not in our own power. . . . therefore they claim that Pharaoh, who was of choic nature, had been 'hardened' by God who 'has mercy' on those who are of pneumatic nature."[157] Yet while he represents the Valentinian theologians as determinists, Origen's account indicates that they use the terms "choic" and "pneumatic" nature to designate the alternative of reprobation and election.[158] This, they claim, is what Paul teaches here through the example of Jacob and Esau: Jacob exemplifies the pneumatic whom God chooses "apart from works" to be among the elect; Esau the choic, excluded from election.

Rom 9:19-26: You will say to me then, "why does he find fault? Who can resist his will?" But who are you, a man, to answer back to God? Shall what is molded (*to plasma*) say to the one who formed it, "why did you make me this way?" Has not the potter the authority to make from the same lump one vessel for honor, another for dishonor? If God . . . has endured with much patience the vessels of wrath made for destruction, to make known the wealth of his glory for the vessels of mercy, which he prepared in advance for glory . . . those of us whom he called . . . will be called "sons of the living God."

The Valentinians might well reply to Origen that the apostle himself has anticipated such objections to the doctrine of election: is God unjust (9:14)? Why does God reject some? Who can resist his will (9:19)? They themselves accept the doctrine of election as a primary theme of their theology.[159] The writer of the Gospel of Truth uses the metaphor of this passage to illustrate the election: certain "vessels" are "filled, supplied, and purified"; others are "emptied, overturned, and broken."[160] Those whom the Father "prepares in advance for glory" (9:23) are the elect, who belong to the "living God," the Father. The same verse is paraphrased in the Gospel of Thomas: "we are his sons, the elect of the living Father."[161]

Rom 9:27-32: And Isaiah cries out concerning Israel, "though the number of the sons of Israel be as the sands of the sea, only a remnant of them will be saved; for the Lord will execute his sentence upon the earth with severity and speed." . . . What then shall we say? That the Gentiles who did not pursue righteousness found righteousness, the righteousness of faith. But Israel, pursuing the law of righteousness, did not fulfill the law. Why? Because it was not from faith but from works.

The initiated reader could take this to mean that while the pneumatic elect receives righteousness "of faith" through election, most of the psychic "sons of Israel," numerous as they are, fail to attain righteousness because they attempt to achieve it through the demiurge's law. Those who fail to fulfill it fall before his ("the Lord's") sentence of condemnation.[162]

Rom 10:1-13: Brethren, my heart's desire and prayer to God for them is for salvation. For I witness of them that they have zeal for God, but not with understanding (*kat' epignōsin*). . . . Moses writes that the one who practices the righteousness of the law will live in it. But the righteousness of faith says . . . "the word is near you, in your mouth and in your heart." This is the statement of faith which we preach: that if you confess with your mouth Jesus as Lord, and believe in your heart that God raised him from the dead, you shall be saved. For with the heart one believes and is justified, and with the mouth one confesses and is saved. . . . For there is no distinction between the Jew and the Greek: the same one is Lord of all, and bestows his wealth upon all who call upon him. For every one who calls on the name of the Lord will be saved.

The psychic "Israelites," however "zealous," lack understanding and remain ignorant (10:2).[163] How can they be saved? According to Valentinian exegesis, Paul discloses that their salvation depends, on the one hand, upon their obedience to "Moses," the demiurge, in "practicing the righteousness of the law" (10:5) and, on the other hand, on their belief in "the statement (*rhēma*) of faith which we preach" (10:8).

The Valentinians apparently infer from 10:10 that Paul intends to discriminate between the psychic and the pneumatic faith. To the psychic he says that "if you confess with your mouth Jesus as Lord," this verbal confession will suffice "for salvation." To the pneumatic he adds that those who "believe in (their) hearts that God (the Father) has raised him from the dead" will receive "justification" (10:10). The Valentinians themselves, apparently heeding Paul's plea in 1 Cor 1:10 ("that you all confess the same thing"),[164] did make a practice of participating in the public, verbal confession in common with other Christians. Irenaeus testifies repeatedly that "they do, indeed, 'confess with the mouth one Jesus Christ,'" but, he complains, they are only "saying one thing and thinking another."[165] Apparently they believe they are following Paul's counsel outwardly to "confess with the mouth" what psychics also confess, yet inwardly to "believe in the heart" on the Father, who "raised him from the dead" in the pneumatic faith that justifies the elect (cf. 10:10). For as Paul says, even those (psychics) who only "call upon the name of the Lord" shall finally "be saved" (10:13).

Rom 10:14-18: But how are they to call upon him in whom they have not believed? How shall they believe in him of whom they have not heard? And how shall they hear without a preacher? . . . but I ask, have they not heard? Indeed, "their sound has gone out to all the earth, and their works to the ends of the world."

The initiated reader could grasp the meaning of Paul's question: how are the psychics to call upon the Father, "upon him in whom they have not believed," or to believe in him "of whom they have not heard"? Heracleon is among the Valentinian theologians who cite Rom 10:15-20 to show that the Father has communicated with the psychic Israel not only through the prophets, but also through the savior.[166] Nevertheless, the majority of Israelites failed to acknowledge the One from whom the revelation came.[167]

Rom 11:1-10: I ask, then, has God rejected his people? By no means! I myself am an Israelite, of the seed of Abraham. . . . God has not rejected his people whom he foreknew. . . . So even at the present time there is a remnant according to the election of grace. But if it is by grace, it is no longer from works . . . what then? Israel failed to obtain what it sought: the elect obtained it. The rest were hardened, as it is written: "God gave them a spirit of deep sleep; eyes that should not see, and ears that should not hear, even to the present time." . . . "let their eyes be darkened so that they cannot see. . . ."

Paul asks, then, has God rejected the psychics? He answers—with careful discernment—that God has *not* rejected them, offering himself as an example: "He did not reject his people *whom he foreknew*" (11:2); that is, he did not reject a "remnant" *elected by grace* from among the psychics, a remnant that includes Paul himself (11:1). But what of the rest—the psychics *not* included among the elect? The apostle answers that God gave to them "a spirit of deep sleep," the demiurge, who, himself "blind" to the higher powers, kept the psychics in the darkness of oblivion.[168]

Rom 11:11-16: So, I ask, have they stumbled so as to fall? By no means! Through their transgression salvation has come to the Gentiles . . . now if their transgression means riches for the cosmos, and if their deficiency means wealth to the Gentiles, how much more will their pleroma mean! . . . If their rejection means the reconciliation of the cosmos, what will their inclusion mean but life from the dead? If the dough offered as first fruit is holy, so is the lump; if the root is holy, so are the branches.

Heracleon cites 11:11 to show that salvation has come "from among the Jews, since (the savior) was born in Judea (the psychic *topos*) but was not in them . . . and from thence salvation and the word came to the Gentiles throughout the whole cosmos."[169] Paul here directs his words specifically to the pneumatic elect ("to you Gentiles," 11:13); but even to the initiate his words might seem absurd, a contradiction in terms. How can the psychics, whose very nature is characterized as deficiency (*usterēma*, or *hettēma*, 11:12),[170] ever attain to fulfillment (pleroma)? Paul admits that he is speaking of a paradox — of nothing less than "life from the dead" (11:15)! To indicate his meaning, he offers the parallel metaphors of 11:16.

Theodotus and Ptolemy both offer exegesis of the secret meaning of Rom 11:16, which serves as a key passage in Valentinian teaching. Ptolemy says that "the term 'first fruit' (*hē aparchē*) denotes that which is *pneumatic*, but 'the lump' (*to phurama*) signifies the psychic ecclesia." In this passage, he continues, the apostle shows how the savior "took up" the psychic ecclesia ("the lump") and "blended it" with himself (and with the "first fruit") as with "leaven," in order to "raise" it.[171] Theodotus similarly explains the connection between the resurrection ("life from the dead" 11:15) and the double metaphor of 11:16:

> After the kingdom of death . . . Jesus Christ . . . received to himself by the power the ecclesia, the elect (*eklogē*) and the called (*klēsis*), the pneumatic from her who bore it (Sophia) and the psychic from the economy (the demiurge), and he raised and saved what he received . . . for "if the first fruits be holy, so is the lump; and if the root be holy, so also the branches."[172]

Theodotus indicates that the second metaphor bears the same symbolic meaning as the first. The "root" signifies what is pneumatic, above all the divine pleroma;[173] the "branches" what is psychic. The writer of Interpretation of the Gnosis calls the elect themselves "the roots," for all are connected with the divine "root," the pleroma.[174]

Rom 11:17-26: But if some of the branches were broken off . . . do not boast over the branches . . . remember that it is not you that bear the root, but the root bears you . . . even the others, unless they persist in unbelief, will be grafted in, for God has the power to graft them in again. . . . I want you to understand this mystery, brethren: a hardening has come upon part of Israel, until the pleroma of the Gentiles comes in; and so all Israel will be saved. . . .

The writer of the Gospel of Truth states that whoever "has no root . . . also has not fruit."[175] Theodotus is even more explicit: referring to Rom 11:17-24, he identifies the psychics as the "branches broken off" (11:17) so that the elect could be engrafted.[176] Yet the gnostic reader would note Paul's warning that the elect are not to boast of this over the psychics: *they* do not bear the root (the *plērōma*), but that divine source that bears them (11:18). Theodotus interprets 11:24 to mean that the psychics ("unless they persist in unbelief") will be "'engrafted onto the olive tree' into faith and incorruption, and 'share the fatness of the olive tree,' so that 'when the Gentiles come in' then 'so shall all Israel'" (11:25).[177] This, indeed, is nothing less than a "mystery" (11:25); it is "life from the dead" (11:15), the "mystery of the resurrection" (1 Cor 15:51): that the psychics ("the dead") shall be "raised" and reunited with the elect, that all may "enter in" to the pleroma together![178] Paul concludes this disclosure marveling at "the depth" (*bythos*, 11:33), the wisdom (*sophia*) and the *gnosis* of God, and praising his "glory among the aions" (11:36).[179]

Rom 12:1-2: I appeal to you, brethren, because of the mercies of God, to present your bodies as a living sacrifice, holy, acceptable to God, your spiritual worship (*logikēn latreian*). And do not be conformed to this aion, but be transformed in the renewing of your minds, that you may prove what is the will of God, good and acceptable and perfect.

Heracleon cites this passage as he expounds Jn 4:24 ("God is spirit, and those who worship him must worship in spirit and in truth"). He says that as the Father's "divine nature is incorruptible, pure and invisible . . . those who worship 'in spirit and in truth,' . . . pneumatically . . . are themselves spirit, of the same nature as the Father. They worship in truth and not in error, as the apostle teaches, saying that such piety is their 'rational service'" (Rom 12:1).[180]

Yet how can Paul say that "spiritual worship" involves the offering of "your bodies" as a "living sacrifice"? The extant text from Heracleon does not answer this question. Elsewhere, however, he states that "the will of the Father" (cf. 12:12) is for men to know the Father and be saved.[181] The homilist of A Valentinian Exposition also explains that "the will of the Father" is for the psychics to be saved.[182] If Heracleon, like other Valentinian teachers, interprets "your bodies" as signifying the psychic believers,[183] he could read in 12:1-2 Paul's appeal to the elect to present the psychics "holy and acceptable" before God. This, one might suggest, is their "rational service" (12:1): in doing this they fulfill the Father's will.

Rom 12:3-6: I say, through the grace given to me, to every one among you, not to think of himself more highly than he ought to think, but to think wisely, as God has measured to each the measure of faith. For as in one body we have many members, and not all the members have the same function, so we, being many, are one body in Christ, and each of us members of each other, having different gifts of grace (*charismata*) according to the grace given to us. . . .

The initiated reader might see in 12:3 Paul's instruction to every believer, whether psychic or pneumatic, to evaluate himself and others according to "the measure of grace" given to him, the psychic "not thinking of lofty things, but led by humble things" (12:16) and the pneumatic putting aside any spiritual pride in the recognition that God has given to him "the measure of faith" he possesses. The author of Interpretation of the Gnosis uses Paul's metaphor of the church as the "one body" (cf. Romans 12, 1 Corinthians 12) to remind all "members of the body" that they all mutually participate in it through the "grace and gift" of Christ. He urges each "member" to share his gift (*charisma*) freely with the others,[184] accepting the diversity of gifts (cf. 12:6) with gratitude, in harmony with all the members.[185]

Rom 13:1-7: Let every soul be subject to the higher powers. For there is no power except from God, and the powers that exist have been instituted by God. Therefore whoever resists any power resists what God has appointed. Those who resist will incur judgment for themselves. For the archons are not a terror to the one who does good, but to the evildoer. Would you not fear the one who has authority? Then do good, and you will gain praise from him. For he is the servant of God for your good. But if you do evil, fear: for he does not bear the sword in vain: he is the servant of God to execute his wrath upon the evildoer. . . . Pay to all of them what is due, tribute to the one who exacts tribute, . . . fear to the one who exacts fear, honor to the one who exacts honor.

What does Paul mean? Is he concerned with the believer's duties toward "actual human authorities" (as Irenaeus insists against Valentinian exegesis)?[186] Heracleon interprets this passage symbolically: "every *soul*" (13:1) that is, every *psychic*, is to remain subject to "the powers," to the cosmic "rulers and authorities," as those "instituted by God"; for, as Paul says, "the archons are not a terror to the one who does good." But evildoers have reason to fear the "servant of God" who "bears the sword" (13:4): for he is "Moses, the lawgiver himself," the demiurge. Heracleon points out the irony of the psychic's situation: "Moses," the one in whom the psychics "placed (their) hope" is the one who "executes wrath."[187] Now, "through necessity" (12:5), they are subjected not only to him, but also to the other cosmic powers, and are to pay to each "what is required," whether *tribute, fear, or honor* (13:6-7).

Rom 13:8-10: Owe nothing to anyone, except to love one another. The one who loves has fulfilled the other law (*ton heteron nomon*). For the law that says, "do not commit adultery, do not murder, do not steal, do not covet," and any other commandment, is summed up in this very word: "you shall love your neighbor as yourself." . . . love is the fulfillment (*plērōma*) of the law.

Having just commanded believers to "pay what is owed" (13:7), Paul now says to "owe nothing to anyone" (13:8)! How could he not be contradicting himself? The initiated reader could resolve this contradiction if he assumes that previously Paul spoke to psychics, but now he speaks to the elect. For they, being subject neither to the "other commandment" (*hetera entolē*) nor to the demiurge nor to his archons, fulfill "the other law" (*ton heteron nomon*)—the pneumatic law of love: as Paul says, "love is the pleroma of the law" (13:10b).

Rom 13:11-13: Knowing the time, that the hour is coming for you to awaken from sleep: for now salvation is nearer than when we first believed. The night is far spent; the day is at hand. Let us cast off the works of darkness, and put on the armor of light. Let us walk as in daylight. . . .

Paul closes the passage with an eschatological warning. The psychic long has remained oblivious of God ("Adam's sleep was the oblivion of the soul") but the savior has come to awaken the soul, whose "awakening" is his salvation.[188] "The day is drawing near"; if the "first day" is past, the *hylic* day, and the second is present, the *psychic* day, the day that "draws near" must be "the third, the *pneumatic* day, the day of resurrection of the ecclesia."[189] On that "day" the psychics shall be roused from sleep, that is, "raised from the dead." The elect already walk "in the day" (13:13), having emerged from the "night" of cosmic existence, "drawn upward by him like the beams by the sun . . . this is the pneumatic resurrection."[190]

Rom 14:1-15:1: As for the one weak in faith, welcome him, but not into disputes over opinions. For one believes that he can eat anything, but the weak eats only vegetables. Let the one who eats not despise the one who abstains, and the one who abstains not judge the one who eats, for God has welcomed him. Who are you to judge one who belongs to another? One stands or falls before his own Lord. . . . One man observes certain days; another considers every day the same. Let each be fully persuaded in his own mind. Whoever observes the day observes it to the Lord. And whoever eats, eats to the Lord, but gives thanks to God. . . . I know . . . that nothing is unclean in itself; but if anyone considers it unclean, for him it is unclean. . . . The faith that you have, keep between yourself and God. Blessed is the one who does not condemn himself for what he approves. But the one who doubts is condemned if he eats, because it is not from faith. Whatever is not from faith is sin. We who are strong should bear with the weaknesses of the weak. . . .

As Paul considers debates over certain observances—dietary laws, holy days—he discriminates between the "weak in faith" (14:1; 15:1) and those who, like himself, are "strong" (15:1). Interpreting this as the contrast between the psychics and the pneumatic elect, the gnostic would note that "the weak," the psychic, observes dietary restrictions and holy days, as Heracleon observes of the psychic "Jews."[191] The "strong" are to welcome the weak, to avoid arguing with them (14:1) but to maintain their own liberty of conscience as those who "know," as Paul does, that nothing is, in itself, unclean (14:14).

Gnostic Christians, identifying themselves with Paul among the "strong," apparently attempted to follow Paul's advice, and cited him as their authority. Irenaeus says that the Valentinians "do not hesitate to eat meat offered to idols, considering that they cannot in that way be defiled": they freely attend pagan meals, festivals, and (if Irenaeus is to be believed) engage freely in diverse sexual practices and magical arts: in all these matters they claim the liberty of those who are pneumatic.[192] Simon of Samaria similarly quotes Paul in defense of his own freedom, saying that "men are saved by grace, and not on account of their own righteous works."[193] The followers of Carpocrates, declaring that they are saved "by faith and love," consider all other things indifferent, "not good or evil in themselves, but only by convention."[194]

Paul warns, however, that those who are "strong," are not to despise the rest for their weakness (14:3), nor are they to allow their own liberty to offend the psychics (14:13-21). He commands the psychics not to presume to judge the pneumatic—"for God has welcomed him": "who are you," he asks the psychic, "to judge one who belongs to another"—to the Father? All are to do what they do "in honor of the Lord," and "giving thanks to God": for finally "each of us shall give his own account to God" (14:12).

In closing he advises the "strong" to keep their faith a secret "between yourselves and God" (14:22), not offending the psychics, so that "together you may glorify the God and Father of our Lord Jesus Christ" (15:6). For he acknowledges to the "Gentiles" whom he praises and blesses (15:13-17) that "you yourselves are full of goodness, having been filled with all gnosis, and are fully capable of admonishing others" (15:14). He praises the "grace" through which he has come to preach "the gospel of God" (15:16), the pneumatic gospel, adding that "I know that when I come to you I shall come in the fullness (*pleroma*) of Christ's blessing (15:29)." Finally, he commends them "to the One Wise God, through Jesus Christ, among the aions" (16:27).

NOTES: ROMANS

1. Valentinian exegetes consistently characterize the psychics as slaves; cf. CJ 6.20 (6.39;20.38); Exc 56.3-57 (cf. F. Sagnard, *Extraits de Théodote* [Paris: Sources Chrétiennes 23, 1948], 175, n. 4). For discussion, see E. Pagels, *The Johannine Gospel in Gnostic Exegesis* (Nashville: Abingdon, 1973), 54-57.

2. On contrast between "the called" (ἡ κλῆσις) and "the elect" (ἡ ἐκλογή) , cf. Exc 21.1; 39; 58.1; CJ 13.31-51.

3. CR 1.1 (*JTS* 13.210). On Paul as pneumatic by birth, see CJ 2.20; cf. AH 1.8.1; 3.13.1.

4. CR 1.1; on Sophia as mother, see references on 1 Cor 15:8.

5. Cf. discussion of Phil 2:7-9.

6. On David as image of the demiurge, cf. Exc 62.1; for discussion see E. Pagels, "The Valentinian Claim to Esoteric Exegesis of Romans," *Vig Chr* 26 (1972), 224, 252-253. On the demiurge as ruler, see CJ 20.38; as "petty king" (βασιλικός) CJ 13.60.

7. On demiurge as "father" of mankind "according to the flesh," see Ref 6.34; AH 1.5.1-6.

8. Exc 23.2-4:

   Ἐν τύπῳ δὲ Παρακλήτου ὁ Παῦλος ἀναστάσεως Ἀπόστολος γέγονεν...Διὸ καὶ καθ᾽ ἑκάτερον ἐκήρυξε τὸν Σωτῆρα • γεννητὸν καὶ παθητὸν διὰ τοὺς ἀριστερούς, ὅτι τοῦτον γνῶναι δυνηθέντες κατὰ τὸν τόπον τοῦτον δεδίασιν • καὶ κατὰ τὸ πνευματικὸν ἐξ ἁγίου Πνεύματος καὶ Παρθένου, ὡς οἱ δεξιοὶ ἄγγελοι γινώσκουσιν.

9. AH 3.12.6-7: The Valentinians claim that Peter's preaching was limited to the demiurgic message addressed to "the Jews," that is, to the psychic church, typified as "Israel" (AH 4.30.3). Peter "was imperfect" (or: uninitiated: imperfectus, ἀτελής) and "did not possess perfect gnosis" (3.12.6-7). This means that he had not received the truth conveyed through secret, oral tradition: for

   > they claim that the truth was not transmitted by means of written documents, but in living speech (*non enim per literas traditam illam, sed per vivam vocem*) and that therefore Paul said, "we speak wisdom among the perfect (or: initiates: Σοφίαν δὲ λαλοῦμεν ἐν τοῖς τελείοις) but not the wisdom of this age" (3.2.1: cf. 1 Cor 2:6).

   Note also EP 99.29-100.19; 103.28-30; cf. discussion of Gal 1:1-8. For discussion see P. Perkins, "Peter in Gnostic Revelation," in: *SBL Seminar Papers*, II, 1974, 1-13.

10. Cf. AH 3.5.1-10.5 for Irenaeus' refutation.

11. AV 2: Tertullian complains that "we are called by them simple" and "are considered foolish because we are simple": he answers that the Valentinians are the fools. Similarly Irenaeus (AH 3.15.2) and Hippolytus (Ref *Praefatio*).

12. AH 1.8.3; Ref 6.34: see discussion of this passage below.

13. CJ 13.25: Heracleon says that only those who are pneumatic, being "of the same nature as the Father" (αὐτοὶ τῆς αὐτῆς φύσεως ὄντες τῷ πατρὶ πνεῦμα εἰσιν...) worship "in spirit and in truth," citing Paul's statement in Rom 12:1: καὶ ὁ ἀπόστολος διδάσκει λέγων λογικὴν λατρείαν τὴν τοιαύτην θεοσέβειαν.

14. AH 3.2.1; cf. n. 9 above.

15. AH 3.3.1: As "the apostles knew 'hidden mysteries' which they used to impart to 'the perfect' apart from the rest, in secret"; so the Valentinians themselves allegedly having received such initiation, offer to disclose to others "in secret, the ineffable mystery of their pleroma" (AH 3.15.2).

16. AH 1.8.2; Ref 6.35.;

Πάντες οὖν οἱ προφῆται καὶ ὁ νόμος ἐλάλησαν ἀπὸ τοῦ δημιουργοῦ, μωροῦ λέγει θεοῦ, μωροὶ οὐδὲν εἰδότες...Ὅτε οὖν τέλος ἔλαβεν ἡ κτίσις, καὶ ἔδει λοιπὸν γενέσθαι τὴν ἀποκάλυψιν τῶν υἱῶν τοῦ θεοῦ, τουτέστι τοῦ δημιουργοῦ, τὴν ἐγπεπαλυμμένην, ἥν, φησίν, ἐγκεκάλυπτο ὁ ψυχικὸς ἄνθρωπος, καὶ εἶχε κάλυμμε ἐπὶ τὴν καρδίαν.

17. Valentinus, Fragment 5 (strom 4.89.6-90.1):

Ὁπόσον ἐλάττων ἡ εἰκὼν τοῦ ζῶντος προσώπου, τοσοῦτον ἥσσων ὁ κόσμος τοῦ ζῶντος αἰῶνος. τίς οὖν αἰτία τῆς εἰκόνος; μεγαλωσύνη τοῦ προσώπου παρεσχημένου τῷ ζωγράφῳ τὸν τύπον, ἵνα τιμηθῇ δι᾽ ὀνόματος αὐτοῦ • οὐ γὰρ αὐθεντικῶς εὑρέθη μορφή, ἀλλὰ τὸ ὄνομα ἐπλήρωσεν τὸ ὑστερῆσαν ἐν πλάσει. συνεργεῖ δὲ καὶ τὸ τοῦ θεοῦ ἀόρατον εἰς πίστιν τοῦ πεπλασμένου.

18. Exc 47.2. According to AH 1.5.1, Sophia, herself "in the image of the invisible Father," formed the demiurge in the image of the Son, or "image of the anthropos" (cf. Rom 1:23).

19. AH 1.17.1-2.

20. AH 1.3.1: "They claim that Paul frequently mentions the divine aions above. . . ." Cf. Eph 3.21.

21. Cf. AH 1.5.1-2; 1.4.5; Exc 47.1:

Πρῶτος μὲν οὖν Δημιουργὸς ὁ Σωτὴρ γίνεται καθολικός• ἡ δὲ Σοφία δευτέρα οἰκοδομεῖ οἶκον ἑαυτῇ...

CG 11,2:35.10-37.36. For discussion, see Sagnard, Extraits, 159: Pagels, "The Valentinian Claim," 246.

22. CJ 13.19:

...οἱ πρότεροι προσκυνηταὶ ἐν σαρκὶ καὶ πλάνῃ προσεκύνουν τῷ μὴ πατρί... ἐλάτρευον τῇ κτίσει, καὶ οὐ τῷ κατ᾽ ἀλήθειαν κτίστῃ, ὅς ἐστιν Χριστός, εἴ γε Πάντα δι᾽ αὐτοῦ ἐγένετο...

On the savior as creator, see AH 1.4.5; Exc 47.1.

23. AH 1.8.5: Aletheia together with the Nous constitutes the second syzygy of the primary tetrad.

24. CJ 20.28 (cf. Jn 8:44): the devil, constituted of error and ignorance, is "of the very nature of the lie."

25. CJ 13.19; 13.51.

26. Cf. AH 1.6.1.

27. AH 1.6.4; cf. discussion of 1 Cor 10:23.

28. These terms include: πάθη (sufferings); ἄρρην/θῆλυς (male/female); φύσις (nature); ἀσχημοσύνη (disgrace); πλάνη (error).

29. Ref 5.7 recounts the Naassene exegesis of Rom 1:20-27; for discussion see E. Pagels, "The Valentinian Claim," 247, n. 24.

30. Cf. Exc 21.1-3; EP 71, 78. Cf. discussion G. Quispel, Makarius, Das Thomasevangelium und Das Lied von der Perle (Leiden: Brill, 1967), 57-60.

31. AH 3.15.2; a course of action that Irenaeus strongly endorses; 4.26.3-4; 5.26.2.

32. Exc 21.1-3.

33. AH 3.14.1-2: Irenaeus objects that Paul never taught (as they claim) esoteric "mysteries" different from his preaching, nor did he practice any duplicity.

34. CJ 20.38.

35. CJ 13.20.

36. AH 1.21.5:

...Ἔρχεσθαι δὲ ἐπὶ τοὺς περὶ τὸν Δημιουργὸν, καὶ λέγειν...Σκεῦός εἰμι ἔντιμον, μᾶλλον παρὰ τὴν θήλειαν τὴν ποιήσασαν ὑμᾶς...καὶ ἐπικαλοῦμαι τὴν ἄφθαρτον Σοφίαν, ἥτις ἐστὶν ἐν τῷ Πατρί...ἐγὼ δὲ ἐπικαλοῦμαι αὐτῆς τὴν μητέρα. Τούτους δὲ τοὺς περὶ τὸν Δημιουργὸν ἀκούσαντας σφόδρα ταραχθῆναι...

37. Ref 7.27; for Valentinian definition of the "inner anthropos," see Tertullian, DR 40:45.
38. Ref 6.34.
39. *JTS* 9.239: EF 5.9-11:

κατὰ μὲν τὸ φαινόμενον καὶ τὸ σωματικῶς ἐκτελεῖσθαι ἀνῃρέθη,. κατὰ δὲ τὸ πνευματικὸν ἀνελήφθη...καὶ περιτομὴν περιτετμῆσθαι ἡμᾶς βούλεται, ἀλλ' οὐχὶ τῆς ἀκροβυστίας τῆς σωματικῆς, ἀλλὰ καρδίας τῆς πνευματικῆς.

Cf. ET 53: . . . "The true circumcision in spirit (ПC̅BBE M̅ME HM̅ ΠN̅A̅) has become profitable in every way."
40. Scherer, 168-169, n. 15.
41. Exc 56.5.
42. *JTS* 9.239; AH 1.8.3; Ref 6.34; see discussion of 1 Cor 2:14.
43. ET 55.
44. AH 1.7.3-4; Ref 6.35; CJ 13.19.
45. For discussion, cf. Pagels, "Valentinian Claim," 249; cf. CJ 2.21.
46. *JTS* 13.218.
47. Scherer, 126.
48. AH 1.19.1:

Ἀναγκαῖον ἡγησάμην προσθεῖναι τούτοις καὶ ὅσα περὶ τοῦ Προπάτορος αὐτῶν, ὃς ἄγνωστος ἦν τοῖς πᾶσι πρὸ τῆς τοῦ Χριστοῦ παρουσίας...ἵν' ἐπιδείξωσι τὸν Κύριον ἡμῶν ἄλλον καταγγέλλοντα Πατέρα παρὰ τὸν ποιητὴν τοῦδε τοῦ παντός...Καὶ διὰ 'Ωσηὲ τὸ εἰρημένον. Οὐκ ἔστιν ἐν αὐτοῖς ἀλήθεια, οὐδὲ ἐπίγνωσις Θεοῦ, εἰς τὸ αὐτὸ συντείνειν βιάζονται. Καὶ, οὐκ ἔστιν ὁ συνιῶν, ἢ ἐκζητῶν τὸν Θεόν • πάντες ἐξέκλιναν, ἅμα ἠχρειώθησαν ἐπὶ τῆς τοῦ Βυθοῦ ἀγνωσίας τάττοοσι.

49. Exc 23.2.
50. EV 17.5-8, 36.15; ET 2, 92; A.H. 1.2.2; CJ 13.26.
51. Scherer, 143, 186; 200-204; EP 122.5-12.
52. AH 1.6.4; Exc 67.1.
53. Scherer, 157-160; cf. Pagels, "Valentinian Claim," 250.
54. CJ 10.19.
55. AH 1.8.2.
56. AH 3.12.7; for discussion, see Pagels, "Valentinian View of Baptism and Eucharist."
57. Scherer, 168: Irenaeus, like Origen, objects to the Valentinian claim that "the god of the Jews" differs from "the god of the Christians"; AH 3.12.6-7.
58. Scherer, 174.
59. Ref 6.34:

Προέβαλε καὶ ὁ δημιουργὸς ψυχάς • αὕτη γὰρ οὐσία ψυχῶν • οὗτός ἐστι κατ' αὐτοὺς Ἀβραὰμ καὶ ταῦτα τοῦ Ἀβραὰμ τὰ τέκνα.

60. ꙋcnerer, 220.
61. CJ 13.51; Exc 36.2.
62. AH 4.8.1-3.
63. CJ 13.60.
64. Scherer, 200-204.
65. AH 1.5.6: for discussion of the two elements of the seed, see: E. Pagels. "Conflicting Versions of Valentinian Eschatology: Irenaeus' Treatise vs. the Excerpts from Theodotus," *HTR* 67.1 (1974): 35-44.
66. Exc 22.1; Ev Ver 28.10; Scherer, 168, n. 15: see discussion of 1 Cor 1:26-27.

67. Exc 68; 79-80. On Valentinian allegorical exegesis of the parable of Gal 4:24ff, see Exc 56.5-57.
68. Scherer, 220: Valentinian exegetes reserve these epithets for the Father.
69. Exc 69.1-74.2.
70. Exc 67.1.
71. Exc 73.1-3; see discussion of Rom 7:14-25.
72. Exc 67.4; 72.1-74.2.
73. Exc 54.1: Abel, "the just" (ὁ δίκαιος)·symbolizes the psychic nature; cf. AH 1.7.5; Ref 5.20.2.
74. CJ 10.19.
75. AH 1.8.2-3.
76. AH 1.6.1.
77. Exc 59.1-3; 23.1-3.
78. CJ 20.38; see discussion of Rom 13:1-7.
79. Ref 7.25.
80. Strom 4.89.
81. Exc 47.1.
82. Exc 58.1.
83. Of these cosmic powers, Theodotus says:

Διάφοροι δ' εἰσὶν καὶ οἱ ἀστέρες καὶ αἱ δυνάμεις, ἀγαθοποιοὶ κακοποιοί, δεξιοὶ ἀριστεροί...οἳ μὲν ὑπὲρ ἡμῶν, οἳ δὲ καθ' ἡμῶν παρατάσσονται. Οἳ μὲν γὰρ στρατιώταις ἐοίκασι, συμμαχοῦντες ἡμῖν, ὡς ἄν ὑπηρέται Θεοῦ • οἱ δὲ λῃσταῖς.

Exc 71.2-72.2; cf. 73.1-2.
84. Exc 58.1-3.
85. CJ 13.51.
86. Ibid., also Exc 36.1-2.
87. Exc 21.1-3.
88. Exc 80.1-3; on death as metaphor of cosmic existence. Cf. Ex. 22.2; CG 11.1:1.38; 3.37; EV 25.12.19; ER 44.20-21.
89. Exc 36.1-2.
90. CJ 13.25; 13.51; 2.21.
91. Strom 4.91.2-4·

...ἐπὶ τὸ καταλῦσαι θάνατον ἀφικνεῖται τὸ διαφέρον γένος...σὺν Χριστῷ καταστρατεύεσθαι τοῦ θανάτου λέγοιεν...ὡς τῆς θείας τοῦ Δημιουργοῦ κατατρέχειν τολμῶσι συνάμεως, τὴν κτίσιν τὴν αὐτοῦ ὡς κρείττους ἐπανορθούμενοι, πειρώμενοι σώζειν τὴν ψυχικὴν εἰκόνα, ἣν αὐτὸς ῥύσασθαι τῆς φθορᾶς οὐ κατίσχυσεν.

92. AH 1.6.1.
93. JTS 10.46f.
94. AH 2.31.2; Tertullian, DR 19.
95. ER 45.14-28.
96. ER 48.31-38.
97. Exc 77.1-2:

Ταύτῃ θάνατος καὶ τέλος λέγεται τοῦ παλαιοῦ βίου τὸ βάπτισμα, ἀποτασσομένων ἡμῶν ταῖς πονηραῖς Ἀρχαῖς, ζωὴ δὲ κατὰ Χριστόν, ἧς μόνος αὐτὸς κυριεύει. Ἡ δύναμις δὲ τῆς μεταβρλῆς τοῦ βαπτισθέντος οὐ περὶ τὸ σῶμα (ὁ αὐτὸς γὰρ ἀναβαίνει), ἀλλὰ περὶ ψυχήν.

98. Exc 80.1:

Ὃν γεννᾷ ἡ Μήτηρ εἰς θάνατον ἄγεται καὶ εἰς κόσμον • ὃν δὲ ἀναγεγγᾷ Χριστὸς εἰς ζωὴν μετατίθεται, εἰς Ὀγδοάδα. Καὶ ἀποθνήσκουσιν μὲν τῷ κόσμῳ, ζῶσι δὲ τῷ Θεῷ, ἵνα θάνατος θανάτῳ λυθῇ, ἀναστάσει δὲ ἡ φθορά.

99. Exc 76.1-2.
100. Exc 80.3; EP 67.

101. AH 1.3.4; CJ 10.33: Tertullian, DR 19.
102. AH 1.21.4:

...εἶναι τὴν γνῶσιν ἀπολύτρωσιν τοῦ ἔνδον ἀνθρώπου...πνευματικὴν οὖν δεῖ καὶ τὴν λύτρωσιν ὑπάρχειν · λυτροῦσθαι...τὸν ἔσω ἄνθρωπον τὸν πνευμετικὸν, καὶ ἀρκεῖσθαι αὐτοὺς τῇ τῶν ὅλων ἐπιγνώσει ·

Tertullian interprets "heretical" exegesis of these terms (inner man, outer man) as a contrast between soul and body: *nactae denique haereses duos homines ab apostolo editos, interiorem, id est animam, et exteriorem, id est carnem, salutem guidem animae, id est interiori homini, exitium vero carni, id est exteriori* (cf. 2 Cor 4:16) . . . DR 40; cf. also DR 45.1-8; 19.14.

103. ER 42.22-40; 49.15-30.
104. Tertullian, DR 19.
105. On the "mortal body" as the throne of sin, *JTS* 9.363; on obedience to the devil as enslavement to passions, *Strom* 2.114; CJ 20.24.
106. EP 125.15-31.
107. EP 127.14-15.
108. AH 1.6.1.
109. CJ 20.24.
110. CJ 13.19; EP 132.21.
111. EP 132.20-133.29.
112. Exc 67.1:

Ὅτε ἦμεν ἐν τῇ σαρκί, φησὶν ὁ Ἀπόστολος, ὥσπερ ἔξω τοῦ σώματος λαλῶν. Σάρκα οὖν λέγειν αὐτοῦ φησιν ἐκείνην τὴν ἀσθένειαν, τὴν ἀπὸ τῆς ἄνω Γυναικὸς προβολήν.

113. Exc 67.1-6.
114. EP 122.3-12.
115. ER 44.20-21.
116. Origen, CR 5:1: *"Ego," inquit (scil. Paulus), "mortuus sum"; coepit enim iam mihi reputari peccatum . . . Dixit enim, inquit apostolus, quia "ego vivebam sine lege aliquando," hoc est, antequam in istud corpus venirem, in ea specie corporis vixi, quae sub lege non esset . . ."*
117. EF 6.6:

ταῦτα δὲ...καὶ ὁ ἀπόστολος Παῦλος ἔδειξε...τὸ δὲ τοῦ συμπεπλεγμένου νόμου τῇ ἀδικίᾳ, εἰπὼν τὸν νόμον τῶν ἐντολῶν ἐν δόγμασι κατηργῆσθαι. τὸ δὲ τοῦ ἀσυμπλόκου τῷ χείρονι, ὁ μὲν νόμος, εἰπών, ἅγιος, καὶ ἡ ἐντολὴ ἁγία καὶ δικαία καὶ ἀγαθή.

118. *Strom* 2.114.3-6.
119. EP 131.25-28.
120. CJ 13.10-15.
121. Exc 52.1:

Τοῦτο τὸ σαρκίον ἀντίδικον ὁ Σωτὴρ εἶπεν καὶ ὁ Παῦλος νόμον ἀντιστρατευόμενον τῷ νόμῳ τοῦ νοός μου · καὶ δῆσαι παραινεῖ καὶ ἁρπάσαι ὡς ἰσχυροῦ τὰ σκεύη τοῦ ἀντιπολεμοῦντος τῇ οὐρανίῳ ψυχῇ......

122. CJ 13.60; ER 44.20-21.
123. ER 57.17-26.
124. CJ 2.21.
125. CJ 13.25.
126. AH 1.13.6:

Εἶναί τε αὐτοὺς ἐν ὕψει ὑπὲρ πᾶσαν δύναμιν · δ ὦ καὶ ἐλευθέρως πάντα πράσσειν... Διὰ γὰρ τὴν ἀπολύτρωσιν ἀκρατήτους καὶ ἀοράτους γίνεσθαι τῷ κριτῇ.

127. CJ 20.38; cf. AH 1.6.1-3.
128. CJ 13.60; ER 44.20-21: the "law of nature" is "death"; cf. 45.23-46.19.

129. See Tertullian, DC 16 for exegetical discussion of Rom 8.3; DC 17 for indication that Alexander follows Valentinus.
130. See discussion of Rom 2:14-15.
131. ER 49.9-16.
132. CJ 13.25.
133. For the heresiologists' refutation of Valentinian exegesis of Rom 8:8-11, see DC 46; AH 5.10.2-13.5. For this term
   (τὸν ἐγείραντα ᾽Ιησοῦν τὸν Κύριον ἡμῶν ἐκ νεκρῶν)
   as an epithet of the Father, see Scherer, 220 on Rom 4:24.
134. Cf. AH 5.3.3; 5.7.1-2; 15.2; Tertullian, DR 46.
135. AH 5.7.1; Ref 6.35; Tertullian, DR 46; Exc 22.2; for references and discussion, see: E. Pagels "The Mystery of the Resurrection," *JBL* 93.2 (1974): 283-287.
136. Tertullian, DR 35; 46.
137. For Tertullian's counter-argument, see DR 18. Cf. Exc 61.5-8; see discussion of 1 Corinthians 15.
138. CJ 13.38; see discussion of Rom 9:10-18.
139. CJ 13.16; for discussion, see Pagels, *Johannine Gospel*, 103-104.
140. CJ 13.19; Exc 49.1-2; Ref. 7.25-27.
141. Exc 49.1-2. The author of the Gospel of Philip, who alludes to Jn 8:32-36 to describe the one who has "gnosis of the truth" as the free man who does not sin (EP 125.15-18), may refer as well to Rom 8:20 when he adds that "whoever is a slave against his will will be able to become free (EP 127.14-15; cf. 133.28-30).
142. Exc 49.2:
   Τεκμήριον δὲ μάλιστα τοῦ ἀκουσίου τὸ εὐλογεῖν τὸ σάββατον καὶ τὴν ἀπὸ τῶν πόνων ἀνάπαυσιν ὑπερασπάξεσθαι.
143. Ref 7.25:
   Καὶ ἡ κτίσις αὐτὴ συστενάξει καὶ συνωδίνει τὴν ἀποκάλυψιν τῶν υἱῶν τοῦ θεοῦ ἐχδεχομένη Ὑιοὶ δέ, φησίν, ἐσμὲν ἡμεῖς οἱ πνευματικοί...
144. Ref 7.26-27.
145. Exc 58.1; AH 1.8.3; see discussion of Rom 11:16.
146. Exc 30.2-31.3.
147. Cf. discussion of Rom 8:10 above.
148. Exc 35.3-4.
149. ER 46.25-32.
150. CJ 20.38.
151. Exc 62.1-2.
152. CJ 13.20-25.
153. AH 1.3.5; CJ 13.19.
154. CJ 10.33.
155. Ref 6.34.
156. De Prin 3.1.18.
157. Ibid., 3.1.7.
158. For discussion, see Pagels "The Valentinian Claim," 241-258.
159. AH 1.6.2; Exc 2.1-3.2; for discussion, see Sagnard, *La Gnose Valentinienne*, 567-618; G. Quispel, "La conception de l'homme dans la gnose valentinienne," in: *Eranos Jahrbuch* 15 (1947): 249-286.
160. EV 26.8-15.
161. ET 50.
162. CJ 20.38.
163. CJ 13.17-19.

164. See discussion of 1 Cor 1:10.
165. AH 3.16.1; 3.16.6; 3.16.8; 4.33.3.
166. Ref 5.7; 6.34; CJ 13.19.
167. AH 1.7.3.
168. Ref 6.34.
169. CJ 13.19.
170. AH 1.16.2-3; 1.21.4; 2.1.1; 2.3.2; 2.28.4.
171. AH 1.8.3:

> Ὅτι ἰδὼν ἤμελλε σώξειν ὁ Σωτήρ, τούτων τὰς ἀπαρχὰς ἀνέλαβε, τὸν Παῦλον εἰρηκέναι· Καὶ ἦν ἡ ἀπαρχὴ ἀγία, καὶ τὸ φύραμα. Ἀπαρχὴν μὲν τὸ πνευματικὸν εἰρῆσθαι διδάσκοντες · φύραμα δὲ ἡμᾶς, τουτέστι τὴν ψυχικὴν Ἐκκλησίαν, ἧς τὸ φύραμα ἀνειληφέναι λέγουσιν αὐτόν. καὶ ἐν αὐτῷ συνεσταλκέναι, ἐπειδὴ ἦν αὐτὸς ζύμη.

Exc 1.2-2.2 describes how the "elect seed" acts as "leaven" to "raise" the rest.
172. Exc 58.1-2.
173. Ref 6.30; AH 1.1.1; 1.2.1; 1.14.21; 1.21.5; CG 11,1:21.32-40; CG 11,2:23.19-23. See Sagnard, Gnose, 654, for other references.
174. CG 11,1:21.32-40.
175. EV 28.16-18.
176. Exc 56.4.
177. Exc 56.4-6:

> Ὅταν οὖν τὰ ψυχικὰ ἐγκεντρισθῇ τῇ καλλιελαίῳ εἰς πίστιν καὶ ἀφθαρσίαν, καὶ μετάσχῃ τῆς πιότητος τῆς ἐλαίας, καὶ ὅταν εἰσέλθη τὰ ἔθνη, τότε οὕτω πᾶς Ἰσραήλ...Ἰσραὴλ δὲ ἀλληγορεῖται ὁ πνευματικός, ὁ ὀψόμενος τὸν Θεόν...

178. See discussion of 1 Cor 15:50-57.
179. AH 1.3.4.
180. CJ 13.25.
181. CJ 13.38.
182. CG 11,2:36.28-34.
183. See discussion of Rom 8:10, 23.
184. CG 11,1:17.28-38.
185. Ibid., 17.20-20.40.
186. AH 5.24.1.
187. CJ 20.38.
188. Exc 2.2-3.1; see discussion of Eph 5:14.
189. CJ 10.37; Exc 61.5.
190. ER 45.28-40.
191. CJ 13.17.
192. AH 1.6.3.
193. AH 1.23.3.
194. AH 1.25.5.

II

1 CORINTHIANS

1 Cor 1:1-3: Paul, called to be an apostle of Jesus Christ through the will of God . . . to the church of God which is (*tē ousē*) in Corinth, to those sanctified in Christ Jesus, to those called to be holy, with all who call upon the name of our Lord Jesus Christ in every place, yours and ours. Grace to you and peace from God our Father and from the Lord Jesus Christ.

Paul's greeting discloses to the Valentinian initiate how he discriminates between the psychic and pneumatic aspects of himself, his audience, and his message. As in his greeting to the Romans, he acknowledges first himself in psychic terms, as one "called," and secondly designates himself as a pneumatic apostle "through the will of God" (1:1).[1]

Next he speaks to "the ecclesia of God which is (being) in Corinth." Is Paul thinking literally—merely specifying geographical location? Valentinian exegetes suggest that the mature reader will recognize the metaphysical meaning of the phrase: those who are "of God," who alone truly "is," themselves participate in true being.[2] Paul distinguishes these as pneumatics from those who are only "called to be holy" (1:2).[3]

Although Paul discriminates again in 1:2 between the "called" and those who "call upon the *name* of our Lord Jesus Christ" (the *name*, Theodotus says, refers to the invisible divine being),[4] he blesses all according to their capacity: "grace" as the gift from "God our Father" to the pneumatics,[5] and "peace" which the "Lord" (1:3) conveys to psychics.[6]

1 Cor 1:4-9: I thank God always because of you, for the grace of God given to you in Jesus Christ, that you were enriched in every way in him, in every logos and every gnosis . . . so that you lack no charismatic gift . . . who also will secure you to the

53

end, blameless in the day of our Lord Jesus Christ. God is faithful, by whom you were called into the communion of his son Jesus Christ our Lord.

Paul speaks first to those who already have been "enriched in every logos and every gnosis" and "lack no charismatic gift." But the Valentinian could infer from 1:8-9 that he speaks to others—apparently psychics—in very different terms. Since they have not yet received gnosis nor have they attained perfection, he prays that God will sustain them until the end, even in the judgment (1:8), assuring them that it is God the Father who has called them into communion with "the Lord Jesus Christ" (1:9).

1 Cor 1:10-12: I entreat you, brothers, through the name of our Lord Jesus Christ, that you all confess the same thing, and there be no schisms among you; that you all be joined in the same mind and the same intention. For it has been shown to me . . . that there are rivalries among you. I mean that each of you says, "I am of Paul," or "I am of Apollos," or "I am of Peter," or "I am of Christ."

Now Paul takes up the concern that motivates his letter — the schisms that divide the Christian community. In the pneumatic "name" of the psychic "Lord" he pleads that "you all make a common confession, and there be no schisms among you" (1:10). What are these schisms?

He explains in 1:12 that some claim allegiance to himself or to Apollos, others to Peter. The Valentinian initiate could recognize these immediately as schisms between pneumatic Christians who follow the secret teaching of Paul, which Paul's disciple Theudas transmitted to Valentinus himself,[7] and the psychic Christians who follow Peter, founder of the psychic church.[8] For although Paul himself discriminates in 2:4 between his *logos* (his pneumatic teaching) and his *kerygma* (the psychic preaching),[9] he insists that all "confess the same thing" in order to end futile and destructive schisms within the community. Valentinian Christians attempt to follow his advice, as Irenaeus admits: "they appear to be like us in public, repeating the same words (of confession) we do."[10] But, he adds, "although they certainly do 'confess Jesus Christ with the mouth' they make fools of themselves, saying one thing and thinking another . . . they keep asking us, how it is that when they confess the same things and hold the same doctrine, we call them heretics!"[11]

1 Cor 1:14-17: I am thankful that I baptized no one . . . for Christ did not send me to baptize but to evangelize, not in wisdom (*sophia*) of logos (*logos*), lest the cross of Christ be emptied.

Here Paul contrasts his own mission with that of the other apostles. For the psychic apostles, notably Peter, preach and baptize "with water," offering to psychics forgiveness of sins,[12] but Paul says that he has been sent "not to baptize but to evangelize." But he admits that when he preaches publicly he refrains from teaching "in*wisdom of logos," that is, concerning Sophia!

1 Cor 1:18-20: For the discourse (*logos*) of the cross is foolishness to those who are perishing, although to those of us who are saved, it is the power of God, for it is written, "I will destroy the wisdom of the wise, and set aside the understanding of those who understand." Where is the wise? Where is the scribe? Where is the investigator of this age? Has not God made foolish the wisdom of this age (*tou aiōnos toutou*)?

Why does Paul withhold the "wisdom of logos" (1:17) from his public preaching? The Valentinians explain (1:18) that the "logos of the cross"— the secret doctrine that reveals how the cross symbolizes Sophia's (wisdom's) fall and restoration[13]—seems only "foolishness to those who are perishing," that is, to psychics. Psychics believe only what they see with their own eyes: they need to witness "works of power." The savior, recognizing this, says to them, "unless you see signs and wonders, you will not believe" (Jn 4:48), showing (as Heracleon explains) they "must be persuaded to believe through sense-perception, and not through *logos.*"[14]

Yet the psychics who regard the divine logos as "foolishness" only show how foolish they are themselves. Paul has explained in Rom 1:25 that the psychics have "become fools," dominated by the foolish demiurge,[15] who has vowed to "destroy the wisdom of the wise, and set aside the understanding of those who understand" (1:19). The "wise," the pneumatics, have no place in the present age: for them the "wisdom of this age," of the demiurge, is itself mere foolishness (1:20).

1 Cor 1:21-24: For since, in the wisdom (*sophia*) of God, the cosmos did not know God through wisdom (*sophia*), God was pleased through the foolishness of the kerygma to save those who believe. Since the Jews ask for signs, and the Greeks seek wisdom (*sophia*), we preach Christ crucified, to the Jews a scandal, to the Gentiles foolishness, but to those who are called, both Jews and Greeks, Christ, the power of God and the wisdom of God.

Is the conflict between the foolish wisdom "of this age" (1:20) and the apparent "foolishness" of God's wisdom irreconcilable? Paul answers no: since the psychic "cosmos" proved incapable of knowing God through his wisdom (*sophia*), God has accommodated his revelation to the psychics' own limited and foolish capacity — he "was pleased through the foolishness of the *kerygma* to save those who believed" (1:21). Because the psychics ("Jews") seek signs, and the pneumatics ("Greeks") seek wisdom (*sophia*), Paul preaches the message in the form accessible to the greatest number: "we preach Christ crucified" (1:23). Although psychics ("the Jews") find his message a scandal, and the pneumatics ("the Greeks") consider it foolish, Paul insists that this kerygmatic message speaks to each of them in different ways. The psychics receive it psychically as the "power of God," and the pneumatic "Gentiles" receive it spiritually as the "wisdom of God" (1:24).

1 Cor 1:26-28: Consider your calling, brothers, that (it includes) not many who are wise, according to the flesh not many who are powerful, not many who are wellborn; but God chose what is foolish in the cosmos to shame the wise, and what is weak in the cosmos to shame the strong. God chose what is nothing in the cosmos, and what was despised, even those that are not, to bring to nothing those who are. . . .

Among the "many" psychics who are "called," only "a few" are "wise, powerful, and wellborn" in human terms (that is, "according to the flesh").[16] But Valentinian exegetes note Paul's ironic inversion of values in 1:27-28: God has elected those that seem "foolish" to shame "the wise," that is, to shame "those who considered themselves wise . . . but were not truly wise."[17] He chose the "hidden ones" who seem "weak" and "despised" in the cosmos, but who, according to the Gospel of Philip, are "those revealed in the truth"; in reality they are "strong and honored."[18] God has chosen those "unbegotten of the cosmos," those who in cosmic terms are "nothing," even those who "do not exist" to shame "those who are." For whoever preceives not "according to the flesh" but "according to the spirit" recognizes that in reality it is the elect who are "wise, powerful, wellborn"; that from the pneumatic viewpoint, it is the psychics who are "foolish, weak, those who are not, are nothing."[19] So, as the author of the Epistle to Rheginos declares· to his fellow pneumatics, "we are elected . . . predestined from the beginning not to fall into the foolishness of those who are without gnosis . . . but we shall enter into the wisdom of those who have known the truth."[20]

1 Cor 1:29-31: . . . so that no one may boast before God. For you are from him in Christ Jesus, who was begotten as wisdom (*sophia*) for us from God, righteousness and sanctification and redemption (*apolytrōsis*). As it is written, "whoever boasts, let him boast in the Lord!"

Why has God chosen in this way to humiliate the pneumatic elect? Paul answers this in 1:29: so that none of them may boast before God the Father. They are to recognize that they are elected only "from him" who alone effects true, pneumatic righteousness, sanctification, and redemption. The gnostic reader might note how the apostle adds with some irony that whoever boasts must boast ·"in the *Lord*" since only psychics, who achieve salvation from their own works done in service to the demiurgic Lord may boast of their own achievement (see discussion of Romans 4). The pneumatic redemption excludes all human boasting "before God" (1:29).

1 Cor 2:1-5: And when I came to you, brothers, I did not come proclaiming the mystery of God among you in the superiority of discourse (*logos*) or wisdom (*sophia*). For I decided to know nothing among you except Jesus Christ, even the one who was crucified. And I came to be among you in weakness and in fear and in much trembling, and my discourse (*logos*) and my preaching (*kerygma*) were not in persuasive words of wisdom (*sophia*), but in demonstrations of the spirit and of power, so that your faith might not be in wisdom (*sophia*) of men but in the power of God.

Paul offers himself as an example of the pneumatic who voluntarily humbles himself by preaching to psychics on their own level: "I did not come to you proclaiming the mystery of God to you in the superiority of logos or wisdom" (2:1). On the contrary, he says he deliberately suppressed what he knew of divine wisdom, having "*decided* not to know anything among you but Jesus Christ crucified" (2:2); accommodating his preaching to the limited capacity of those still enslaved to the demiurge.[21] Besides preaching this psychic message, Paul expressed the corresponding psychic emotional attitudes: "I came to be with you in weakness, in fear and trembling" (2:3). Although the apostle discriminates between his pneumatic message (*logos*) and the psychic preaching (*kerygma*), as Origen's Valentinian opponents note, he says he refrained from speaking "in persuasive words (*logoi*) of wisdom (*sophia*)," confining his expression instead to "demonstrations of the spirit and of power" (2:4) so that their faith "might not be in the wisdom of the *anthropoi* but in the *power* of God" (2:5).

1 Cor 2:6-8: We do speak wisdom (*sophia*) among the initiates (the mature, *teleioi*), but not the wisdom of this age or of the archons of this age, who are passing away. But we speak the hidden wisdom (*sophia*) of God in a mystery, which God ordained before the aions for our glory. None of the archons of this age knew this: had they known it, they would not have crucified the Lord of glory.

Valentinian exegetes claim that in these words Paul acknowledges and authorizes the secret wisdom tradition which they themselves have received. For although he decided to preach only "Christ crucified" among the psychics he addresses in 2:2, the apostle himself reveals that "among the initiates we *do speak wisdom*" (2:6). For the apostle knows that "truth cannot be communicated by means of written documents"; it must be spoken—orally communicated—to those who are ready to receive it. The Valentinians cite this passage to explain that for this reason no one who only reads the written scriptures (i.e., the letters of Paul) without having received this oral tradition can understand the deeper meaning.[22]

Yet the wisdom that initiates receive through oral teaching is "not a wisdom of this age or of its archons, who are passing away"; for this, unknown to the demiurge (2:8), is "a secret and hidden wisdom of God" — of the Father: it is the secret mystery of Sophia.[23] The Father ordained this wisdom before the aions (2:7). Basilides explains Paul's statement that "none of the archons of this age knew this" (2:8a) by saying that when the Great Archon (the demiurge) heard the mystery of the divine Mother Sophia, who had brought forth and sustained his power while he ignorantly believed he was the sole "god of the universe," he "was filled with terror, and was silent."[24] Had the archons known this mystery "they would not have crucified the Lord of Glory" (2:8b) for that crucifixion revealed symbolically the fall and restoration of Sophia.[25]

As Paul himself revealed such "wisdom" in secret to such "mature" Christians as Theudas, who in turn initiated Valentinus, so the Valentinians claim they also reveal these mysteries in secret meetings with those who are "initiates."[26]

1 Cor 2:9: But as it is written, "eye has not seen, nor has ear heard, nor has it entered into the heart of man, what God has prepared for those who love him."

The initiated reader would recognize the words of 2:9a, in all probability, as the formula pronounced at his own initiation into gnosis. Hippolytus records the oath of secrecy required of candidates for initiation in Justinus' group:

> If you wish to know "what eye has not seen and ear has not heard, and what has not entered into the heart," that is, if you wish to know Him who is good (*agathos*) above all, Him who is more highly exalted, swear that you will keep the secrets of the discipline as those that are to be kept in silence.[27]

This passage also occurs in the Gospel of Thomas, where Jesus offers the pneumatic initiation: "I will give you 'what eye has not seen, and what ear has not heard,' what has not been touched, and what 'has not arisen in the heart of man.' "[28]

1 Cor 2:10-13: God has revealed this to us through the spirit. For the spirit searches all things, even the deep things (*ta bathe*) of God. For who knows the things of man, but the spirit of mankind that is in him? So also, no one knows the things of God but the spirit of God. Now we have not received the spirit of the cosmos, but the spirit which is from God, that we may perceive the gifts of grace (*charisthenta*) given to us by God. And we speak these things not in words taught by human wisdom, but taught by the spirit, interpreting pneumatic things to those who are pneumatic.

These secret mysteries are revealed "through the spirit" which "searches all things, even the deep things of God" (2:10), which, according to Valentinian exegesis, suggests the mysteries of the divine pleroma.[29] The "soul," being psychic, cannot comprehend these mysteries; only "the spirit" can know them. Paul continues, "We have not received the spirit of the cosmos (i.e., the demiurge) but the spirit of God (the Father)" who alone reveals the "deep things of God," as the Naassenes, Basilides, and the Valentinians agree.[30]

1 Cor 2:14-16: For the psychic (*ho psychichos*) does not receive the things of the spirit of God: they are foolishness to him, and he cannot know them, because they are pneumatically discerned. The pneumatic (*ho pneumatikos*) on the other hand discerns all things, but himself is discerned by no one. For "who has known the mind of the Lord, and who may instruct him?" But we have the mind of Christ!

This passage commands great attention from gnostic theologians. Here, they claim, Paul clearly distinguishes the *psychic* from the *pneumatic* nature. He declares that the demiurge, being psychic, "does not comprehend the things of the spirit," since he, "being psychic, knew neither his Mother, who was pneumatic, nor her seeds, nor the aions of the pleroma";[31] he was "foolish, and lacked understanding, imagining that he himself made the cosmos. But he was ignorant that Sophia, the Mother, the Ogdoad, was really the cause of his activity.[32] Those who, like the demiurge, are psychic have received only the "spirit of the cosmos" (2:12) and consequently lack understanding of pneumatic realities.

Who, then, has "known the mind of the Lord, and who may instruct him?" Who, indeed, but the spirit who instructed the demiurgic "Lord"—and those who have received the same "initiation into gnosis" that "the Lord" himself received?[33] Paul's answer in 2:16 suggests that the *elect* know the "mind of the Lord" because, as he says, "we have the mind of Christ."

1 Cor 3:1-3: And I, brothers, was not able to speak to you as to pneumatics, but as to sarkics, as to those immature in Christ. I fed you milk, not meat, for you were not yet able (to take it). Nor are you now—you are still sarkic. For where there is strife and envy among you, are you not sarkic . . . ?

Paul turns abruptly from praising the pneumatics' spiritual potential to criticizing their actual situation. Although gifted with the spirit, they are still "sarkic, immature in Christ": they are not ready to receive the secret, oral teaching he could offer them.

1 Cor 3:4-9: For when one says, "I am of Paul," and another, "I am of Apollos," are you not merely human? What, then, is Apollos, and what is Paul? Servants through whom you believed, each one as the Lord gave. I planted, Apollos watered, but God increased the growth. The one who plants and the one who waters are one, and each will receive his own reward for his own labor. For we are co-workers with God: you are God's field.

As long as the pneumatics argue about which of the apostles has "generated them in Christ" they demonstrate their spiritual immaturity—failing to realize that they have been generated "from above."[34] As Heracleon says, the pneumatic seed is not sown by the apostles but by the Logos himself.[35] This seed, generated in a state of immaturity, must be clothed with the sarkic garment of materiality,[36] in order to grow in wisdom and strength to maturity.[37]

What Paul says in 3:6-8 can be read pneumatically in terms of this metaphor. The task of planting and watering the seed (cf. 3:5) is entrusted to the demiurge ("the Lord") and to his servants,[38] so that the savior will find it "ripe and ready for harvest" when he comes to reap.[39] The Valentinian could see in 3:6 Paul's allusion to this threefold process of planting, watering, and growth. In this process, Sophia, the savior, and the Father all participate ("I planted, Apollos watered, but God gave the increase"). Yet God the Father alone enacts the entire process, and rewards all who share in the "labor" (3:8).[40] Paul recognizes that he, as an apostle, shares in the process, for those whom he cultivates are "God's field" (3:9). The author of *A Valentinian Exposition* explains that the Father's will is that "every field'" be cultivated and bear fruit;[41] Ptolemy, writing to Flora, expresses hope that the "seed" sown in her as in "good ground" will grow and bear fruit for God.[42]

1 Cor 3:9b-11: . . . you are God's temple. According to the grace of God given to me as a wise architect, I set down a foundation: another builds upon it. Let each one consider how he builds. No one can lay any other foundation than the one that has been set down, which is Christ Jesus.

How is this second metaphor—the construction of the temple—to be interpreted pneumatically? Basilides perceives in this a warning to the demiurge, "for he was ignorant that there is another wiser and more powerful and greater than himself. Recognizing himself as Lord and master and 'wise architect,' he turns to the creation of everything in the cosmos."[43] Yet "another" is actually "building" through him—and this is Sophia, who "built a house for herself"[44] having already "laid the foundation" (3:11). Through the demiurge's creation, Sophia is constructing the "temple"—that is, the *ecclesia*, the totality of those who are to be restored to God.[45]

1 Cor 3:12-15: If anyone builds on the foundation with gold, silver, precious stones, or with wood, hay, and stubble, the work of each shall be revealed, for the day will disclose it. If the work that anyone builds on the foundation survives, he shall receive a reward. If anyone's work is burned up, he shall suffer loss, but himself be saved, as if through fire.

What does Paul mean? Most Christians, taking this literally, anticipate a catastrophic event that will consume the world in flames. Yet according to the Valentinians, only the initiated reader discerns its true, symbolic meaning. Fire symbolizes *ignorance of God*—the source of destruction and death that lies concealed in the elements of the cosmos. At the consummation, this "fire that lies hidden in the cosmos will blaze up and burn," destroying "all materiality."[46] Those wholly involved in materiality (the hylics) will be consumed; the psychics, although they "feel the fire" (cf. 2:13-15),[47] may escape destruction if they pass through the "fiery place" which is the cosmos, stripping off from themselves all "flammable materials"—not only the material body, but also the psychic soul.[48] Paul warns in 3:12-14 that the psychics will be judged on that day for their works—whether they have built with hylic and psychic materials ("wood, hay, stubble") or with the pneumatic substances ("gold, silver, precious stones") that can survive the fire, so that they may progress from the cosmos into the pleroma.[49]

1 Cor 3:16-17: Do you not know that you are the temple of God, and the spirit of God dwells in you? If anyone destroys God's temple, God will destroy him. For God's temple is holy—you are that temple.

To whom is Paul speaking? The initiate would note that now he is speaking to those "in whom God's spirit dwells" (3:16), that is, to the elect. Heracleon offers a detailed interpretation of the temple symbolism. He says that the outer court signifies the cosmos, where psychics worship the demiurge; the inner sanctuary—the holy of holies—signifies the pleroma, where the pneumatics worship the Father "in spirit and in truth."[50]

1 Cor 3:18-23: Let no one deceive himself. If anyone among you seems to be wise in this age, let him become a fool, that he may become wise. For the wisdom of this cosmos is foolishness before God. . . . Let no one boast humanly. For all things are yours, and you are of Christ, and Christ is of God.

Paul concludes by warning the psychics that anyone who considers himself "wise in this age" is "a fool before God" the Father: even the demiurge knows this (3:20; "the Lord knows that the reasonings of the wise are futile"). The apostle admonishes the pneumatics not to boast in any way of their spiritual superiority: what need have they to boast when "all things" are theirs, even the psychic cosmos and its archons? "You are of Christ, and Christ is of God" (3:23).[51]

1 Cor 4:1-5: This is how we should be considered, as servants of Christ, and as administrators of the mysteries of God. Moreover, it is required of administrators that they be found faithful. . . . it is the Lord who judges me. So do not judge anyone before the time when the Lord comes, who will also enlighten the hidden things of darkness and manifest the intentions of the hearts. And then every man shall receive his praise from God.

Here Paul explains apparently, how the elect are to be regarded in the community: both as "servants (*douloi*) of Christ," that is, as psychics, and as "administrators of the mysteries of God," as pneumatic teachers. Those entrusted with these secret mysteries, however, are to be "found faithful," as if they were psychics. Yet they, unlike the psychics, need not fear the judgment of the demiurge ("the Lord"); when the "hidden things" are manifest,[52] they shall receive praise from God (4:5).

1 Cor 4:6: I have spoken metaphorically of myself and Apollos (*meteschematisa eis emauton kai Apollōn*) for your sake, brothers, that you may learn from us not to go beyond what is written (*mathēte to mē hyper ha gegraptai*) so that no one may be puffed up, one against another.

Previously Paul has insisted that the pneumatics make a public confession in common with psychics (1:10); now he tells them that they are "not to go beyond what is written." What is Paul saying? Having admitted already that he himself communicates secret oral teaching to initiates (2:6), he cannot intend to prohibit such teaching in private. He must mean that the pneumatics are not to speak openly of it among psychics, or to allow any difference between themselves and the psychics to become publicly visible (4:7) "so that no one may become arrogant in regard to another" (4:6). The Valentinians read his meaning in this way, at any rate; and Irenaeus testifies that they conduct themselves accordingly. He says that "such persons seem to outward appearance to be sheep; for they appear to be like us, from what they say in public,"[53] but "in private they describe the ineffable mysteries of their pleroma."[54] They themselves could defend such practice as obedience to Paul's counsel of humility.

1 Cor 4:7-8: For who discerns you? What do you have that you did not receive? If you received it, why do you boast as if you had not received it? Already you have been filled; already you have become rich; apart from us you reign. . . .

Since it is the Father who "discerns you" (4:7), and who bestows every blessing pneumatics receive, Paul reminds them that they—unlike the psychics—have no grounds at all for "boasting." The gnostic initiate could read 4:7-8 not as Paul's irony, but as his presentation of the criteria by which the pneumatics recognize their election. For, as Heracleon says, the elect have become "rich" in the "wealth poured down from above";[55] they have become "filled," having received their "fulfillment" (*teleiōsis*);[56] already they "reign" over the demiurge and the archons.[57] If (according to their exegesis) Paul acknowledges that they have received these pneumatic blessings, why does he urge them to keep these blessings secret? The apostle explains that he is using himself, Apollos, and Christ as examples to show that in the present age, the pneumatic is not to enjoy his wealth, but instead is to become poor;[58] not to be "filled," but to "empty" himself;[59] not to reign, but to serve.[60]

1 Cor 4:9-13: I think that God has exhibited us apostles last of all, as those sentenced to death, because we have become a spectacle to the cosmos and to angels and to men . . . We are weak, but you are strong. We are despised, but you are honored. Even to the present time we hunger and thirst and are naked and buffeted and homeless, and we labor, working with our own hands. . . . we have become like the refuse of the cosmos, the offscouring of all things.

Paul himself exemplifies the paradox of the pneumatic's situation: God the Father has exhibited the apostles as men subject "to death" (4:9), that is, to the demiurge's power:[61] "we have become a spectacle to the cosmos, and to angels and to men," that is, to the whole psychic order. While his fellow pneumatics are "wise, strong, and glorious" in Christ, Paul and his companions have become "fools, weak, dishonored." The apostles themselves "work" (4:12) and suffer as psychics, having become "like the refuse of the cosmos," that is, of the psychic order—and even "the offscouring of all things" (that is, apparently, the *abortion* excluded from the pleroma, *ta panta*).[62]

1 Cor 4:14-21: I do not write to shame you, but to admonish you, as my beloved children. . . . I urge you, then, to imitate me. Therefore I sent you Timothy, my beloved and faithful child in the Lord, to remind you of my ways in Christ, as I teach them everywhere in every church. Some are puffed up, as though I were not coming to you, but I will come to you soon, if the Lord wills, and find out not the discourse (*logos*) of those who are puffed up, but their power (*dynamis*). . . . Shall I come to you with a rod, or with love, in the spirit of gentleness?

Why does Paul do this? He explains in 1 Corinthians 9 that he does it for the sake of the psychics; and he urges the elect to imitate him in his labor of love (4:15). Apparently unwilling to commit such a secret teaching to writing, he says he is sending Timothy to show them what he means (4:17). For although Timothy is a Gentile and his "beloved child" (therefore pneumatic like themselves, his "beloved children," 4:14) he, like Paul, conducts himself publicly as a psychic ("faithful in the Lord," 4:17). Timothy will be able to teach them Paul's methods of reaching the psychics. Paul promises to come to them in person as soon as possible, presumably to see how well they have learned this method, since he says that in this case he wants to know what they understand pneumatically (not their *logos*; 4:19) but how effectively they communicate it in psychic terms (their *dynamis*; 4:19). Paul reminds them that he can come either as one sent from the demiurge "with a rod"[63] or as a pneumatic to his brethren, "in the spirit of love" (4:21).

1 Cor 5:1-2: It is actually reported that there is fornication among you, such fornication that is not found among the Gentiles: someone has his father's wife. And you are arrogant! Should not you grieve instead, so that the one who has done this may be removed from your midst?

Paul next takes up a case of "fornication." What does he mean? Heracleon suggests from a different context that the term bears a pneumatic meaning. Interpreting the account of the Samaritan woman in John 4 as an allegory of the pneumatic elect, he explains that her "fornication" signifies her "ignorance of God, of true worship, and of the needs of her own life."[64] Having involved herself with the "six men" who symbolize her involvement with "all material evil,"[65] she participates in an illegitimate, inauthentic relationship that substitutes for her true, pneumatic relationship to her "own husband," her spiritual identity.[66]

Yet in the passage above, Paul declares that this case of "fornication" differs entirely from that found "among the Gentiles," that is, among those who are pneumatic (like the Samaritan woman). The term could not be taken literally in regard to pneumatics, since they need not observe actual sexual prohibitions.[67] "Among the Gentiles," then, the term may signify the immature involvement with materiality that precedes mature spiritual self-realization. But here Paul condemns those he addresses for tolerating libertine behavior, even for being *proud* of it (5:2), as if attempting to prove that they too are free from the law, as are the elect. Since they are psychics, they ought to "grieve instead," for they, being "of the world," must practice continence and good works to attain salvation.[68] Paul therefore prescribes strong discipline.

1 Cor 5:3-5: For I, absent in (relation to) the body, but present in the spirit, already have judged the one who has done this in the name of the Lord Jesus. When you are gathered together, and my spirit is with you, with the power of our Lord Jesus, you are to deliver this man to Satan for the destruction of the flesh, so that his spirit may be saved in the day of the Lord.

Paul, being pneumatic, lives apart from the body and its concerns, "present in the spirit" alone.[69] He decides that the community is to join with his "spirit" and with the demiurgic judge ("the *power* of our Lord Jesus") to deliver the guilty one to Satan, the power of materiality. Since they claim that the evil plaguing the psychic resides in the "flesh,"[70] the Valentinians take this to mean that both the *flesh* and the *psychic body* (the lower element of the soul)[71] must be destroyed so that the "spirit" hidden within can be released at the judgment.[72]

1 Cor 5:6-8: Your boasting is not good. Do you not know that a little leaven raises the whole lump? Cleanse out the old leaven, that you may be a new lump, as you are unleavened. For our passover was sacrificed—Christ. So let us feast not in the old leaven, the leaven of evil and wickedness, but in unleavened bread of simplicity and truth.

How can the "spirit" be saved? Paul tells the psychics not to boast for (as the Valentinians read in the metaphor of Rom 11:16) it is *Christ* and the *elect* who are the "leaven" that raises the "whole lump" of psychics.[73] Yet the psychics must be purified before they can partake of the new "divine Passover,"[74] the eschatological "great feast" that shall celebrate their passage from the slavery of cosmic existence into the freedom of pleromic life.[75]

1 Cor 5:9-13: I wrote to you in my letter not to mingle with fornicators, but I did not mean the fornicators of the cosmos . . . since you would have had to go out of the cosmos. . . . What is it to me to judge those outside? Do you not judge those inside? Those outside God judges. . . .

Paul now explains to the pneumatics that although he wrote to them not to mingle with "fornicators," he did not mean that they should avoid the "fornicators of this cosmos," the psychics guilty of immorality.[76] In that case they would have to leave the cosmos! But they are to judge "those within" the church, and to "cleanse out the evil" they find among the psychics, as he himself has done. Yet Paul, as one of the elect, has nothing to do with judging those who already have passed *beyond* the cosmos—the elect: these are left to the providence of God the Father (5:13).

1 Cor 6:1-5: Does any one of you, having something against another, dare to be judged before the unholy, and not before the holy ones? Or do you not know that the holy shall judge the cosmos? And if the cosmos is to be judged by you, are you unworthy to judge the most trivial matters? Do you not know that we shall judge angels? Shall one not, then, judge matters that concern this life? If you judge matters of this life, do you seat as judges those who are nothing in the church? I speak to shame you. Is there not even one wise man among you, who will be able to judge between his brothers?

What concerns Paul when he discusses judgment? Is he merely giving advice on settling everyday legal disputes? Valentinian exegetes reject such literal interpretation, and claim that here Paul again shows that "the pneumatic judges all things, but himself is judged by no one" (1 Cor 2:15). He insists that "the holy," the pneumatics, are to judge "the cosmos;" all who are psychic, not only human beings, but even the angels of the demiurge! He argues in 6:4 (according to Valentinian exegesis) that "you would not seat as judges those who are *nothing* in the church"—that is, the psychics—but only "the one who is wise." [77]

1 Cor 6:7-9: Now it is a deficiency among you that have litigations with each other. Why not rather allow yourself to be treated unjustly; why not rather allow yourselves to be deprived? . . . Do you not know that the unjust will not inherit the kingdom of God?

Although he has stated that judgment properly belongs to the pneumatics, Paul now argues that they are not to insist on their prerogatives. He advises them instead to give up their rights and defer to the psychics, even if they risk being treated unjustly or deprived of what belongs to them. He offers them consolation for such temporary deprivations in 6:9: those who mistreat the elect "shall not inherit the kingdom of God," since to attain it, psychics must become just and righteous. [78] He reminds the elect in 6:11 that even they themselves had done such things before they were "redeemed, sanctified, and justified . . . in the spirit of our God."

1 Cor 6:12: All things are authorized for me, but not all things ae beneficial. All things are authorized for me, but I will not be subjected to the authority of any(one).

While the psychics are bound to the law, and must avoid especially sexual sins, idolatry, greed, thievery, and drunkenness (6:9), Paul declares that for him—as for all the elect—"all things are authorized" precisely because the pneumatic "will not be subjected to authority by anyone" (*hypo tinos*, 6:12). From what authority does Paul pronounce his own liberty? Specifically, from the authority of the demiurge who stands as ruler, lawgiver, and judge! [79] The Valentinians claim that those who receive the sacrament of "redemption" (cf. 6:11) thereby come to "stand at a height above any power; therefore they are free to do anything, having no fear of anyone in any way," for "through the redemption they have transcended the authority of the (demiurgic) judge."[80] The Marcosians say that through the sacrament of redemption the initiate simultaneously realizes his own pneumatic freedom and becomes independent of the demiurge's authority.[81] Simon Magus also connects the gnostic's freedom from the demiurgic powers with his freedom from the restrictions of the law: those who know the Father above are freed from subjection to "the angels who made the cosmos" and are now "free to live as they please," being saved through (the Father's) grace, and not through good works."[82] Basilides too claims that the pneumatics, no longer subject to the cosmic powers, therefore are free from the sexual, ethical, and dietary practices the law prescribes.[83] Carpocrates declares that the gnostic initiates themselves "already have authority to rule over the archons and makers of the cosmos" (cf. 1 Cor 6:2-3), and therefore are released from any legal constraints on sexual and magical practices.[84] Each of these gnostic teachers emphasizes the connection that they claim Paul makes in 1 Cor 6:12: that "all things are authorized" for those who are released from the demiurge's authority.

1 Cor 6:13: Meats are for the stomach, and the stomach for meats; but God will destroy both (the stomach and meats). The body is not for fornication, but for the Lord, and the Lord for the body.

Since pneumatics have authority over the devil, the region he rules—materiality[85]—no longer has any power to enslave them. The followers of Valentinus, Basilides, Simon, and Carpocrates claim, therefore, that they are free to regard bodily things with indifference. The gnostic might read 6:13b as saying that the body (which includes the psychic body as well as the material one)[86] belongs to the demiurgic "Lord" as he himself belongs to it. Those who belong to God, however, belong to One who has power over "the Lord" and over "all bodies" (6:14) that he made.[87]

1 Cor 6:14-20: But God has raised the Lord and ourselves through his power. Do you not know that your bodies are members of Christ? Shall I take the members of Christ and make them members of a prostitute? Whoever is joined to the Lord becomes one spirit with him. . . . Avoid fornication . . . whoever commits fornication sins against his own body. Do you not know that your body is the temple of the holy spirit, which is in you, which is of God, and you are not your own? . . . therefore glorify God in your Body and your spirit, which are of God.

What can Paul mean? Most Christians assume the literal meaning—that the actual body forms an essential element of the relation to Christ.[88] The gnostic reader, finding this interpretation absurd, could argue that the whole passage is absurd if taken literally. Valentinian exegetes offer instead a symbolic interpretation: the pneumatics' "bodies" signify those "members of Christ" who are, as yet, only psychic.[89] In the same way, when Paul speaks of actual sexual union, they explain, he is using this symbolically to describe spiritual relationships.[90]

What Paul reveals in 6:15 is that the *psychics* ("your bodies") are *also* "members of Christ."[91] The psychic "body" that joins itself to "a prostitute"—to materiality—becomes "one flesh" with matter and is destroyed along with it; but the psychic who joins with the pneumatic becomes with it "one spirit."[92] The Valentinian might infer from 6:17-20, then, that the pneumatic who remains involved with materiality ("fornication"; see 5:1-2 above) neglects his relationship with the psychic who is his "own body" (6:17). The elect are to recognize that they are not their own; they have been redeemed (6:20) not for their own sake but for the sake of redeeming the psychics. The elect is to bring his "body"—the psychic—as well as his "spirit" to "glorify God" (6:20).

1 Cor 7:1-2: Concerning the matter of which you wrote: it is good for a man not to touch a woman. Yet, to avoid fornication, let every man have his own wife, and every woman her own husband.

Paul's advice, read literally by psychics, would encourage them in their efforts to observe a strict code of sexual ethics.[93] But how are the pneumatics to understand Paul's discussion of sexual ethics and of marriage in 1 Corinthians 7? Heracleon offers a clue in his exegesis of John 4: he explains that the woman fallen into fornication symbolizes the pneumatic elect, immersed in materiality, ignorant of God. To be freed from "fornication," the woman (the pneumatic elect) must be joined to "her own husband" (cf. 1 Cor 7:2), her spiritual identity. The savior reveals her husband to her and marries the two "in power and unity and conjunction." Human marriage (as Paul describes it here) becomes a symbol of the process through which the pneumatic comes into relation to the divine syzygos, to Christ, and to the Father.[94] Heracleon interprets the story of the marriage at Cana, where the savior transforms water into wine, as a symbol of that "divine marriage" which transforms what is merely human into the divine.[95]

More than one form of the secret Valentinian sacrament of redemption enacts this divine marriage. The writer of the Gospel of Philip regards the bridechamber as the "true mystery," the sacrament revealed through Jesus.[96] Fragments of such a liturgy may survive in the final section of A Valentinian Exposition from Nag Hammadi.[97] Among the Marcosians, the celebrant, speaking as the savior, joins the initiate as a bride with her divine bridegroom:

> Prepare yourself as a bride expecting her husband, that you may be what I am, and I what you are: place the seed of light in your marriage chamber; receive from me a husband, and be received by him. [98]

Those who receive the sacrament say that "therefore in every way they must continually concern themselves with the mystery of conjunction." Whoever is "in the cosmos" but not "of it"—whoever is pneumatic—must "love a woman so that he is joined with her." [99] What does this mean? Irenaeus seizes upon this as a gnostic attempt to justify sexual licentiousness. Yet the context and parallels suggest that the statement is a symbolic one: it refers to the *pneumatics*, who are to join themselves with the *psychics* as husbands to their wives. The author of Philip contrasts the "marriage of uncleanness" (which involves sarkic desire) with the "true mystery" of marriage, which involves the pure will. [100]

Since the sexual terms, taken allegorically, may denote modes of relationship, the Valentinians, like Philo, can describe the same person as either male or female in the context of different relationships. In relation to the divine, the pneumatic is receptive, and therefore female; the bride, the woman receiving her divine husband "from above." Yet in relation to the psychic, apparently, the pneumatic takes the active role: in terms of this relationship, the pneumatic is male (the man, the husband) and the receptive psychic, in turn, is female. [101] Theodotus describes how the pneumatic "males" and the psychic "females," originally part of the same being, have become separated from one another, as Eve separated from Adam. [102] So, according to the Gospel of Philip,

> If the woman had not separated from the man, she would not die with the man. His separation became the beginning of death. Because of this Christ came, in order that he might remove the separation, and again unite the two. . . . But the woman is united to her husband in the bridal chamber. Those who have been united in the bridal chamber will no longer be separated! [103]

The marriage symbolism of 1 Cor 7:2-3, then, could be interpreted pneumatically on two different levels. First, the elect are delivered from spiritual "fornication" by joining with their divine syzygies; second, the psychics, in turn, are delivered from actual fornication by joining with the elect. The Valentinians teach that the pneumatic, therefore, must join with his psychic partner in order to protect and to strengthen the psychic against bodily temptations (7:4-5). Paul adds in 7:7 that he wishes that all were "as he is" (that is, pneumatic) yet concedes that "each one has his own gift from God, one in this way, another in that way."

1 Cor 7:10-14: Let not the woman leave her husband, but if she leaves, let her remain unmarried, or be reconciled with her husband. Let not the husband divorce his wife. . . . otherwise, your children would be unholy, but now they are holy.

Like his advice on marriage, Paul's counsel on divorce could be interpreted symbolically in either of two ways. Taken in reference to the *pneumatic's* "marriage" with the divine syzygos, Paul counsels her not to abandon her newly discovered relationship with God which was consummated in the *apolytrosis* sacrament. Alternatively, in reference to the *psychics's* union with her pneumatic "husband," he instructs her not to leave her divinely given syzygos. For each of these forms of "marriage" bears the potential for producing a new being "as human intercourse in marriage produces a child."[104] In the relationship between believers, the "unbelieving one," the psychic, can be saved through the association with the pneumatic (cf. 7:14-16).

1 Cor 7:17-31: Only let each walk as the Lord has assigned to him, as God has called. . . . For neither circumcision nor uncircumcision matters, but to keep the commandments of God. Let each one remain in the calling in which he was called. . . . for the schema of this cosmos is passing away.

Paul advises each person to accept his own situation, whether assigned to the psychic place by "the Lord" (7:17a) or called to election by "God" (7:17b). He reminds all Christians that "the schema of the cosmos is passing away"—and with it all such distinctions. For the differences between the psychic and the pneumatic—characterized as male and female, slavery and freedom, circumcision and uncircumcision—belong only to "the schema of this cosmos" and will pass away with the cosmos. Finally the psychics who are now slaves shall be transformed into pneumatic freedom (7:21-22):[105] those circumcised in the flesh shall receive pneumatic "circumcision of the heart"; the females shall be transformed, united, and identified with the males.[106] As Theodotus describes the eschaton, all shall be equal and identical when "God shall be all in all." This shall take place when "the schema of the cosmos" (7:31) has passed away. The author of the Gospel of Truth explains that "the schema *is* the cosmos" which is annihilated when its deficiency is filled.[107]

1 Cor 8:1-8: Concerning what is offered to idols, we know that we all have gnosis. Gnosis puffs up, but love builds up. . . . If anyone loves God, he himself is known of God. Concerning the eating of things offered to idols, we know that the idol in the cosmos is nothing, and that there is no God but the One God. And if there are many called gods in the heavens or on earth, as there are many gods and many lords, yet to us there is One God, the Father, of whom are all things, and we in him . . . but this gnosis is not in all. Some in the usual way even now eat it as something offered to an idol, and their conscience, being weak, is defiled. But meat does not commend us to God; if we eat we are not better for it, nor, if we do not, are we the worse for it.

Paul speaks to the elect as those who "all have gnosis," reminding them that those who "know God" are also known by him (8:3). The author of the Gospel of Truth, citing this passage, says "the little children who had gnosis of the Father . . . knew and were known; they were glorified, and they glorified."[108] Heracleon says that only "his own" know the "one God" (8:4) as their Father (8:6). They know that from him "are all things," that is, the divine pleroma,[109] "and we in him," as the elect recognize themselves.[110]

Yet Paul goes on to remind the elect that "this gnosis is not in all" (8.7). Those who lack gnosis, he says, "have accustomed themselves to the idol in the cosmos," to "those called gods in the heavens or on earth," that is, to the demiurge and the archons, whom they ignorantly worship.[111] Heracleon calls them idolators, who "worship in flesh and error the one who is not the Father."[112] Because they remain "in the weakness of the flesh,"[113] Paul says that "their conscience, being weak, is defiled" (8:7). The Valentinians cite this passage to show that those who *do* have gnosis need not hesitate to eat meat sacrificed to idols, "since they cannot incur defilement."[114]

1 Cor 8:9-13: But beware that your authority may not become a stumbling block to the weak. For if anyone sees you—you who have gnosis—seated in the pagan temple . . . shall not the weaker brother, for whom Christ died, be destroyed because of your gnosis? . . . Therefore, if meat makes my brother to offend, I shall not eat meat in this age, lest I cause my brother to offend.

Now Paul warns the gnostics not to allow their gnosis and their authority to become an obstacle to "the weak," to psychics.[115] Instead they are to help the psychics whom Christ came to save,[116] even if this means giving up the freedom their gnosis affords them. Paul himself, the pneumatic apostle, chooses to give up his liberty in this age (8:13) rather than to harm his "weaker brother" by asserting it.

1 Cor 9:1-23: Am I not free? Am I not an apostle? . . . have we not authority to eat and drink? Have we not authority to take a sister as wife? . . . If others share in this authority of yours, do not we share in it? Yet we have not used this authority, but instead endure all things, lest we should hinder the gospel of Christ . . . . What, then, is my reward? That when I preach I set forth the gospel free, so that I do not misuse my power in the gospel. For though I am free from all, I have made myself a slave to all, that I might gain the many; and I became as a Jew to the Jews, that I might gain the Jews; to those under law I became as one under law: to those without law I became as one without law—not being without the law of God, but within the law of Christ—that I might gain those without the law. To the weak I became weak so that I might gain the weak. I have become all things to all, so that by all means I might save some. I do all things for the sake of the gospel, that I might become a partaker in it.

Here Paul sums up his whole message to the elect. Proclaiming himself free in dietary and sexual matters (9:4-5), he is "free from all" (9:19), free from the demiurge's psychic law. Yet he stands in the pneumatic law, that of God the Father and of Christ (9:21), which is the law of love. For this reason, he refuses to assert his own freedom and authority, so that he may not offend the psychics to whom he preaches the gospel (9:18). What is his reward for this? His reward, as Heracleon says of the savior, is "the salvation and restoration to rest"[117] of those to whom he ministers.

Paul describes how he, like the savior, although pneumatic, has taken upon himself a psychic role. Being "free" he has made himself a "slave" to work among the psychic slaves; he has become "a Jew to the Jews," "as one under the law to those under the law," even "weak" to those who are the weak. In every way he accommodates himself in order to "become all things to all, so that by all means I might save some" (9:22). For it is through the ministry of the pneumatics (as Heracleon says) that psychics hear the gospel and are saved.[118]

1 Cor 10:1-6: I do not want you to be ignorant, brothers, that all our fathers were under the cloud, and all passed through the sea, and all were baptized unto Moses in the cloud and in the sea, and all ate the same pneumatic food, and all drank the same pneumatic drink. For they drank from the pneumatic rock; and the rock was Christ. But God was not pleased with the majority of them, for they were overthrown in the wilderness. These things were types for us . . . .

So that the elect may not lack gnosis (10:1), Paul discloses to them his own pneumatic exegesis, revealing the symbolic meaning hidden in Israel's history. Those baptized "unto Moses" typify those who are baptized unto the demiurge.[119] Having come from Egypt, which symbolizes the region of materiality, they passed through the sea, the "immersion in materiality."[120] Yet the Israelites remained "under a cloud," as the psychics remain under the "obscurity in which the psychic was hidden."[121] Although all shared of the same food and drink (as all Christians partake of the pneumatic food and drink, Christ) God is not pleased with "the many," that is, with the psychics (10:5). Heracleon sees in 10:5 evidence that God has rejected the psychics because they, like the Jews, "worship the demiurge in flesh and error."[122]

That the Israelites perished in the desert signifies that the psychics are perishing "in the desert" which symbolizes "the material region."[123]

1 Cor 10:11-15: These things happened to them typologically, and were written to admonish us, on whom the last of the aions (*ta telē tōn aiōnōn*) have come. . . . Therefore, beloved ones, flee from idolatry. I speak to those who understand (*hōs phronimois*). . . .

Paul demonstrates here (according to Ptolemy) that "the law, which was exemplary and pneumatic, was transformed by the savior from the perceptible and phenomenal level to the pneumatic and invisible one."[124] He speaks specifically to those who are pneumatic, "on whom the last of the aions have come,"[125] his "beloved ones," those "who understand." For the account from Israel's history warns them against the psychics' error, idolatrous worship of the demiurge instead of the true God.

1 Cor 10:16-19: The cup of blessing which we bless—is it not communion in the blood of Christ? The bread we break—is it not communion in the body of Christ? For we, being many, are one bread, and one body, for we all partake of the same bread.

Beware of Israel according to the flesh: are not those who eat the sacrifice participants of the altar? What shall I say? That what is offered in sacrifice to idols is anything, or that the idol is anything?

What does Paul mean when he warns against "Israel according to the flesh," and connects this with a warning against *idolatry* in the Christian communion meal? Valentinian teachers offer various interpretations of the meal and of its elements. One interprets the bread as a symbol of "his body," the *ecclesia*[126] (cf. 6:17: "we, being many, are one bread, and one body"). In the Marcosian sacrament, the wine symbolizes grace,[127] as the mingling of water and wine suggests the transformation of the human into the divine. The writer of the Gospel of Philip offers another interpretation: "his flesh is his logos, and his blood the holy spirit."[128]

Valentinian teachers agree, however, that those who refer the bread and wine to Jesus' sacrificial passion and death interpret the elements only psychically. The writer of the Gospel of Philip suggests ironically that "their God is a man-eater. Because of this they kill the man for him. Before they killed the man they were killing the animals. Those for whom they killed them are no gods."[129] Would not participation in such a psychic "sacrifice of the altar" (10:18) involve the pneumatic in eating "food offered to idols" (10:19), that is, to the demiurge and the cosmic archons?

1 Cor 10:23-29: All things are permissible to me, but not all are advantageous. All things are lawful, but not all build up. Let no one seek his own good, but what is good for his neighbor. . . . If any of the unbelievers invites you to eat and you want to go, eat whatever is set before you, asking no question for the sake of conscience. But if anyone says to you, "This has been offered in sacrifice to idols," then do not eat, for the sake of the one who said it, and for the sake of conscience—I mean his conscience, not yours. . . .

Paul reminds the elect that for them "all things are permissible," even though not all are advantageous. He advises them not to consider themselves or their own welfare in this matter, but the welfare of their psychic brothers. Those invited to share in the psychic communion should go, if they want to, and eat with the psychics. Yet if one of them cautions the pneumatic that the feast has been offered "to idols" (recognizing the demiurge as an idol) he is to abstain for the sake of the psychic who warned him against "idolatry." So the initiate might read this passage.

1 Cor 10:29b-33: Why is my freedom judged by another man's conscience? If I partake of grace (*chariti metechō*), why should I be denounced for that which I eucharize? Whether you eat or drink or whatever you do, do all to the glory of God. Do not offend either the Jews or the Greeks or the ecclesia of God, just as I please all men in all things, not seeking my own advantage, but that of the many (*tōn pollōn*) that they may be saved.

Paul anticipates that the gnostic will resist his advice: why should he be judged by another man's conscience—especially when the other is only psychic, and has no right to judge him at all? Why should he refuse to offend the psychics, who present to judge his own pneumatic celebration of the eucharist, which symbolizes the participation in grace (10:29b; in *charis*)?[130]

Paul replies as he has before (6:20) that the pneumatic must do all "for the glory of God," since both the psychic "Jews" and the pneumatic "Greeks" are members of "the ecclesia of God" (10:32). The Valentinians apparently attempt to put Paul's advice (as they understand it) into practice. Irenaeus indicates that while they participate willingly in the communion celebration with the "psychic church" they reserve the pneumatic eucharistic celebration for private meetings among initiates.[131]

1 Cor 11:1-12: Become imitators of me, as I myself imitate Christ, I praise you that you remember me in all things, and so you observe the traditions I passed on to you. I want you to know that the head of every man is Christ; the head of the woman is the man; and the head of Christ is God. Every man who prays or prophesies having something over his head shames his head. Every woman who prays or prophesies with her head unveiled shames her head. . . . For the man should not have anything over his head, since he is the image and glory of God. The woman is the glory of the man. For the man is not from the woman but the woman from the man. And the man was not created for the woman, but the woman for the man. Therefore the woman should have authority over her head, on account of the angels. Yet there is neither woman without man, nor man without woman in the Lord. For as the woman is from the man, so also man is through the woman: . . . and all things are from God.

Paul urges the elect to imitate him: they are to "remember" what he taught them (11:1-2; apparently the secret, oral teaching) and on that basis to observe "the traditions" transmitted to them. Why, then, does he abruptly break off his discussion in 11:3 and turn to consider such trivial matters as the social relationship between men and women, and the question of proper dress? The initiated reader could perceive that Paul has not changed the subject, but now he chooses to continue it in symbolic language, so that the elect alone are able to follow his hidden meaning.

When the apostle speaks of the relationship between *man* and *woman*, the Valentinians explain, he is speaking symbolically first of the relationship between *Christ* and the *ecclesia*, and secondly of the relationship between the *elect* and the *called*.[132] As God is the head of Christ, so Christ is the head of the man (that is, of the *pneumatic elect*) and the man the head of the woman (the *psychic ecclesia*). Through this metaphor Paul reveals the hierachy of divine relationship: God, Christ, the elect, the called (cf. 11:3).

In this passage the Valentinians apparently see reference to the two pre-cosmic stages of creation: 11:12 refers to Sophia's creation of Adam, and 11:9 to the prior creation of Sophia herself. Although Sophia brought forth as her "finest emanation" both the male and female in the image of God (cf. Gen 1:26) only the male, pneumatic element—Adam—retained it, "bearing the image and glory of God" (11:7). The female, Eve, separating from the male, became the merely derivative, psychic element.[133]

Why does Paul insist that the man should have "nothing over his head" (11:4, 7)? The veil symbolizes authority, as Paul reveals in 11:10. He intends to show that the elect is *not* to acknowledge any authority "over his head"; "any man" (that is, any *pneumatic*) who *does* acknowledge the demiurge's authority over him "shames his head," which is Christ.[134] But every *woman*—every psychic—who *fails* to acknowledge the demiurge's authority "shames *her* head," that is, her "man" (the pneumatic). So Paul explains in 11:7 that the pneumatic "man" bears "the image and glory of God"; but the psychic "woman" bears only, his reflected glory. Through this symbolic language, the Valentinians might claim, Paul shows that the pneumatic is not derived from the psychic, but the psychic from the pneumatic (11:8).

What can Paul mean when he says in 11:9 that "the man was not created for the woman, but the woman for the man," and goes on to declare in 11:12 that "the woman is from the man, as the man is through the woman"? Valentinian exegetes could suggest that these two passages refer to different stages of the process of creation. The first (11:9) describes the creation of Sophia herself: "the man"—Christ and the elect—did not originate "for the woman," that is, for Sophia, "the woman above"; instead, Sophia ("the woman") was created "for the man," that is, for the savior, who is the "first universal creator."[135] The second passage (11:12), then, describes the second stage of creation. As "the woman" (Sophia) is "from the man" (the savior) so also "the man" (Christ and the elect) is generated into the cosmos "through the woman" (through Sophia).[136] Similarly, Ptolemy explains that 11:10 applies first to Sophia and secondly to the ecclesia. For when Sophia, separated from the light, rejoiced to see the savior coming toward her, she veiled her head in shame "on account of the (male) angels."[137] So also the demiurge ("Moses") veiled himself, acknowledging the authority over *him*; this veil signifying the demiurgic authority that rules over psychics, and "remains over the heart of the psychic even now."[138]

1 Cor 11:11-15: Yet there is neither the woman without the man nor the man without the woman in the Lord. . . . Judge for yourselves. Is it appropriate for a woman to pray to God unveiled? Does not the very nature (*hē physis autē*) teach you that if a man has long hair it is a disgrace to him, but if a woman has long hair, it is her glory? For her hair is given to her as a covering.

Paul teaches here that for the present—"in the *Lord*"—psychics and pneumatics belong together: only in conjunction with one another can either gain access into the pleroma.[139] But, he asks, is it appropriate for a psychic (i.e., a "woman") to pray "to *God*" the Father apart from the authority of the demiurge (unveiled, 11:13)? Does not "the very nature" (*physis*) of each teach that for the pneumatic to submit to demiurgic authority is for him "a disgrace," but the psychic's subjection is "her glory" (11:14-15)? For this reason, the apostle explains, "the women"—the psychics—"should remain silent in the assemblies of the holy ones" (the *elect*; 14:33-34): "it is not appropriate for them to speak, but to be subjected, as the law (of the demiurge) says." Through this symbolic language he directs to the elect, the Valentinian could read Paul's explanation of how proper church order depends on insight concerning the divine hierarchy: God, Christ, the elect, the called.

1 Cor 11:17-21: In this I do not praise you: that you gather together not for the better but for the worse. For first, indeed, when you gather together in the ecclesia, I hear that there are schisms among you; and in part I believe it. For there must be sects (*haireseis*) among you, so that those who are revered may be revealed to you. When you gather together in the same place, therefore, it is not to eat the Lord's supper.·For each one partakes of his own supper in eating; one is hungry, and another is drunk.

Paul admits that "there must be sects among you, so that those who are revered (that is, the elect) may be revealed to you."[140] Even when they meet with psychics "in the same place" the elect do not come "to eat the Lord's supper" (11:20). For how can those released from his authority celebrate the feast of the demiurgic "Lord"? The diversity among Christians means that "each one (whether psychic or pneumatic) eats his own supper," just as "each one knows the Lord in his own way, and not all know him alike:" one "hungers" spiritually; another "is drunk," oblivious to spiritual needs.[141]

1 Cor 11:23-32: For what I received from the Lord I also passed on to you, that the Lord Jesus, on the night he was betrayed, took bread, and giving thanks, he broke it, and said, "This is my body, which is for you; do this for the recalling of me" . . . For as often as you eat this bread and drink this cup you proclaim the death of the Lord, until he comes. Therefore whoever eats and drinks unworthily, eats and drinks condemnation to himself . . . . when we are judged, we are chastened by the Lord, so that we should not be condemned along with the cosmos.

Paul reminds them of the tradition he received "from the Lord" and passed on to the whole community in common. The meal of bread and wine, recalling the "body and blood" of the Lord, "demonstrates his death" and anticipates his return. The initiated reader, recognizing this interpretation of the eucharist as psychic teaching, would perceive that Paul directs his warning to the psychics (11:27-34): they are to fear "unworthy" participation, realizing that they face "the Lord's" judgment, and risk condemnation along with "the cosmos."[142]

1 Cor 12:1-7: Now concerning pneumatic gifts, brothers, I do not want you to be ignorant. You know that no one, speaking in the spirit of God, says, "Cursed be Jesus," and no one can say, "Jesus is Lord" except by the holy spirit. There are different charismata, but the same spirit; differences of service, but the same Lord. There are different modes of activity, but the same God energizes all in all. To each one is given the revelation of the spirit as it is beneficial.

Having spoken before in psychic terms to the majority, Paul now speaks to the elect: they are not to lack gnosis of pneumatic gifts. They must realize first that no pneumatic, speaking through the holy spirit, can despise the psychic Jesus: and secondly, that no psychic can recognize the psychic Jesus "as Lord" except through the holy spirit (12:3). Although pneumatics receive "different charismata" the "same spirit" bestows them all; and although the psychics receive "different services," the "same Lord" appoints them all. Although these pneumatic *charismata* and psychic *services* are "different modes of activity," Paul insists that "it is the same God," the Father, who energizes all of them, giving "to each one," whether psychic or pneumatic, "that manifestation of the spirit" that benefits each (12:7).

1 Cor 12:8-11: For (*men*; on the one hand) to one is given through the spirit the logos of wisdom (*sophia*); to another the logos of gnosis according to the same spirit; to another faith in the same spirit; to another charismata of healing in the one spirit; (*de*, on the other hand) to another is given prophecy, discerning of spirits, different tongues, interpretation of tongues; but one and the same spirit energizes all of these, distributing to each one as he wills.

Valentinian exegetes would note that in the first clause, where Paul describes the "higher gifts"—(logos of wisdom, logos of gnosis, faith, *charismata*)—he says specifically in each case that the charismatic gifts (12:4) come from "the one spirit" (12: 8-9). But in the second clause (12:10), where he enumerates the "services" (12:5), he declines to attribute these to "the same spirit." The Valentinians infer from this that these "services" are appointed by "the Lord" (12:5), the *demiurge* (an exegesis Origen contests).[143] Yet the apostle insists that "one and the same spirit" works in all, whether directly or through the demiurge, "distributing to each one as he wills" (12:11).

1 Cor 12:12-27: For as the body is one, and has many members, and all members of the body, being many, are one body, so also is Christ. For in one spirit we have all been baptized into one body, whether Jews or Greeks, slaves or free, and we have all been made to drink from one spirit. For the body is not one member but many. If the foot shall say, "Because I am not the hand, I am not part of the body," is it not part of the body? . . . Now God has set the members, each one of them, into the body as he willed. . . . The eye cannot say to the hand, "I do not need you," nor the head to the feet, "I do not need you." . . . Our more harmonious members have no need; but God has mingled the body together, giving greater honor to the more deficient part, so that there might be no schism in the body. but the members should care for one another in the same way. Now you are the body of Christ, and members in different parts.

Theodotus offers a unique exegesis of this metaphor: he suggests that the elect constitute "one spirit" headed by Christ while the psychics constitute "the body" of Jesus.[144] The Valentinian homilist of The Interpretation of the Gnosis exegetes this passage in terms more consistent with Paul's text: he cites it to encourage his pneumatic brothers to love the psychics, since all together, "Jews" as well as "Gentiles," "slaves" as well as "free," constitute the one "body of Christ." Correlating this passage with Rom 12:4-5, he urges that the lesser, psychic members—the foot in relation to the hand, the ear in relation to the eye (12:15-16)—not complain at their inferiority to the greater, pneumatic members.[145] Conversely, the greater members must not despise the lesser ones as if they were unnecessary to the whole (12:21-22).[146] On the contrary, the psychic members *are* necessary: the "body of Christ" was constituted for their sake (12:24). Without them the elect cannot become complete,[147] for God has "mingled the body" so that the psychics, "the many, having become one, might be mingled in the one that was divided for our sake."[148] Therefore, as the Valentinian homilist concludes, all are to live together in love as members of one body headed by Christ, mutually sustaining each other, praising God who has willed the participation of each member.[149]

1 Cor 12:28-31: And God set some in the ecclesia first, as apostles; second, prophets; third, teachers; then powers, then gifts of healing, then ministers, administrators, different tongues. . . . earnestly seek the greater *charismata:* yet I will show you a superior way.

The initiate recognizes here that Paul discriminates between the different levels of function in "the body," encouraging them to seek the "greater charismata."

1 Cor 13:1-2: Though I speak with the tongues of men and of angels, and have not love, I am become as a sounding gong, or a clanging cymbal. And though I have prophecy, and understand all mysteries, and all gnosis, and have all faith . . . and have not love, I am nothing.

What is that "superior way"? It is the way superior to the demiurge, who confesses that although he speaks "with the tongues of men and of angels" he lacks divine love: therefore all his utterance is merely "sound."[150] He admits that even if he understood "all mysteries and all gnosis" (which, according to Heracleon, he does not),[151] he would be "nothing" apart from the Father's divine love.

1 Cor 13:7-10: Love bears all things, believes all things, hopes all things, suffers all things. Love never fails. If there are prophecies, they shall cease; if there are tongues, they shall cease; if there is gnosis, it will disappear. For now we know in part and we prophecy in part. But when the perfect comes, what is partial shall disappear.

Since they claim that only pneumatics truly have love, the Valentinians read this passage as the psychics' admission that their prophecies, their tongues, their gnosis, are only limited: what is psychic, and therefore only partial, must give way to what is pneumatic and perfect.[152]

1 Cor 13:11-13: When I was an infant, I spoke as an infant, I understood as an infant, I thought as an infant; but when I became a man, I put away infantile things. Even now we see through a mirror, in an enigma; then face to face. Now I know in part; then I shall know as I am known. Now faith, hope, and love remain, these three: but the greatest of these is love.

Is the pneumatics' gnosis also limited? Paul reveals here that the pneumatic's gnosis may be limited temporarily by his own immaturity. The pneumatic seed, sown "in a state of infancy" (cf. 13:11a), must grow into the mature, rational understanding of "a man" (13:11b).[153] At first the pneumatic sees only "in a mirror, in an enigma"; but gradually he grows into insight (*gnōsis*) and maturity (*teleiōsis*). Finally, Paul mentions faith and hope—qualities that psychics may share with the elect—but praises love as the "greatest of these," the pneumatic "superior way" known to the elect alone.[154] The writer of the Gospel of Philip contrasts *faith*, through which one receives divine gifts, with *love,* through which one also gives them.[155] Apparently commenting on the three qualities Paul mentions (13:13), he says, "the husbandry of God is . . . through *four*: faith, hope, love, and gnosis. Our earth is faith, in which we take root. The water is hope, through which we are nourished. The wind is love, through which we grow. But the light is *gnosis,* through which we ripen to maturity."[156]

1 Cor 15:1-7: I remind you, brothers, of the gospel I preached to you, which you received, in which you stand, by which you are saved, if you hold to it, unless you believed in vain. For I transmitted to you at first what I too received, that Christ died for our sins according to the scriptures, that he was buried, and that he was raised on the third day according to the scriptures, and appeared to Peter, then to the twelve. . . . he appeared to James, then to all the apostles.

Now that Paul is ready to "speak a mystery" (15:51) he begins by showing how his own pneumatic message differs from the psychic preaching he shares with the other apostles (15:1-11). First he reminds his psychic hearers of "the gospel which I preached, in which you stand, through which you are saved" (15:1).[157] "At first," he says, he transmitted what he himself received—namely, the *kerygma*—that "Christ died for our sins according to the scriptures, that he was buried, and that he was raised on the third day" (15:3-4), and then appeared to Peter, to the twelve, and to many others, including James and "all the apostles" (15:5-7). He promises that their faith will not be "in vain" if they receive it "in the logos" through which he spoke (15:2).

1 Cor 15:8-10: Last of all he appeared to me, as to an abortion. For I am the least of the apostles, not worthy to be called an apostle, because I persecuted the church of

God. But by the grace of God I am what I am, and his grace in me was not empty, but I labored more than any of them, not I, but the grace of God with me.

But now Paul describes his own unique experience: "Last of all he appeared to me, as a kind of abortion" (15:8). Here he alludes symbolically to the pneumatic election to show how the savior appeared to Achamoth "when she was outside the pleroma, 'as a kind of abortion.'"[158] Basilides explains that the whole elect has undergone the same experience, having remained "in formlessness, 'like an abortion.'"[159] Theodotus says that "as long as we were children only of the female (Sophia), as of a shameful syzygy, we were incomplete, infants, mindless, weak, unformed, brought forth like abortions."[160]

From this amorphous state, Paul—symbolizing the elect—is redeemed by grace: "his grace in me was not empty" (since grace, *charis,* is an aion of the "fullness," the pleroma).[161] Taking 15:10 as Paul's account of how he was "spiritually born," delivered through the "labor" of "the grace (*charis*) of God,"[162] the Valentinians explain that Paul alone received "the mystery of God" through the pleromic aion *charis,* while the other apostles received only what was transmitted through the psychic demiurge.[163] From this they conclude that Paul alone received the pneumatic gospel, while the preaching of the rest remained only psychic.[164]

1 Cor 15:12: If Christ is preached as having been raised from the dead, how can some of you say there is no resurrection of the dead?

What does Paul mean when he speaks of "the resurrection of the dead"? The other apostles clearly proclaim this as the future, bodily resurrection of those who have died.[165] But the gnostic initiate rejects this preaching as crude literalism, as error typical of psychic preaching, the "faith of fools"![166] For who are "the dead"? The initiate knows that these are the psychics, who have been "deadened in this existence."[167] What, then, concerns Paul in 1 Cor 15:12? He says that "some" are saying "there is no resurrection of the dead," that is, that the psychics *cannot* be raised from the "deadness of this existence" to spiritual life![168] For according to Valentinian exegesis, the "resurrection of the dead" is "the recognition of the truth" spoken by those who have gnosis.[169]

1 Cor 15:13-19: If there is no resurrection of the dead, then Christ is not raised; if Christ is not raised, then our kerygma is empty, and your faith is empty. We are found even to be false witnesses of God, for we testified of God that he raised Christ from the dead, whom he did not raise, if the dead are not raised. For if the dead are not raised, then Christ has not been raised. If Christ is not raised, your faith is in vain, and you are still in your sins. Then those who have fallen asleep in Christ have perished. If in this life we alone have hoped in Christ then we are the most miserable of all mankind.

Paul argues that "if there is no resurrection of the dead" (15:13), then Christ, who came in psychic form to save the psychic element,[170] has not been raised to pneumatic life. In that case, he declares, "our kerygma is empty, and your faith is empty." For "if there is no resurrection of the dead," that is, if psychics can never attain "recognition of the truth," Paul sees that his whole activity in preaching the kerygma to psychics[171]—and their faith in believing it—would all be futile. In that case, if the psychics, who are "dead,"[172] cannot be "raised," those who have "fallen asleep" (15:18) held under the power of the "spirit of deep sleep" (cf. Rom 11:8) have perished. Paul even says that "if in this life we (the elect) *alone* have hoped in Christ, then we are the most miserable of all mankind," for the elect alone would see the hopelessness of the psychics' situation.

1 Cor 15:20-23: But now Christ is risen from the dead, the first fruits of those who have fallen asleep. For since by man came death, so also through man came the resurrection of the dead. For as in Adam all die, even so in Christ shall all be made alive, each in his own order, the first fruit, Christ, then those of Christ in his presence.

Yet Paul proclaims in 15:20 that "now Christ is raised from the dead, the first fruits of those who have fallen asleep." For Christ and the elect are the "first fruits" through whom the psychics ("those who have fallen asleep") shall be "raised and saved."[173]

While psychics mistake Christ's resurrection as a literal, past event, pneumatic Christians understand it symbolically: Christ's resurrection signifies the "resurrection of the ecclesia."[174] That he rose "on the third day" (15:4) means that the psychic church shall be raised only when the first two days—the *hylic* and *psychic* days, are over,[175] and the demiurge's creation, the "kingdom of death" has ended. On the "third day, that is, the pneumatic day,"[176] Christ shall "raise" the psychics and lead them from the cosmos into the pleroma.[177]

Those generated "in Adam all die" (15:22), being born "into death and into the cosmos," but "he whom Christ regenerates is transferred to life in the Ogdoad."[178] Each receives life "in his own order": "Christ, the first fruits" (that is, the elect);[179] and second, "those who belong to Christ at his coming," the psychics who receive him through his cosmic appearance.

1 Cor 15:24-28: Then comes the end, when he delivers the kingdom to God the Father, when every rule and every authority and power is destroyed. For he must reign until he puts all his enemies under his feet. The last enemy to be destroyed is death. . . . when all things are subjected to him, then even the son himself will be subjected to him who subjected all things, that God may be all in all.

At the consummation of this age, Christ delivers "the kingdom" of the demiurge "to God the Father" (15:24), after destroying "every archon, every authority, and every power," even the "last enemy, death" (15:26).[180] The demiurge's "kingdom of death"[181] finally shall be destroyed entirely. "He must reign until he has put all his enemies under his feet" (15:25): the Valentinians explain from this that Christ reigns "at the right hand" of the demiurge for the duration of the present age "until the final consummation."[182] Then Christ will subject all things to the Father—even himself—that "God may be all in all" (15:28).

1 Cor 15:29: Otherwise why are some baptized in behalf of the dead? If, indeed, the dead are not raised, why are some baptized for their sake?

Paul now argues his case for the resurrection from the practice of baptism for the dead. The meaning of this passage, which has puzzled so many exegetes, must have seemed obvious to the Valentinians. According to their own sacramental practice, the pneumatic elect receive baptism for "the dead" that is, for the psychics. The purpose of this proxy baptism is to ensure that the psychics will receive the power to transcend the region of the demiurge, and to enter into the pleroma.[183] Since psychics cannot receive this sacrament themselves (as long as they remain "dead" in ignorance of the truth), the elect take on the responsibility of performing this baptism for them. The elect receive the "laying on of hands" for the "angelic redemption" in the name of the psychics, so that the psychics may receive the redemption effected through the divine name. Paul is asking what purpose there could be in performing such baptism for "the dead" unless the psychics indeed *can* be "raised from the dead."

1 Cor 15:30-34: Why are we in danger every hour? I die every day. . . . What advantage is it to me, humanly speaking, if I have fought with wild beasts in Ephesus? . . . Do not be deceived. . . . Become sober, and do not sin. For some are ignorant of God. I say this to shame you.

Paul continues: if the psychics cannot be raised, why is he taking risks to evangelize them (15:30)? Why is he "dying," participating in psychic existence, for their sake (15:31)? Why does he enter into their conflicts, fighting the "wild beasts" of the passions as they do (15:32)?[184] Paul warns the psychics to "become sober," overcoming the drunkenness of their oblivion. They must be righteous and not sin (15:34); since they are yet ignorant of God (15:34), their salvation depends on their own works.[185]

1 Cor 15:35-40: But some one will say, "How are the dead raised? With what body do they come?" You fool—what you sow does not come to life until it dies, and what you sow is not the body which it is to become. . . . God has given to each of the seeds a body as he willed, and to each of the seeds its own body. Not all flesh is the same flesh. . . . There are heavenly bodies and earthly bodies. And the glory of the heavenly is one (kind of glory), and of the earthly, another.

Here Paul castigates as "fools" those who ask "how the dead are raised" or "with what body they come." Such literal-minded questions betray the naive belief in bodily resurrection which the Valentinians call the "faith of fools" (that is, of psychics).[186] He offers instead a pneumatic (that is, symbolic) interpretation of the resurrection. He begins with his metaphor of the seeds: "what you sow is not the body which it is to become. . . . But God gives to each . . . a body as he willed, and to each of the seeds its own body" (15:38).

What is "sown," and what are the "seeds"? The Valentinians explain that these are the two different types of seed produced by Sophia—the pneumatic seed of the elect[187] and the psychic seed of the called![188] Although God has willed that the two types of seed—psychic and pneumatic (15:43-47)—differ in "body" (15:38), in "flesh," (15:39), and in "glory" (15:41), he will raise "each in its own order" (15:23).

1 Cor 15:42-49: So is the resurrection of the dead. What is sown in corruption is raised in incorruption; what is sown in dishonor is raised in glory. What is sown in weakness is raised in power. Sown a psychic body, it is raised a pneumatic body. For so it is written: "the first man Adam became a living soul"; the last Adam, a life-giving spirit. But the pneumatic is not the first, but the psychic, and then the pneumatic. The first man is from earth, choic; the second man from heaven. Those who are choic are like the choic, and those who are heavenly, like the heavenly. And as we have borne the earthly image, so also we shall bear the heavenly image.

Now Paul reveals the great "mystery" (15:51). Although the psychic has been sown into "corruption, dishonor, and weakness" (15:42-43), into "death and the cosmos,"[189] as Theodotus says, it shall be raised in "incorruption, glory, and power" (15:42-43). "Sown a *psychic* body, it shall be raised a *pneumatic* body; for if there is a *psychic* body, there is also a *pneumatic* body" (15:44).[190] Theodotus explains that elements of the pneumatic seed were sown even into the psychics.[191] The Valentinians explain from 15:45 that the "first Adam," the demiurge's creation, was made a "living soul."[192] Yet secretly "Sophia put forth pneumatic seed into

Adam," concealing it within the psychic creation as living marrow is concealed within the structure of bone.[193] Therefore the "last Adam"—the transformed psychic—shall be a "life-giving spirit."

Paul goes on to say that "the pneumatic is not first, but the psychic. . . . the first anthropos was from earth, choic, but the second from heaven" (15:46-48). The author of the Gospel of Philip, interpreting this passage, says of

the "man from heaven," many more are his sons than of the "man of earth." If the sons of Adam are many, but nonetheless die, how much more are the sons of the Perfect Man, those who do not die, but continually are begotten. [194]

Because of this act of "ineffable providence"—Sophia's sowing the divine seed into the psychic creation[195]—the psychic, although he bears the *choic* image, shall also bear the *pneumatic* image! So Theodotus interprets this passage:

Whomever the Mother generates is led into death and into the cosmos; but he whom Christ regenerates is transferred to life in the Ogdoad . . . they die to the cosmos, but live to God, death having been released by death, and corruption by resurrection . . . "having borne the image of the choic," they then bear "the image of the heavenly."

1 Cor 15:50-52: This I declare, brothers: that flesh and blood cannot inherit the kingdom of God, nor can corruption inherit incorruption. Behold, I tell you a mystery: we shall not all sleep, but we shall all be changed, in a moment, in the twinkling of an eye, at the last trumpet. The trumpet shall sound, and the dead shall be raised incorruptible, and we shall be changed.

Who, then, receives the resurrection? Is it the "first Adam," the demiurge's creation, mortal in soul and body,[197] who is resurrected? The Valentinians claim that Paul shows that the "first Adam" must put off the material bodies which bear the "choic image," and be transformed. They insist that Paul states this clearly in 15:50 when he declares that "flesh and blood cannot inherit the kingdom of God, nor can corruption inherit incorruption." They consider this decisive evidence against the church's claim of bodily resurrection—resurrection "in this flesh," as Tertullian says.[198] Irenaeus says that "all the heretics always introduce this passage" into debates on this issue.[199] Tertullian complains that they perversely insist on their own exegesis of it.[200] The gnostics claim that it was the psychic apostles—whose understanding was (and remained) merely "literalistic"—who proclaimed Christ's bodily resurrection.[201] Paul alone, they claim, as "apostle of the resurrection," taught the pneumatic doctrine of resurrection: that "flesh and blood cannot inherit the kingdom of God, nor can corruption inherit incorruption." Nothing that is psychic, nothing that comes from the demiurge, can enter into the kingdom of God the Father.[202] Instead, "what is corruptible must put on incorruption" and "what is mortal must put on immortality" (15:53). Heracleon cites this verse to show that the psychic, "corruptible" in body and "mortal" in soul (cf. Mt 10:28), can only receive salvation after he has "put off" the psychic "garments" of body and soul.[203]

1 Cor 15:54-56: For this corruptible must put on incorruption; and this mortal must put on immortality. When this corruptible puts on incorruption, and this mortal puts on immortality, then shall come to pass the saying that is written: "death is swallowed up in victory. O death, where is your victory? O grave, where is your sting?" The sting of death is sin, and the strength of sin is the law.

How can the psychic be transformed into the pneumatic? The author of Philip cites 15:54 to refute the error of "those who wish to arise in the flesh": he says they are afraid that they will be "naked" without the body, but they fail to realize that, while "clothed" in the body, they are "naked" of the spiritual garments.[204] Heracleon and Theodotus explain that the psychic shall "put off" the garments of body and soul when the demiurge's "reign of death" is ended and "swallowed up in victory." As the savior was "divested of perishable rags," and was "dressed with incorruption,"[205] so for others matter shall be "swallowed up," plurality in unity, "obscurity by light, death by life."[206] Then, "the psychic elements are raised and saved," and, taking off their former garments, share in the "nakedness" of those who enter the pleromic bride chamber.[207]

1 Cor 15:57-58: But thanks be to God, who gives us the victory through our Lord Jesus Christ. Therefore, my beloved brothers, be strong, immovable, always abounding in the work of the Lord, knowing that your labor in the Lord is not in vain.

Finally Paul praises God the Father who gives the victory through "our Lord Jesus Christ," whom Theodotus calls the "great champion, who received to himself the church, the elect and the called, the one (pneumatic) from the mother, the other (psychic) from the dispensation, and he saved and raised what he had received."[208]

Having revealed this great mystery, the resurrection of the dead, that those who are "dead" (the psychics) are to be "raised," Paul assures the elect that their present labor—their work of preaching and ministering to psychics "in the Lord"—is not in vain (15:58).

NOTES: 1 CORINTHIANS

1. On significance of the preposition (per/ διά),, see discussion of Rom 3:30; Scherer, 170-174; cf. AH 1.7.2; 3.16.1; compare Naassene and docetic exegesis of Jn 3:5-6, in Ref 5.7, 8.10; Tertullian's attack on Valentinian and other exegetes (DC 20):

   > To what shifts you resort in your attempt to rob the syllable *ex* of its proper effect as a preposition, and to substitute for it another (*per*) not found in the Holy Scriptures. You say that he (Christ) was born *through* (*per*) a virgin, not of (*ex*) a virgin. . . .

2. τὸ ὄν : *JTS* 9.232; EV 27.30-28.16; cf. Scherer, 210; on Rom 1:7: " ἐν ῥώμῃ " om. G 1908 mg Orig.

3. *JTS* 9.232: A suggestion that Origen rejects, arguing that all included in ἐκκλησία are "called."

4. Exc 26.1; 22.4-6; EV 38.6-41.3.

5. AH 1.13.2-3.

6. Exc 74.1.

7. AV 4; *Strom* 7.17.

8. AH 3.12.1-14.1: cf. Irenaeus' refutation of the Valentinian account of Paul as a pneumatic teacher and Peter as a psychic one; for Origen's response to this claim, cf. Scherer, 177 (n. 12).

9. *JTS* 9.233, 238; see discussion of 1 Cor 2:4.

10. AH 3.16.8.

11. AH 3.16.1; 16.6; 3.15.2; 4.33.3; N. Brox, *Offenbarung*, 22-35.

12. Cf. CJ 6.20; AH 1.21.1-2: on pneumatic baptism, E. Segelberg, "Evangelium Veritatis: A Confirmation Homily and Its Relation to the Odes of Solomon," *Orientalia Suecana VIII* (1959): 3-42; E. Pagels, "A Valentinian Interpretation of Baptism and Eucharist," *HTR* 65 (1972): 154-162.

13. AH 1.3.5:

    > καὶ διὰ τούτου τὴν ἐνέργειαν τοῦ Ὅρου μεμηνυκέναι πτύον γὰρ ἐκεῖνον τὸν Σταυρὸν ἑρμηνεύουσιν εἶναι...Παῦλον δὲ τὸν Ἀπόστολον καὶ αὐτοῦ ἐπιμιμνήσκεσθαι τούτου τοῦ Σταυροῦ λέγουσιν οὕτως ·ὁ λόγος γὰρ ὁ τοῦ σταυροῦ τοῖς μὲν ἀπολλυμένοις μωρία ἐστι, τοῖς δὲ σωζομένοις ἡμῖν δύναμις Θεοῦ · καὶ πάλιν. [Gal 4:14]

    Cf. AH 1.8.3; CJ 10.33.

14. CJ 13.60.

15. Ref 6.35; see discussion of Rom 1:25.

16. CJ 13.51; cf. Mt 22:9.

17. EV 19.22-27.

18. EP 132.14-20:

    > Now we have the manifest things of the creation. We say they are the strong which are honored. But the hidden are the weak which are despised. So it is with the revealed in the truth: they are weak and despised, but the hidden are the strong and are honored.

    See note, Wilson, 188.

19. These occur as technical terms for psychics and pneumatics respectively: see EV 27.30-28.16; Scherer, 210.

20. ER 46.25-32: here, according to M. L. Peel, *The Epistle to Rheginos, A Valentinian Letter on the Resurrection*, (London: SCM/Philadelphia: Westminster, 1969), 80, 151n: "The abstract noun TMNTAΘHT translates the Greek ἀφροσύνα or ἀνοία (Crum 715a) but it can translate μωρία."

21. Cf. AH 3.14.1-2; cf. AH 1.24.4.

22. AH 3.2.1:

When they refuted from the scriptures, they . . . claim that the scriptures are ambiguous (*convertuntur ipsarum Scripturarum, quia varie sint dictae*) and that the truth cannot be derived from them by those who are ignorant of tradition (*et quia non possit ex his inveniri veritas ab his qui nesciant traditionem*). For they allege that the truth was not delivered by means of written documents, but in living speech, wherefore Paul also declared, "But we speak wisdom among those that are perfect, but not the wisdom of this cosmos," (1 Cor 2:6—*Non enim per literas traditam illam, sed per vivam vocem: ob quam causam et Paulum dixisse: "Sapientiam autem loquimur inter perfectos: sapientiam autem non mundi hujus." Et hanc sapientiam unusquisque eorum esse dicit . . . ut digne secundum eos sit veritas . . .*).

Cf. also 1.8.4; 3.3.1; 3.14.1-2; AV I.

23. AH 1.8.4; 3.3.1; 3.15.2; Ref 7.26.
24. Ref 7.26; cf. AH 1.24.4.
25. AH 1.3.5; 1.8.3. J. Ménard (*L'Évangile de Vérité*, 88) notes that in EV 18.21-24, "*L'Erreur . . . serait à assimiler aux Archontes de I Cor 2.8 qui ont crucifié le Christ.*"
26. AH 3.3.1-2; 3.15.2; AV I.
27. Ref 5.24:

Ὄμνυε δέ, φησὶν Ἰουστῖνος, εἰ γνῶναι θέλεις ἃ ὀφθαλμὸς οὐκ εἶδε, καὶ οὓς οὐκ ἤκουσεν, οὐδὲ ἐπί καρδίαν ἀνθρώπου ἀνέβη, τὸν ἐπάνω πάντων ἀγαθόν. τὸν ἀνώτερον, ἄρρητα φυλάξαι τὰ τῆς διδασκαλίας σιγώμενα.

This formula (apparently the oath of secrecy required of those being initiated into "the gnosis of the Father") may have been repeated both at the beginning of the ritual and again at its conclusion; cf. Ref 5.26-27. The account indicates that the initiate undergoes the same process of initiation that the demiurge himself has undergone.

28. ET 17. Strikingly, both citations of 1 Cor 2:9 omit the final phrase. Exc 86.3 may suggest the reason: the final phrase may have been taken to refer to the divine "marriage of syzygies," the vision of God (cf. Exc 64) which is revealed only eschatologically. The extant *Excerpta ex Theodoto* conclude with this phrase, apparently in anticipation of the final entrance into the *pleroma*, when "συνεισῆλθον εἰς τὰ ἡτοιμασμένα ἀγαθά, εἰς ἃ ἐπιθυμοῦσιν Ἄγγελοι παρακύψαι." Exc 86.3; cf. 1 Cor 2:9a.

29. τὰ βάθη τοῦ θεοῦ: AH 1.2.2; praef, 2; EV 24.10-12; Ref 5.6:

Μετὰ δὲ ταῦτα ἐπεκάλεσαν ἑαυτοὺς γνωστικούς, φάσκοντες μόνοι τὰ Βάθη γινώσκειν·

For references, cf. Sagnard, *Gnose*, 634.

30. *JTS* 9.239. The Naassenes apply 1 Cor 2:12 specifically to initiation into the "secret mysteries" of the *Anthropos* (cf. 1 Cor 2:11), which remain incomprehensible to the uninitiated; Ref 5.8. Basilides also interprets the "wisdom" of 2:7 as secret, oral initiation that answers such questions as:

τίς ἐστιν ὁ οὐκ ὤν, τίς ἡ υἱότης τί τὸ ἅγιον πνεῦμα, τίς ἡ τῶν ὅλων κατασκευή, ποῦ ταῦτα ἀποκατασταθήσεται· αὕτη ἐστὶν ἡ σοφία ἐν μυστερίῳ λεγομένον, περὶ ἧς...ἡ γραφὴ λέγει·   [1 Cor 2:13].

31. AH 1.8.3.
32. Ref 6.34. For Naassene exegesis of 2:14, Ref 5.8.
33. Ref 6.24-27.
34. AH 1.8.3; 2.19.2-7.
35. CJ 2.21; alternatively, they can be said to be generated by "the son of man beyond the *topos*," CJ 13.48-49.

36. AH 1.6.4; 2.19.4.
37. CJ 13.49-51; AH 1.5.3-6; 2.19.4.
38. CJ 13.51.
39. CJ 13.46.
40. CJ 13.44; for discussion, see Sagnard, *Gnose,* 489-494; Pagels, *Johannine Gospel,* 98-113.
41. CG 11,2:36.28-36.
42. EF 7.10; EV 127.18-30; AH 1.13.2.
43. Ref 7.23:

    ἠγνόει γὰρ ὅτι ἐστὶν αὐτοῦ σοφωτέρα καὶ δυνατωτέρα καὶ κρείττων. νομίσας οὖν αὐτὸς εἶναι κύριος καὶ δεσπότης καὶ σοφὸς ἀρχιτέκτων τρέπεται εἰς τὴν καθ᾽ ἕκασται κτίσιν τοῦ κόσμου.

44. Exc 47.1:

    Πρῶτος μὲν οὖν Δημιουργὸς ὁ Σωτὴρ γίνεται καθολικός· ἡ δὲ Σοφία δευτέρα οἰκοδομεῖ οἶκον ἑαυτῇ καὶ ὑπήρεισεν στύλους ἑπτα.

45. CJ 10.33: on temple as *ecclesia,* see discussion of Hebrews 9.
46. AH 1.7.1; Exc 48.4.
47. Exc 37.
48. Exc 38.1-4.
49. *JTS* 9.244-245: Origen, protesting this exegesis, offers a polemical one instead: those who build with gold, silver, and precious stones are the "orthodox," while "those of the heresies who blaspheme are 'wood,' and the others are 'hay and stubble.' "
50. CJ 10.33.
51. On "boasting," see discussion of Romans 4.
52. Cf. EV 18.15-18.
53. AH 3.16.8; 4.33.3.
54. AH 3.15.2; so, they claim, Paul accommodated his teaching, whether exoteric or esoteric, to his audience; AH 1.14.1-2.
55. CJ 13.10; AH 1.6.4.
56. AH 1.6.4; 3.15.2; CJ 13.16-17.
57. AH 1.13.6; so Carpocrates teaches that the gnostic, being liberated from the cosmic archons, becomes superior to them (AH 1.25.2).
58. See discussion of 2 Cor 8:9.
59. See discussion of Phil 2:7-9.
60. See discussion of 1 Corinthians 9.
61. Exc 58.1.
62. On *ta panta* as epithet of the pleroma, see AH 1.3.4; on the abortion expelled from it, AH 1.8.3.
63. Ref 5.7.
64. CJ 13.15:

    ...ἐξεπόρνευσεν, ὅτι δι ἄγνοιαν θεοῦ καὶ τῆς κατὰ τὸν θεὸν λατρείας ἀμελήσασαν καὶ πάντων τῶν κατὰ τὸν βίον αὐτῇ ἀναγκαίων, καὶ ἄλλως ἀεὶ τὴν ἐν τῷ βίῳ τυγχάνουσαν.

65. CJ 13.11: Heracleon takes the term of Jn 4:18 as *six* instead of *five,* since six symbolizes materiality, as he explains (CJ 10.38).
66. CJ 13.11; *JTS* 9.242.
67. AH 1.6.3-4; cf. 1.25.1-4; 1.23.3.
68. AH 1.6.2-4.
69. Exc 67.1.
70. *JTS* 9.363-364. Tertullian (DR 45-47) explains that the heretics identify the *flesh* with the *body,* in which they say that sin resides.

71. Exc 51.1-2.
72. *JTS* 9.364.
73. *AH 1.8.3:* Exc 58.2; 1.3: see discussion of Rom 11:16.
74. CJ 10.19; EF 5.8, 15.
75. CJ 10.19; Exc 57-58; 63.1-2.
76. On *cosmos* as technical term for psychics, see Pagels, *Johannine Gospel,* 93-94.
77. *JTS* 9.360; Origen protests this exegesis. For technical terms, cf. EV 27.35-28.24.
78. AH 1.6.2; cf CJ 13.60.
79. CJ 20.38: note Heracleon's exegesis of Rom 13:1: "every soul" (psychic) remains subject to "the powers."
80. AH 1.13.6.
81. AH 1.21.5.
82. AH 1.23.3; Haer Fab 1.1.
83. AH 1.24.4-5.
84. AH 1.25.4-5.
85. Cf. CJ 13.16.
86. Exc 52.1-2.
87. *JTS* 9.371.
88. So Origen; cf. *JTS* 9.370-372; and Irenaeus, cf. AH 5.1-8.1.
89. Ref 6.34; AH 5.7.1; see Tertullian, DR 18-19; 35.
90. AH 1.8.4.
91. Ref 6.34; Irenaeus contests this exegesis, AH 5.7.1.
92. AH 1.6.1.
93. CJ 13.11.
94. AH 1.8.4 (n. 81 above); CJ 13.11-15; AH 1.13.1-6; Exc 36.1; EP 112.29-114.4; 115.9-30; 118.9-119.15; 129.34-130.26; CG 11,2:39.10-38.
95. CJ Frag 39.
96. For discussion, see: R. M. Grant, "The Mystery of Marriage in the Gospel of Philip" *Vig Chr* 7 (1961): 129-140; E. Segelberg, "The Coptic Gnostic Gospel According to Philip and Its Sacramental System," *Numen* 7 (1960): 189-200; E. Pagels, "Valentinian Interpretation of Baptism and Eucharist," *HTR* 65:2 (April, 1972): 153-169.
97. CG 11,2:39.10-38; 43.1-44.37.
98. AH 1.13.3:

> Εὐτρέπισον σεαυτήν, ὡς νύμφη ἐκδεχομένη τὸν νυμφίον ἑαυτῆς ἵνα ἔσῃ ὃ ἐγώ, καὶ ἐγὼ ὃ σύ. Καθίδρυσον ἐν τῷ νυμφῶνί σου τὸ σπέρμα τοῦ φωτός. Λάβε παρ' ἐμοῦ τὸν νυμφίον καὶ χώρησον αὐτον, καὶ χωρήθητι ἐν αὐτῷ. Ἰδοὺ ἡ χάρις κατῆλθεν ἐπὶ σέ.

99. AH 1.6.4.
100. EP 130.2-8:

> For marriage in the cosmos is a mystery for those who have taken a wife. But if the marriage of uncleanness be hid, how much more is the marriage undefiled a pure mystery. It is not sarkic but pure, and does not belong to desire but to the will.

Cf. CG 11,2:36.29-31: "For this is the will of the Father: not to allow anything to happen in the *pleroma* without a *syzygy.*"
101. Cf. R. A. Baer, Jr., *Philo's Use of the Categories Male and Female* (Leiden: Brill, 1970).
102. Exc 21.1-2; 22.4; 36.1.
103. EP 118.9-22.

104. Exc 17.2.
105. Exc 57.1.
106. Exc 21.1-22.4; 63.1-3; CG11,2:39.28-39; for discussion, see Pagels, "Conflicting Versions of Valentinian Eschatology," *HTR* 67.1 (1974): 35-53.
107. EV 19.28-34; 24.20-24; compare ER 45.16-17: "He put aside the cosmos which is perishing. . . ."
108. EV 19.28-34.
109. AH 1.3.4; EV 18.33-35; see Sagnard, *Gnose,* 650, for references to the pleroma as τὰ πάντα.
110. CJ 13.25.
111. CJ 13.17:

μὴ δεῖν...κα: ι 'Ιουδαίους· σέβειν τὸ θεῶν, ἐπείπερ καὶ αὐτοὶ μόνοι οἰόμενοι ἐπίστασθαι θεοῦ ἀγνοοῦσιν αὐτόν, λατρεύοντες ἀγγέλοις καὶ μηνὶ καὶ σελήνη.

112. CJ 13.19; EP 110.35-111.4.
113. Exc 67.1-4.
114. AH 1.6.3.
115. EV 33.22; Ménard, *L' Évangile de Vérité,* 157-158.
116. AH 1.6.1.
117. CJ 13.46.
118. CJ 13.30; 10.33.
119. CJ 20.38; compare ER 45.14-15.
120. Ref 5.21; CJ 13.60.
121. Ref 6.34.
122. CJ 13.19:

...τὸ "Ότι η σωτηρία ἐκ τῶν 'Ιουδαίων ἐστίν...ἐπεὶ ἐν τῇ Ιουδαια...ἐγενήθη, ἀλλ οὐκ ἐν αὐτοῖς (οὐ γὰρ εἰς πάντας αὐτοὺς εὐδόκησεν)...ὅτι...προσεκύνουν τῷ μὴ πατρὶ...ἐλάτρευον τῇ κτίσει, καὶ οὐ τῷ κατ' ἀλήθειαν κτίστη, ὅς ἐστιν Χριστός...

123. CJ 13.16; Exc 85.1.
124. EF 5.9.
125. Ref 5.3.
126. Exc 42.3.
127. AH 1.13.1-3.
128. EP 105.6-7; cf. AH 4.18.4-5.
129. EP 110.35-111.4; CJ 10.19.
130. AH 1.13.1-3; CG 11,2:43.21-44.36.
131. AH 4.18.4-5; cf. 3.15.2.
132. AH 1.8.4; Exc 21.1-4.
133. EP 116.22-26; 118.17-22.
134. Exc 33.2; 42.2; On Christ (or the Logos) as "Head," cf. CG 11,*1*:13.33-36; 16.28-31; 17.28-31; 18.28-38; 21.33-34.
135. Exc 47.1; AH 1.4.5; CG 11,2:35.10-32.
136. Ref 6.34-36; AH 1.7.2; Scherer, 173.
137. AH 1.8.2; Exc 44.1-2.
138. AH 1.8.2; Ref 6.34.
139. Exc 35.3-4. The same principle is expressed in CG 11,2:36.28-30: "This is the will of the Father: not to allow anything to happen in the pleroma without a syzygy."
140. Tertullian deplores Valentinian exegesis of this passage; DP 4-5.
141. Exc 2.3-4; on *drunkenness* as metaphor for oblivion, see H. Jonas *The Gnostic Religion,* 68-73; G. MacRae, "Sleep and Awakening in Gnostic Texts," in *Le Origini dello Gnosticismo,* ed. U. Bianchi (Leiden: Brill, 1967).

142. So the Simonians interpret this verse; Ref 6.14.
143. *JTS* 10.31.
144. Exc 42.1.
145. CG 11,1:20.30-40.
146. Ibid, 19.29-30.
147. Exc 35.4-36.1.
148. Exc 36.2.
149. CG 11,1:18.40; 19.36-40.
150. CJ 6.20.
151. CJ 6.39.
152. AH 2.26.1; 2.28.4-9.
153. AH 1.6.4: τὸ σπέρμα τὸ ἐκεῖθεν νήπιον ἐκπεμπόμενον, ἐνθὰ δὲ τελειούμενον;   2.19.1-6.
154. AH 2.26.1; *JTS* 10.34-35.
155. EP 109.36-110.5.
156. EP 127.18-30.
157. ER 43.33-44, 15; see Peel, *Epistle,* 53 n.
158. AH 1.8.2:

> Ὅτι δὲ αὐτῇ ἐπέφανεν ὁ Σωτὴρ ἐκτὸς οὔσης τοῦ Πληρώματος, ἐν ἐκτρώματος
> μοίρα, τὸν Παῦλον λέγουσιν εἰφηκέναι ἐν τῇ πρώτῃ πρὸς Κορινθίους · Ἔσχατον δὲ
> πάντων, ὡσπερεὶ τῷ ἐκτρώματι, ὤφθη κἀμοί...ὁμοίως πεφανερωκέναι αὐτὸν ἐν τῇ
> αὐτῇ ἐπιστολῇ, εἰπόντα · Δεῖ τὴν γυναῖκα κάλυμμα ἔχειν ἐπὶ τῆς κεφαλῆς διὰ τοὺς
> ἀγγέλους.

Cf. discussion of 1 Cor 15.8; 11.10.
159. Ref 7.26.
160. Exc 68.
161. AH 1.13.2-3.
162. *JTS* 10.44: Origen challenges this exegesis of 1 Cor 15:10.
163. AH 3.13.1: Against "those who say that Paul alone knew the truth, to whom the mystery was revealed through revelation" (*Eos autem qui dicunt, solum Paulum veritatem cognivisse, cui per revelationem manifestatum est mysterium*), Irenaeus argues that Peter and the other apostles equally received divine revelation (3.13.2; cf. discussion of Gal 2:5).
164. AH 3.12.7: Here Irenaeus outlines the Valentinian view: Peter, who still lacked perfect gnosis, preached to the circumcised (i.e., to psychics) the "God of the Jews" (the demiurge). Paul, on the other hand, having received gnosis, proclaimed to the Gentiles (to pneumatics) the One God, the Father (AH 3.13.2-5).
165. Irenaeus, AH 5.2-7; Tertullian, DR (passim); Origen, *JTS* 10.44-46. In Origen's discussion a Valentinian reader could hardly fail to note the following: while Paul invariably refers (in 1 Corinthians 15) to the resurrection of *Christ,* Origen insists on discussing (in his exegesis of 1 Corinthians 15) the resurrection of *Jesus.*
166. *JTS* 10.45-46.
167. Exc 22.2:

> Νεκροὶ δὲ ἡμεῖς οἱ νεκρωθέντες τῇ συστάσει ταύτῃ · ζῶντες δὲ οἱ ἄρρενες οἱ μὴ
> μεταβαλόντες τῆς συστάσεως ταύτης.

Scherer, 168 n. For Tertullian's account of Valentinian allegorizing, see DR 19.
168. *JTS* 44-46: Origen's argument demonstrates that his Valentinian opponents clearly do not "deny the resurrection": Origen says that, on the contrary, "every heresy agrees" that Christ was raised from the dead. What the heretics emphatically *do* deny is the orthodox interpretation of that doctrine which

includes the hope of *bodily* resurrection. Origen complains that "the heterodox want to allegorize" this doctrine, and to interpret it as signifying "the resurrection of human beings"! According to H. Ch. Puech and G. Quispel (DR) xi-xii:

> Les Valentines ne niaient pas tout uniment la résurrection des morts, mais l'avouaient. . . . La résurrection d'entre les "morts," accomplie au sein du baptême, était, d'ailleurs, liée, selon eux, à la réception de la "gnose," de la γνῶσις , d'une Connaissance illuminative révélant à l'initié ce qu'il était avant de venir ici-bas, ce qu'il y est devenue, c'est à dire ce qu'il est présentement, ce qu'il sera, une fois sauvé, délivré du corps et du monde: son origine et, par là, sa nature transcendante; son actuelle et provisoire déchéance; la certitude de son retour au lieu d'où il tire le principe de son être et où celui-ci existe en totalité, en plénitude, au "Plérôme" qui embrasse en lui son propre "plérôme." . . . Résurrection et régénération spirituelle se confondent.

169. AH 2.31.2; DR 19.
170. AH 1.6.1; Exc 30-35.4; 59.1-4.
171. Exc 23.1-4.
172. Exc 22.1-2.
173. AH 1.8.3:

> Ὅτι ἰδὼν ἤμελλε σώξειν ὁ Σωτὴρ, τούτων τὰς ἀπαρχὰς ἀνέλαβε, τὸν Παῦλον εἰρηκέναι · Καὶ ἦν ἡ ἀπαρχὴ ἀγία, καὶ τὸ φύραμα. Ἀπαρχὴν μὲν τὸ πνευματικὸν εἰρῆσθαι διδάσκοντες · φύραμα δὲ ἡμᾶς, τουτέστι τὴν ψυκικὴν Ἐκκλησίαν, ἧς τὸ φύραμα ἀνειληφέναι λέγουσιν αὐτὸν, καὶ ἐν αὐτῷ συνεσταλκέναι, ἐπειδὴ ἦν αὐτὸς ξύμη.

Cf. Exc 58.1-2; discussion of Rom 11:16.
174. CJ 10.37; cf. Tertullian, DR 19.
175. CJ 10.37; Exc 61.5; 58.1-2; *JTS* 10.44-46.
176. CJ 13.51.
177. CJ 10.35; Exc 61.5-8; CG 11,2:41.28-38.
178. Exc 61.5-8; 58.1-2.
179. AH 1.8.3; Exc 58.1.
180. Exc 80.1-3.
181. Exc 58.1; 62.1-2.
182. Ibid.
183. Exc 22.1-7:

> Εἰ νεκροὶ οὐκ ἐγείρονται, τί καὶ βαπτιξόμεθα;...Οἱ βαπτιξόμενοι δέ, φασίν, ὑπὲρ ἡμῶν τῶν νεκρῶν, οἱ ἄγγελοί εἰσιν οἱ ὑπὲρ ἡμῶν βαπτιξόμενοι, ἵνα ἔχοντες καὶ ἡμεῖς τὸ Ὄνομα μὴ ἐπισχεθῶμεν κωλυθέντες εἰς τὸ Πλήρωμα παρελθεῖν τῷ Ὄρῳ καὶ τῷ Σταυρῷ.

See discussion of Eph 5:31.
184. On θήριον, as metaphor for the passions, see CJ 13.16; Exc 85.1.
185. AH 1.6.1-4; EV 16.38-17.1; see discussion of Romans 1-4.
186. *JTS* 10.45-46; EP 104.26-105.19; ER 47.30-36; for discussion, see Malinine, Puech, Quispel, Till, *De Resurrectione,* 36; Peel, *Epistle,* 186.
187. AH 1.4.5; 1.6.4; Exc 1.3-2.2; 39.40.
188. Exc 21.1-3; 68: On the two types of seed, see: Pagels, "Conflicting Versions of Valentinian Eschatology," *HTR* 67.1 (1974): 35-44.
189. Exc 80.1-2.
190. Irenaeus' opponents consider this passage decisive evidence for their interpretation: AH 5.7.1-2; see also Tertullian, DR 53; ER 45.39-46.2: "This is the pneumatic resurrection (πνευματικὴ ἀνάστασις) which swallows up the psychic (ψυχικὴ) alike with the other fleshly (σαρκικὴ)": see Peel, *Epistle,* 75.

191. Exc 39-40; 50.1-53.5.
192. Exc 50.3; AH 1,5.5; Tertullian, DR 53.
193. Exc 53.4-5.
194. EP 106.17-22.
195. AH 1.5.6; 2.19.1-9; EV 27.30-31; see Ménard, *L'Évangile de Vérité*, 132-133.
196. Exc 80.1-3;EP 123.22; ER 45.28-40. For discussion see Malinine, Puech, Quispel, Till, *De Resurrectione*, 27-28; for Tertullian's argument against the Valentinian exegesis, see DR 49-53.
197. CJ 13.60.
198. DR 19.1-7.
199. AH 5.9.1-4; 5.13.1-2.
200. DR 49-50.
201. AH 3.3.1; 5.3.1-13.5.
202. AH 1.7.1.
203. CJ 13.60; Tertullian's opponents offer, apparently, a similar exegesis; see DR 51, 54-55.
204. EP 104.26-105.3.
205. EV 20.30-34; AH 5.9.9; ER 45.14-15. Malinine, Puech, Quispel, and Till (*De Resurrectione*, xxi, 39), Van Unnik (*JEH* XV, 21, 1964, 151) and Peel (*Epistle*, 93) agree that the expression "the transformation (μεταβολή) of things" in ER 48.35-36 distinctly echoes the Pauline theme of the "change" or "transformation" of the "resurrection body" (cf. 1 Cor 15:51-52).
206. EV 25.15-19; CJ 13.60; cf. Exc 80.2.2; ER 48.38-49.5; Tertullian, DR 54.
207. Exc 58.1-2; 61.7-8.
208. Ibid.

III

2 CORINTHIANS

2 Cor 2:14-17: Grace be to God, who in everything leads us in triumph in Christ, and through us reveals the fragrance of his gnosis everywhere. For we are the aroma of Christ to God among those who are being saved and those who are perishing, to some fragrance from death unto death, to others fragrance from life unto life. And who is sufficient for these things? We are not, like the many, merchandizing the word of God, but speak from sincerity, as from God, confronting (*katenanti*) God, we speak in Christ.

The Valentinians signify the "fragrance of gnosis" (2:14) in the fragrant oil they use in the apolytrosis sacrament. Ptolemy says that this symbolizes the "fragrance above all things."[1] Those who receive it themselves become "the aroma of Christ" to those in the cosmos (2:15). According to the writer of the Gospel of Truth, "the children of the Father are his aroma, for they are of the grace of his face. Therefore the Father loves his aroma, and manifests it everywhere. And if it is mingled with matter, he gives his aroma to the light, and, in his silence, he allows it to assume every form, every sound."[2]

Nevertheless, Paul continues, "we" the elect "are not merchandising the word of God (*logos toū theoū*)" like "the many" (2:17), that is, the psychics.[3] Heracleon describes how the psychics, like the merchants in the temple courtyard, "merchandise" the message of salvation "attributing nothing to grace, but considering the entrance of strangers into the temple in terms of their own advantage and gain."[4] Paul continues, "we speak sincerely, as from God, confronting God, we speak in Christ" (2:17). What does he mean? Origen's Valentinian opponents take this to mean that Paul here distinguishes the Father from the demiurge: therefore he says that he speaks

95

both *from* God, the "good Father," and *confronting* or *contrary to* (*katenanti*) god, that is, to the demiurge.[5]

2 Cor 3:1-6: Are we beginning to commend ourselves again? Or do we need, as some do, letters of recommendation to you or from you? You yourselves are our letter, written on our hearts, to be known and read by all mankind; revealing that you are a letter from Christ, having received our ministry, written not in ink, but in the spirit of the living God; not in stone tablets, but on fleshly tablets of hearts.

We have such confidence through Christ toward God. Not that we are sufficient of ourselves to claim anything as from ourselves, but our sufficiency is from God, who has sufficed us to become ministers of a new covenant, not in letter but in spirit. For the letter kills, but the spirit makes alive.

Valentinian exegetes correlate this passage with Rom 2:14-15, where Paul describes the "natural law" which the spirit has "written upon the hearts" of the elect.[6] This he contrasts with the law of Moses written "in letters" on "stone tablets." Paul rejects any claim of credit for himself or for his own works; he claims only that the "law of works" has been abolished, and the "law of faith," the law of the new covenant, offers life to him, as to all the elect.[7]

2 Cor 3:7-15: Now if the service of death, engraved in letters of stone, became so glorious that the sons of Israel could not look upon Moses' face because of its brightness, fading as it was, will not the service of the spirit be much more glorious? . . . Since we have such a hope, we are very bold, unlike Moses, who put a veil over his face so that the Israelites might not see the end of the fading glory. But their hearts were hardened: for to this day, when they read the old covenant, the same veil remains. . . . to this day whenever Moses is read, a veil lies over their heart. . . .

What does Paul mean? The Valentinians, rejecting the literal interpretation, recognize Moses as "the lawgiver himself," the demiurge. Service to his law is "service of death" (cf. 1 Cor 7:3).[8] The veiling of his face, pneumatically interpreted, symbolizes the veil with which Sophia covered her shame in her exile from the pleroma.[9] But in the present time (cf. 3:14-15) the veil has another meaning: it signifies that Christ's glory has been hidden from the "sons of Israel," that is, from psychics. Valentinian exegetes explain from this passage that "the psychic was hidden in darkness, and has a veil upon his heart."[10]

2 Cor 3:17-18: Where the spirit of the Lord is, there is freedom. We all with unveiled faces reflect the glory of the Lord, and are being changed in that likeness from glory to glory. . . .

Paul includes the elect with himself when he declares that "we" with "unveiled faces reflect the glory of the Lord" and are being transformed "from glory to glory," that is, from the psychic "glory" of the demiurgic

"Lord" and from the fading glory of his old covenant (3:7) to the "much greater glory" of the new, pneumatic covenant.[11]

2 Cor 4:1-6: Therefore, having such a service, as we received the mercy of God . . . in the revelation of truth we commend ourselves to every man's conscience before God. If our gospel is veiled, it is veiled to those that are perishing, in whom the god of this age has blinded the minds of those who do not believe, to prevent them from seeing the enlightenment of the gospel of the glory of Christ, who is the image of God. . . : for God has said, "Let light shine from darkness," who shone in our hearts for the enlightenment of gnosis of the glory of God in the face of Christ.

Paul speaks as if answering an accusation—the charge that he himself has kept hidden "his gospel" (4:3) or has deliberately obscured it. The gnostic reader would recognize that his accusers probably refer to the apostle's practice of secretly instructing "the initiates" in "wisdom" (cf. 1 Cor 2:6-9), in the pneumatic version of the gospel.[12] The apostle answers with a counter accusation: he, having received his ministry "from God" (4:1), has preached "in the openness of the truth" (4:2). If "his gospel" is obscure it is so only "to those who are perishing." He refuses to accept blame for its obscurity; instead, Valentinian exegetes claim, Paul accuses "the god of this age"—the demiurge—of "blinding the minds of those who do not believe." For the demiurge seeks to hinder men from receiving the "enlightenment of the gospel," the revelation of the Father, who is "beyond every principality and rule and power."[13] The Father "is he who said, 'Let light shine out of darkness' " (4:6); but the demiurge attempts to obscure the "enlightenment of the gnosis of God's glory" (4:6), to the gnosis that would reveal to them the Father! Paul insists that the fault lies not in his preaching but in their perception. He then defends his preaching of a psychic version of the gospel ("what we preach is . . . *Jesus Christ as Lord*"), with the claim that he is forced to accommodate his teaching to the psychics' limited capacity.[14] For Paul himself claims to have been enlightened, to have received gnosis "from God" (4:6); but, as he goes on to explain, he has been compelled to hide that "glory" from the psychics, who could not even bear to look upon the "fading glory" of the *old* covenant (3:7).

2 Cor 4:7-16: But we have this treasure in earthen vessels, that the transcendence of power may be from God, and not from ourselves. . . . we always bear the deadness of Jesus in the body, that the life of Jesus might be revealed in our body. For we, the living, are continually given over to death through Jesus, that the life of Jesus might be manifested in our mortal flesh. . . . knowing that he who raised the Lord Jesus will raise us also with Jesus and bring us with you into his presence. For it is all for your sake. . . . though our outer man is destroyed, our inner man is renewed from day to day.

For the psychics' sake, Paul says, he consents to hide the treasure—"enlightenment of the gnosis of glory" (4:6)—in the "earthen vessels" of his human flesh. Tertullian indicates that heretical exegetes interpret 4:10 to mean that "the deadness of Jesus"—the somatic counterpart of the pneumatic Christ—is manifested also in the fleshly existence of the elect.[15] For although the apostle is among "the living" (4:11)[16] (the elect being, as Valentinus says, "by nature immortal and deathless")[17] he is "given up continually to death," that is, to the power that reigns over the present cosmos.[18] Yet Paul anticipates that the Father, "who raised the Lord Jesus, will raise us also with Jesus" from "the deadness of this existence"[19] and will "bring us *with you* into his presence," so that psychics, although dead, may be resurrected to pneumatic "life in Christ" together with the elect.[20] The sarkic, "outer man" perishes, but the pneumatic "inner man" is renewed continually: according to Tertullian's gnostic opponents, that although the flesh, the "old man" perishes, the spirit within the flesh, the "new man," continually is renewed.[21]

2 Cor 5:1-8: For we know that if our earthly dwelling of this tent (*skēnous*) is destroyed, we have a dwelling place from God—a house not made with hands, eternal in the heavens. And indeed we groan for this, earnestly longing to be clothed with our heavenly dwelling; if indeed, although unclothed, we shall not be found naked. For indeed we groan, being oppressed in this tent, not that we want to be unclothed, but to be clothed, so that the mortal may be swallowed up by life. The one who works this in us is God, who has given us the deposit of the spirit. Therefore we are confident in every way, and we know that while we dwell in the body we dwell apart from the Lord; for we walk by faith, not by sight. For we are confident, and willing rather to dwell apart from the body and present with the Lord.

The writer of the Gospel of Truth marvels how Jesus, being "clothed with eternal life . . . divested himself of these perishable rags" and "clothed himself with incorruptibility."[22] So, he explains, for each one who receives gnosis, "obscurity is swallowed up by light, and death by life."[23] The teacher of Rheginos apparently assumes this meaning as he agrees with the author of the Gospel of Truth that "the savior has swallowed up death (you should not remain in ignorance) for he has abandoned the perishable cosmos, and has become an imperishable aion; and he raised himself up, having swallowed up the visible with the invisible . . . this is the pneumatic resurrection, which swallows up the psychic alike along with the sarkic."[24]

Rheginos is encouraged to "depart" from the body (cf. 5:8): "for you" his teacher says, "absence (from the body) is a gain."[25] How can this be? "Some are afraid that they will arise naked," explains the author of the Gospel of

Philip (apparently referring to 5:3-4). To allay such fears he offers a gnostic exegesis of the passage:

> . . . therefore they want to arise in flesh (*sarx*). They do not know that those who bear flesh are already naked! But those who unclothe themselves are not naked. "No flesh and blood shall inherit the kingdom of God." What is the flesh that shall not inherit? That which we have. What is that which shall inherit? It is the flesh and blood of Jesus: for this reason he said, "whoever does not eat my flesh and drink my blood has no life in him." What is it? His flesh is the logos and his drink the holy spirit. Whoever has these has nourishment, and has drink and clothing. [26]

2 Cor 5:11-18: Knowing the fear of the Lord, we persuade men: but we are revealed before God; and I hope that we are revealed also in your consciences. . . . If we are ecstatic (*exestēmen*) it is before God: if we are moderate (*sōphronoumen*) it is before you. For the love of Christ constrains us. . . . henceforth we know no one according to the flesh. If once we knew Christ according to the flesh, now we know him so no longer. Therefore if anyone is in Christ—a new creation! Behold, old things have passed away; all things have become new; and all things are of God. . . .

The apostle explains that the elect preach psychically to psychics who fear the demiurge: "knowing the fear of the *Lord*, we persuade men" (5:11).[27] Yet "we"—the elect—"are revealed before *God*" the Father, and before him "we are ecstatic," even though he admits that "before you" psychics the elect restrain and moderate their behavior (5:14). Even those of the elect who once knew Christ "according to the flesh" (5:16) now know him pneumatically, "according to the spirit."[28] The apostle who previously bore "the deadness of Jesus" (4:10-11) now knows only the living Christ (5:14-16). For the elect the "old things" of the demiurgic creation have already "passed away": now "all things are become new, and all things are of God."[29]

NOTES: 2 CORINTHIANS

1. AH 1.21.3.
2. EV 33.39-34.9.
3. On "the many" (οἱ πολλοί) as technical term for the psychics see, for example, CJ 13.51; Exc 36.2.
4. CJ 10.33.
5. Scherer, 220.
6. Cf. discussion of Rom 2:14-15.
7. Scherer, 174-178.
8. On *Moses* as the demiurge, cf. CJ 20.38; on βασιλείαν τοῦ θανάτου, Exc 58.1; ER 44.17-21.
9. AH 1.8.2:

> Καὶ ὅτι ἥκοντος τοῦ Σωτῆρος πρὸς αὐτήν, δι αἰδῶ κάλυμμα ἐπέθετο ἡ Ἀχαμώθ, Μωσέα πεποιηκέναι φανερόν, κάλυμμα θέμενον ἐπὶ τὸ πρόσωπον εὐτοῦ.

10. Ref 6.35:

> ...ἐγκεκάλυπτο ὁ ψυχικὸς ἄνθρωπος, καὶ εἶχε κάλυμμα ἐπὶ τὴν καρδίαν.

11. CJ 6.10; Exc 57.
12. AH 1.2.1-3.1; cf. discussion of 1 Cor 2:6-9.
13. AH 3.7.1-2.
14. AH 3.13.1-14.4.
15. Tertullian, DR 44; cf. CJ 6.60.
16. Exc 22.1; Scherer, 196-204.
17. *Strom* 4.89.1-3.
18. Exc 58.1; 80.1-3.
19. Exc 59.1-3; CJ 13.60.
20. Exc 22.2.
21. Tertulian, DR 45; cf. CJ 6.60.
22. EV 20.38-32.
23. EV 25.15-19.
24. ER 45.14-46.2; cf CJ 13.60; Exc 80.1-3.
25. ER 47.19-20; cf. Tertullian, DR 43.
26. EP 104.26-105.8.
27. Exc 23.1-3.
28. Cf. discussion of Rom 1:3.
29. Cf. discussion of Gal 3:28.

IV

GALATIANS

Gal 1:1-5: Paul, an apostle, not from men nor through man, but through Jesus Christ and God the Father who raised him from the dead . . . grace to you and peace from God our Father and from the Lord Jesus Christ, who gave himself for our sins that he might deliver us from the present aion, according to the will of God and of our Father, to whom be glory unto the aions of the aions.

Paul intends in Galatians to distinguish his own pneumatic teaching of the gospel from the merely psychic preaching of the other apostles; so Valentinian exegetes claim. Irenaeus devotes the third book of his treatise to refute their exegesis, arguing that Paul's account in his letter to the Galatians agrees with the harmonizing account in Acts 15. Irenaeus insists, indeed, that Paul's message agrees not only with that of the Jerusalem apostles, but also with the traditions of Israel. Yet the Valentinians make a plausible exegetical case for their interpretation, which contrasts the liberty that Paul, the pneumatic teacher, reveals "to the Gentiles"[1] with the psychic kerygma that Peter, who "lacked perfect gnosis," preaches "to the Jews."[2] The author of the Gospel of Philip, who frequently cites Galatians, contrasts the "Hebrews" whom he identifies as "the apostles and apostolic men" and characterizes as "the dead," with the "Gentile" who is "alive."[3]

Such exegetes infer from Gal 1:1, for example, that Paul intends to contrast the commission the other apostles receive "from men and through man" with that which he himself receives from "God the Father." They point out that Paul identifies the Father as the one who receives "glory among the aions of aions," as he "clearly names the aions" in their pleromic order.[4] The Father wills "to deliver us from the present evil aion" which is ruled by the demiurge, whom Paul calls "the god of this aion" (cf. 2 Cor 4:4).[5]

101

Gal 1:6-8: I am astonished that you are so quickly deserting him who called you in the grace of Christ for another gospel—not that there is another, but there are some who trouble you and want to pervert the gospel of Christ. But even if we or an angel from heaven should preach to you a gospel contrary to that which we preached among you, let him be accursed.

Paul is astonished and dismayed that the Galatians have deserted the Father, "the one who has called you in the grace of Christ" for "another gospel." What is this "other gospel"? The Valentinians claim that the other apostles—including Peter and Luke—preached another gospel,[6] even another god[7] than Paul proclaimed. Knowing neither the truth nor the Father themselves, "the apostles preached the gospel still in some way under the influence of Jewish opinions."[8] Paul warns that whoever preaches anything other than what he himself has preached, even if that "other" is an "angel from heaven" (the demiurge himself!)[9] he is "accursed." (Irenaeus calls such exegesis blasphemy, "the madness of those who . . . have imagined that they themselves have discovered more than the apostles, by discovering another god . . . and that they themselves are purer in doctrine and more insightful than the apostles."[10]

Gal 1:11-17: For I would have you know, brethren, that the gospel I preached is not a human one. For I did not receive it from man, nor was I taught it, but received it through revelation of Jesus Christ. For you have heard of my former conduct in Judaism, how I violently persecuted the church of God and tried to destroy it; and I was advanced in Judaism beyond many of my age among my people. . . . But when it pleased the One who separated me from my mother's womb, and called me through his grace, to reveal his son in me, that I might proclaim him among the Gentiles, immediately I did not confer with flesh and blood, nor did I go into Jerusalem to those who were apostles before me, but I went into Arabia, and returned again to Damascus.

Paul says that once he preached "what I also received" (1 Cor 15:3ff) in common with the other apostles; but here he discloses "what I did not receive from men" (1:12). This means, according to Valentinian exegetes, that of all the apostles, Paul "alone knew the truth, since to him the mystery was revealed by revelation" (cf. 1:12).[11] He admits that he himself, like the others, formerly was ignorant of the Father: he too had been taught "in Judaism." According to Valentinian symbolism, this means that Paul too once worshiped the demiurge "in flesh and error" along with the psychic "Jews."[12]

Paul continues: "but . . . the one who separated me from my mother's womb . . . was pleased to reveal his son in me." The Father, then, is the one who "separated" Paul: but what did he "separate"? Valentinian exegetes, citing 1 Cor 15:46 ("the first anthropos is psychic, the second pneumatic") answer that he separated Paul the psychic "outer anthropos" from the pneumatic "inner anthropos."[13] The "old anthropos" must be "put off" (cf. Col 3:9-10) in order to "put on" the new, pneumatic anthropos. Psychics must effect this transformation through their own efforts; but the Father himself already has "separated" the pneumatic "from the womb of (his) mother," that is from Sophia, through his will in pre-election.[14]

The apostle goes on to say that God has chosen "to reveal his son in me (*en emoi*)"; as Heracleon explains, the elect receive him *within* themselves (*en autois*) while psychics receive him only externally *among* themselves (*par' autois*).[15] Recognizing that he was to communicate his pneumatic revelation not to the psychic "Jews" but to the pneumatic "Gentiles," Paul says that he avoided going to "Jerusalem," to the psychic region (*topos*),[16] and he shunned "those who were apostles before me" (1:17). The gnostic author of the Gospel of Philip characterizes "the apostles who were before us," as "Hebrews, the apostles and apostolic men."[17] He went instead into Gentile lands (1:17), that is, into the pneumatic region. He remained "unknown by sight" to the assemblies in Jerusalem; this might remind the gnostic reader that the psychics, limited to sense-perception alone, are incapable of perceiving what is pneumatic.[18]

Gal 2:1-5: Then, after fourteen years, I went up to Jerusalem with Barnabas, taking Titus with me. I went up according to revelation, and I set forth—in private before those who were respected—the gospel which I preach among the Gentiles, lest in any way I should be running or had run in vain. But even Titus, who was with me, was not required to be circumcised, although he was a Greek. But because of false brethren secretly brought in, who came in to spy out our freedom which we have in Christ Jesus, so that they might enslave us—to them we did not yield in submission even for a moment, so that the truth of the gospel might be preserved for you.

Here Paul clarifies his relationship to the apostles "before him"—those who preach the psychic version of the gospel.[19] To stress his independence from them, he states first that he visited them only when he had completed fourteen years of evangelistic activity; second, that he went accompanied by Barnabas and Titus (a "Greek," i.e., pneumatic like himself). Third, he declares that he went "according to revelation" (2:2) and not out of any sense of subjection to their authority.

Why, then, did he present the gospel he preached among the Gentiles "in private" to prominent members of the Jerusalem community? And why does he say that, had he not, he might have "run in vain"? The initiated reader could understand his reasoning: Paul knows that such privacy is the essential precondition for communicating the pneumatic gospel.[20] Although Paul says that Titus, his pneumatic companion, was not compelled to submit to psychic practices (to "circumcision," 2:3), he notes that certain "false brethren" among the psychic Christians wanted to "enslave" their pneumatic brethren, apparently envying their freedom in Christ (2:4). Paul declares that he "did not yield in submission to them—not even for a moment" (2:5). Paul knows that his opposition to the "Judaizers" (as the Valentinians understand it) is essential to preserve the pneumatic's spiritual autonomy and liberty of conscience against the authoritarian and moralizing psychics.[21]

Irenaeus, confronted with this "heretical" exegesis of the passage, offers an opposite interpretation: that Paul's private disclosure of his gospel to Peter, James, and John expresses his need for them to authorize his teaching.[22] Strikingly, Irenaeus and Tertullian, attempting to refute heretical exegesis of the passage, both reject the usual reading of the text. Both follow an infrequent variant reading that *omits* the negative, to read 2:5a "for a time we *did* yield to subjection, so that the truth of the gospel might be preserved for your sake." On this basis they claim that Paul *did* submit to the authority of the Jerusalem apostles. Irenaeus compares his reading of Gal 2:5 with Acts 15 to conclude that "Paul's statement harmonizes with and is identical with Luke's testimony concerning the other apostles."[23] Both Irenaeus and Tertullian intend their exegesis of this passage to refute the distinction between Paul's gospel and that of the other apostles.

Gal. 2:6-10: Those who were of reputation (what they were does not matter to me—God shows no partiality), those, I say, who were of repute added nothing to me; but on the contrary, when they saw that I had been entrusted with the gospel to the uncircumcised, as Peter had been entrusted with the gospel to the circumcised (for the one who has energized Peter for the apostleship to the circumcised also energized me for the Gentiles), and when they perceived the grace that was given to me, James and Cephas and John, who were reputed to be pillars, gave to me and to Barnabas the right hand of communion, that we should go to the Gentiles, and they to the circumcised. Only they wanted us to remember the poor, which I myself was eager to do.

From this passage the Valentinians could infer that even the leaders of the psychic community recognized that Paul was sent to proclaim the perfect gnosis he received through grace to the "Gentile" elect.[24] Peter (whom the emerging "orthodox" majority was coming to claim as the primary founder of their church) was sent to preach specifically to the "circumcised," that is, to psychics. Peter, "lacking perfect gnosis," himself remained "ignorant" and "imperfect" (ateles: uninitiated):[25] as the apostle "to the Jews" he was sent from the demiurge[26] (the "god of the Jews")[27] to preach the kerygmatic message of "Jesus."[28]

While the contrast between Paul's pneumatic gospel and Peter's psychic preaching remains a fundamental premise in much of their theology,[29] the Valentinians apparently acknowledge from 2:8 that the same One energizes *both* types of preaching. Some, it seems, anticipate that even the psychics finally shall come into perfect gnosis and come to know the true Father.[30] Those among the psychic community who understood that Paul had received a higher gnosis than their own gave him "the right hand of communion," apparently signifying his special responsibility "to those on the right," the pneumatic "Gentiles," as they themselves took primary responsibility to preach "to those on the left," the psychic "circumcised" (2:9).[31] They only remind Paul to "remember the poor," that is, apparently, the psychics among his audience; so that, as Theodotus says, he willingly preaches "in each of two ways," in one way for pneumatics, and in another for psychics.

Gal 2:11-16: But when Cephas came to Antioch, I opposed him to his face, for he stood condemned. For before certain men came from James, he ate with the Gentiles; but when they came, he withdrew and seprarated himself, fearing the circumcision party. . . . we ourselves, knowing that a man is not justified from works of the law, but through faith in Jesus Christ, have believed in Jesus Christ, in order to be justified from faith in Christ, and not from works of the law, for all flesh shall not be justified from works of the law.

Paul now explains his confrontation with Peter. When Peter ventured into Gentle territory ("into Antioch") even he, for a time, disregarded the moral scruples that characterize psychics. Yet when certain psychics were present, he apparently tried to compel even some of the pneumatic "Gentiles" to "act like Jews" (2:14). For the psychic apostles, being "still under the influence of Jewish opinions," still observe the "law of Moses"[32] in obedience to the demiurge.

Gal 2:19-21: For through the law I died to the law, that I might live to God. I have been crucified with Christ; I live, yet it is no longer I, but Christ who lives in me. What I now live in the flesh, I live in faith in the son of God, who has loved me, and has given himself for me. I do not reject the grace of God; for if righteousness is through the law, Christ died in vain.

The initiated reader could see here Paul's affirmation that he has "died" to law, having been redeemed from the cosmos and from its demiurgic ruler.[33] For crucifixion symbolizes the process separation described in Gal 6:14 ("the cosmos has been crucified to me, and I to the cosmos"). Valentinian exegetes explain what Paul means; that what in him was hylic has been consumed, and what is psychic has been purified.[34] He now "lives" pneumatically or, rather, Christ lives "in him."[35] Instead of rejecting "grace," he rejects the "righteousness through the law" in which psychics place their hope.[36]

Gal 3:1-5: O foolish Galatians! Who has bewitched you, before whose eyes Jesus Christ was publicly portrayed as crucified? This alone I want to learn from you: did you receive the spirit from works of the law or from hearing in faith? Are you so foolish? . . . does he who gives the spirit to you and works miracles among you do so from works of the law, or from hearing from faith?

Paul chastises the "foolish," that is, in gnostic terminology, the psychics who reject the pneumatic gospel for an inferior version of it.[37] Basilides says that those who confess Jesus as the crucified one are still enslaved to the "God of the Jews";[38] the Naassenes say that such persons have been "bewitched" by the demiurge, whose spell has the opposite effect of the Logos' divine enchantment.[39] The Sethians agree that only the unknown Father supplies the spirit and works miracles (3:5).[40]

Gal 3:6-11: As Abraham "believed in God, and it was accounted to him for righteousness," know that those who are from faith are the sons of Abraham . . . so those who are of faith are blessed with faithful Abraham. For all who depend upon works of the law are under a curse. . . . Therefore it is clear that in the law no one is justified before God, because "the just shall live by faith."

Why does Paul refer to Abraham, Israel's ancestor, as an example of faith? The initiated reader would recognize that Paul's reference to Abraham is no more to be taken literally than his previous references to the Jews. Hippolytus explains that "Abraham" signifies the demiurge, as the "children of Abraham" are the psychics.[41] Characterized as Abraham, the demiurge exemplifies faith in God (3:6), as Heracleon says; "the demiurge believes well."[42] Only those of the psychic creation who share his faith are blessed along with him, men and angels alike. Those who reject his faith "in God" are consigned to the outer darkness. Heracleon explains that the psychics, apart from faith in the Father, stand "under a curse": they stand under the demiurgic "law of sin and death" (cf. Rom 7:21).[43] Therefore, as Paul says in 3:11, "it is clear that in the law no one is just before *God*"—in the law one can be justified only before the demiurge. But the psychic ("the just")[44] cannot receive divine life from the demiurge; he can only receive it as the demiurge does, from God the Father.[45]

Gal 3:13-14: Christ redeemed us from the curse of the law, having become a curse for us; as it is written, "cursed be everyone who hangs on a tree," so that in Christ Jesus. the blessing of Abraham might come upon the Gentiles, that we might receive the promise of the spirit through faith.

What is "accursed" is the fleshly body, which involves mankind in the curse upon materiality.[46] The crucifixion signifies the giving up of the material body to destruction; simultaneously the inner man is released for reunion with God.[47] Paul adds that this release from materiality ("the blessing of Abraham") comes "to the Gentiles (the elect) so that we may receive the promise of the spirit through faith" (3:14). Heracleon explains that the savior reveals himself first to the elect; they, in turn, proclaim him to the psychics, "for through the spirit (the pneumatic elect) and by the spirit the soul (the psychic) is led to the savior."[48] The psychics first apprehend the savior in a limited way; later they come fully to recognize and receive him.[49] To illustrate this Paul gives a "human example" in 3:15-18.

Gal 3:15-18: No one cancels or adds to a human will, once it has been ratified: now the promises were made to Abraham "and to his seed." It does not say, "and to his seeds," as to many, but as to one, "and to your seed," which is Christ. This is what I mean: the law, which came four hundred and thirty years later, does not cancel the will previously ratified by God, to nullify the promise. . . . God gave it to Abraham by a promise.

Paul stresses here the singularity of the seed that has received God's promise. It was not given "to many," which to the initiate might suggest "the many psychics," but specifically "to one," that is, to the "elect nature, single formed and unified."[50] That this "one seed" is "Christ," might be taken to indicate that Christ and the elect are essentially one.[51]

Gal 3:19-20: Why, then, the law? It was added because of transgressions, until the seed should come to whom the promise had been made, having been transmitted through angels, in the hand of a mediator. Yet the mediator is not one; God is one.

Paul must answer the obvious question: why was the law given? He reveals that it was given "for transgressions," as a provision "until the seed should come" (3:19). Heracleon interprets 3:19b in reference to the pneumatic seed, which he says was sown and raised through the mediation of the demiurge's angels.[52] Another Valentinian agrees, citing 3:19 to show that "the seed was sown imperceptibly into Adam by Sophia" by means of the demiurgic angels. Yet the mediator—apparently the demiurge—is "not of one" as God the Father "is one."[53]

Gal 3:23-28: Now before faith came, we were constrained under the law, kept in restraint until the faith that was to come should be revealed. So the law became our instuctor (*paidagōgos*) for Christ, so that we should be justified from faith. But now that faith has come, we are no longer under an instructor; for in Christ Jesus you are all sons of God through faith. For as many of you as were baptized into Christ have put on Christ. There is neither Jew nor Greek, neither slave nor free, neither male nor female; for you are all one in Christ Jesus.

The initiated reader could see in 3:23-25 Paul's declaration of the liberation of the elect—as "sons of God" (cf. 3:26) from the restraints and tutelege of the demiurge's law. One Valentinian teacher describes how those "baptized into God" (cf. 3:27) in the name of the Father, Son, and holy spirit, are "reborn" and "become higher than all the other powers."[54] Apparently referring to 3:27, the author of the Gospel of Philip says that "the living water is a body. It is fitting that we put on the living man. Because of this, when he is about to go down to the water he unclothes himself, so that he may put on this one."[55] Rheginos' teacher adds that those who have died and been raised with the savior in baptism now "wear him."[56] Those who still identify themselves in terms of racial and social distinctions, however (as Jews, Greeks, slaves, or free; cf. 3:28) are not yet truly Christian.[57]

Gal 4:1-7: I mean that the heir, so long as he is immature (*nēpios*) is no better than a slave . . . but he is under guardians and administrators appointed by the father. So also we, when we were immature (*nēpioi*), were enslaved to the elements of the cosmos. When the pleroma of time came, God sent his son, having come into being from a woman, under law, so that he might redeem those held under law, so that we might receive the adoption. Because you are sons, God has sent the spirit of his son into our hearts crying "Abba, Father!" So you are no longer a slave but a son, and, if a son, an heir through God.

Paul reveals in Galatians 4 two distinct "sonships." The pneumatic, born as the "child of God," develops naturally toward his mature status as "God's son" through a process of continual growth. The author of Philip apparently has this in mind as he contrasts the psychic "slave" with the pneumatic "son":

The slave seeks only to be free, but he does not seek after the possessions (*ousia*) of his master. But the son is not only the son, but claims the inheritance (*klēronomia*) of the father. . . . what the father possesses belongs to the son, and he also, the son, so long as he is small, is not entrusted with what is his. But when he becomes a man his father gives him all that he possesses.[58]

The psychics, on the other hand, are "fatherless," but not, it seems, without hope: even the "fatherless orphans" can "obtain a father and mother."[59] Those born "as children only of the female" can become "children of a man."[60] Heracleon says that the psychics can become "sons of God" by adoption.[61] What belongs to the pneumatic by birth he can attain by voluntary choice and an act of will.

The apostle suggests that as long as God's son, the pneumatic, remains "immature," he finds his situation identical with that of the psychic "slave": he too remains subjected to the cosmic powers until the Father acknowledges his maturity (4:1-3). But the psychics are not so much disciplined as "enslaved to the elements of the cosmos" (*stoicheia tou kosmou* 4:3) — to the demiurge and his archons, who formed the elements (*stoicheia*) of Sophia's passion into the "weak and impoverished elements" of cosmic creation.[62]

To redeem the psychics ("those under the law," 4:5), "God sent forth his son in the pleroma of times" (for, as Theodotus says, he bore within himself the whole pleroma).[63] The savior "came into existence from woman" (4:4b) taking on himself the psychic nature generated from Sophia.[64] For according to the *Excerpts from Theodotus,* Paul

> refers to the woman above, whose passions became creation. . . . because of her the savior came to draw us from the passion and adopt us to himself. As long as we were children only of the female, as of a shameful syzygy, we were incomplete (*atelē*), immature (*nēpia*), senseless, weak, and formless, brought forth like abortions . . . but when we have received form from the savior, we became the children of a husband and a bridechamber.[65]

Through those who are sons of God "by nature," the pneumatic elect, God "sends his spirit" into the hearts of the psychics, so that they too may become his sons by adoption (4:6-7), as Heracleon also explains.[66]

Gal 4:8-11: Before, when you did not know God, you were in bondage to those that by nature are not gods; but now that you have come to know God, or, rather, to be known by God, how can you turn back again to the weak and impoverished elements (*stoicheia*), to whom you want to be enslaved again? You observe days, and months, and seasons, and years! I am afraid that I have labored over you in vain.

The apostle is concerned lest believers return to their former worship of the "weak and impoverished elements" which involves observing stars, the planets—elements that gnostic exegetes interpret as the cosmic powers. "The archons wanted to deceive man"; they contrived to make him offer animal sacrifices; yet in reality "no gods were they for whom they killed."[67] The savior offers to deliver mankind from this captivity and deception.[68] Heracleon says that the psychic "Jews," who "think that they alone know God, do not know him"; in their error and ignorance they worship "angels, the months, and the moon."[69] Paul now offers an allegory to illustrate the liberation his message offers.

Gal 4:21-26: Tell me, you who want to be under law, do you not heed the law? For it is written that Abraham had two sons, one from the slave woman, and one from the free. But the son of the slave was generated according to the flesh, and the son of the free woman through the promise. These things are an allegory: for there are two covenants, one from Mt. Sinai, bearing children for slavery, which is Hagar. Now Hagar is Mt. Sinai . . . she corresponds to the present Jerusalem. But the Jerusalem above is free, and she is our mother.

Valentinian exegetes give careful attention to this passage. For Paul says that Hagar is "Mt. Sinai," the "present Jerusalem" which signifies the "psychic region" where the psychic "Jews" worship the "god of the Jews." Theodotus says that her son, Ishmael, the "son of the slave woman" represents the "transformation of the psychic from slavery to freedom." But Sarah's son Isaac "represents allegorically the pneumatic," as Sarah herself represents "the Jerusalem above,"[70] the pneumatic region where the elect "worship God in spirit and in truth."[71] The Valentinians, like the Naassenes, praise the pneumatic Sophia as "Eve," the mother of all living, that is, of all who belong to "the Jerusalem above."[72]

Gal 4:27: For it is written: "Rejoice, O barren one that does not bear; break forth and shout, you who are in labor; for the barren one has more children than she who has a husband."

Here the initiated reader could recognize Paul's joy over the restoration of the lower Sophia: although she had become "barren" in separation from her syzygos[73] and brought forth only aborted offspring stillborn,[74] now she shall have "many children," the "many psychics" who are to be regenerated through Christ.[75]

Gal 5:1-24: For freedom Christ has freed us: stand, then, and do not submit again to a yoke of slavery. . . . I witness again that everyone who is circumcised is obligated to fulfill the entire law. . . . for the whole law is fulfilled in one word, in "you shall love your neighbour as yourself." . . . But I say, walk by the spirit and do not gratify the desire of the flesh. For the desires of the flesh are against the spirit, and the desires of the spirit are against the flesh; these are opposed to each other. . . . If you are led by the spirit, you are not under the law. . . . the fruit of the spirit is love, joy, peace, patience, kindness, goodness, faithfulness, gentleness, self-control: against such there is no law. Those who belong to Christ Jesus have crucified the flesh with its passions and desires.

Paul again contrasts the pneumatic's freedom (1:1) with the psychics' obligation to the law (1:3). Justinus the gnostic interprets 5:16-17 to mean that the psychic "soul" opposes the divine "spirit," and the spirit opposes the soul.[76] Theodotus says that the "flesh" of 5:16f signifies the "hylic soul," the lower element of the soul that resists the spirit.[77] According to Theodotus,

Paul here describes the conflict internal to the psychic, for the pneumatics, being "led by the spirit" are "not under the law" (5:18); "against such there is no law" (5:23). Those who "belong to Christ" have "crucified the flesh" with its passions (*pathēmata*), as the crucifixion symbolizes the release of the pneumatic from the hylic and cosmic elements. [78]

Gal 6:1-5: Brethren, if anyone should be overtaken in any transgression you who are pneumatic should restore him in a spirit of gentleness. . . . bear one another's burdens, and so fulfill the law of Christ. But if anyone thinks he is something when he is nothing, he deceives himself. Let each one test his own work, and then his reason to boast will be in himself alone, and not in another. For each one will have to bear his own burden.

What does Paul mean when he contradicts himself in 6:2 and 6:5? The initiated reader could see that Paul addresses in each passage a very different situation. First (6:2) he directs the pneumatics specifically to restore the psychics who are caught in sin and need (6:1-2). In doing this they "fulfill the law of Christ," the only law the pneumatics recognize, the "law of love" (5:14). But the apostle speaks to psychics in a very different tone: those who are "nothing"[79] are not to imagine that *they* are being addressed as pneumatics! While the pneumatics' concern for others involves a constructive, loving care for their needs, the psychics' concern involves a destructive anxiety lest others surpass them in merit (6:4). Therefore Paul warns each psychic to concern himself only with his *own* work, and to bear only his *own* burden (6:5).

Gal 6:7-9: Do not be deceived: God is not mocked. Whatever a man sows from the flesh that he also shall reap. For the one who sows in his own flesh shall reap corruption from the flesh, but the one who sows in the spirit shall reap eternal life from the spirit. Let us not weary in doing good: in due time we shall reap, if we do not lose heart.

Theodotus explains that Adam, the demiurge's creation, sows "neither from the spirit nor from the psyche, for both are divine, and both are put forth through him but not by him. But his hylic nature is active in seed and generation."[80] Adam sows "from the flesh," and reaps only corruption; but the elect (as Heracleon says) sow "from the spirit," and reap the fruit of eternal life. [81]

Gal 6:14-16: Far be it from me to glory, except in the cross of our Lord Jesus Christ, by whom the cosmos has been crucified to me, and I to the cosmos. For neither circumcision nor uncircumcision count for anything, but a new creation. Peace and mercy . . . be upon the Israel of God.

Finally Paul rejects any "boasting": as one of the elect, he owes his redemption entirely to "the cross" which signifies his separation from the material and the psychic cosmos.[82] So, according to the author of Philip, "Jesus came crucifying the cosmos," separating the hylic and psychic from the pneumatic elements.[83] He concludes by reminding the Galatians that finally "neither circumcision nor uncircumcision means anything but a new creation" (6:15). All who recognize the eschatological hope common to psychics and pneumatics alike are blessed with "peace and mercy," but especially the elect, the "Israel of God,"[84] whom he commends to grace (6:18).

NOTES: GALATIANS

1. AH 3.13.1.
2. AH 3.12.6-7: The Valentinians apparently contrast the "God of the Jews," that is, of the *psychics* with the "God of the Christians," that is, of the pneumatic "Gentiles"; cf. Scherer, 168-170; AH 3.12.8.
3. EP 99.29-100.19; 103.28-30.
4. AH 1.3.1.
5. AH 3.7.1.
6. AH 3.12.12-15.
7. AH 3.12.6-7.
8. AH 3.12.12
9. AH 1.5.2:

    ἑπτὰ γὰρ οὐρανοὺς κατεσκευακέναι, ὧν ἐπάνω τὸν Δημιουργὸν εἶναι λέγουσι... Ἀγγέλους δὲ αὐτοὺς ὑποτίθενται, καὶ τὸν δημιουργὸν δὲ καὶ αὐτὸν ἄγγελον Θεῷ ἐοικότα.

10. AH 3.12.12.
11. AH 3.13.1.
12. CJ 13.19: AH 3.12.6-8: Irenaeus contradicts the Valentinian exegesis of Gal 1:7: These exegetes are, he says, "perverse" when they "oppose the Mosaic law, and consider it to be different from and contrary to the preaching of the gospels" (3.12.12).
13. AH 5.12.1-5.
14. CJ 13.27; 12.24; AH 5.12.5; cf. Rom 1:1.
15. CJ 13.52; 13.19.
16. CJ 10.33; Scherer, 196.
17. EP 110.5-7; 103.29-30. In the latter passage the author explains that such believers erroneously claim that "Mary conceived of the holy spirit," failing to comprehend the virgin birth as a symbolic reference to Sophia (cf. 103.23-36).
18. CJ 13.60; cf. discussion of 1 Cor 2:14.
19. Cf. note 17.
20. AH 3.2.1-3.1.
21. AH 3.13.3; 1.6.4.
22. AH 3.13.3.

23. AH 3.13.3; AM 5.3.
24. AH 3.13.2.
25. AH 3.12.7.
26. AH 3.13.1.
27. AH 3.12.6-7; Scherer, 168-170.
28. AH 3.16.1.
29. AH 3.13.1; AM 16.17, 16.19; Jer Hom 17.2; Scherer, 176-177, n. 2
30. As some anticipate that Peter and others may attain perfection; cf. AH 3.12.7. See discussion of Rom 3:29-31.
31. Cf. Exc 23.3-5; see Pagels, "Conflicting Versions of Valentinian Eschatology," *HTR* 67.1 (1974): 35-53.
32. AH 3.12.12-15.
33. Cf. Exc 77-80; Tertullian, DR 19; ER 45.24-27.
34. AH 1.3.5:

Παῦλον δὲ τὸν Ἀπόστολον καὶ αὐτὸν ἐπιμιμνήσκεσθαι τούτου τοῦ Σταυροῦ λέγουσιν... ἐμοὶ δὲ μὴ γένοιτο ἐν μηδενὶ καυχᾶσθαι, εἰ μὴ ἐν τῷ σταυρῷ τοῦ Ἰησοῦ, δι᾽ οὗ ἐμοὶ κόσμος ἐσταύρωται, κἀγὼ τῷ κοσμῳ • Τοιαῦτα μὲν οὖν περὶ τοῦ πληρώματος αὐτῶν...λέγουσιν.

35. CJ 13.15; ER 45.24-27.
36. Cf. CJ 20.38: it is "Moses," the "lawgiver" in whom the psychics "hope."
37. Ref 6.35.1-3.
38. AH 1.23.4.
39. Ref 5.2.
40. AH 1.30.13.
41. Ref. 6.34.
42. CJ 13.60: on "Abraham" as the demiurge, Ref. 6.36; as exemplar for the psychic church, AH 1.7.4; see discussion of Romans 4.
43. CJ 13.60.
44. Exc 53.1-3.
45. CJ 13.60.
46. Ref. 6.30.
47. CJ 6.60; AH 1.3.4; 1.21.4.
48. CJ 13.31.
49. CJ 13.35.
50. CJ 13.51; Exc 36.1-2.
51. CJ 2.21.
52. CJ 13.50.
53. Exc 53.2-3.
54. Exc 76.2-4.
55. EP 123.21-25.
56. ER 45.24-31.
57. EP 110.26-35.
58. EP 100.2-6; 108.1-6.
59. EP 100.21-24.
60. Exc 68; cf. 76.4, 79-80.3.
61. CJ 20.24: See discussion of Rom 8.14ff.
62. Exc 46.1-49.2; AH 1.4.3.
63. Exc 31.1.
64. Exc 59-60, 68-79.
65. Exc 67.4-68.
66. CJ 20.24.

67. EP 102.18-103.5; 110.35-111.4.
68. Exc 72.1; 69-74.
69. CJ 13.17.
70. Exc 56.5-57.
71. CJ 13.16; 13.19; 10.13; 13.60.
72. Ref 6.34; AH 5.35.2; for Naassene exegesis, cf. Ref 5.2.
73. AH 1.4.1-5; Exc. 67.1-68; CG 11,2:34.22-35.17; EP 107.31-108.1.
74. Exc 67.4-68; 80.1-2.
75. Exc 80.1-3; 67.1-68.
76. Ref 5.21.
77. Exc 51.1-52.2.
78. AH 1.3.5; cf. EP 111.21-24.
79. EV 27.35-28.24.
80. Exc 56.2.
81. CJ 13.49.
82. AH 1.3.5; CJ 10.33.
83. EP 111.21-24; see note Schenke and Till on this passage.
84. Exc 56.3.

V

EPHESIANS

Valentinian exegetes agree with their "orthodox" opponents in assuming Paul's authorship of Ephesians, Colossians, and Hebrews.[1] By contrast with the heresiologists, they virtually omit reference to the pastoral letters:[2] the lack of extant evidence suggests that they do not consider them authentically Pauline. For the gnostics, however, the question of authenticity is based upon criteria that are explicitly theological rather than historical.[3] For theological reasons they especially value Ephesians: for here, they claim, Paul unfolds the mystery of the pneumatic redemption.

Origen's commentary on Ephesians offers striking and detailed evidence of Valentinian exegesis,[4] which other sources often confirm. According to the Valentinians, Paul discusses the pneumatic election in Ephesians 1, and the psychic calling in Ephesians 2. In Ephesians 3 he explains his own pneumatic mission; in 4-5:30 he describes the present structure of the Christian community, and reveals in 5:31 the "great mystery" of the church's eschatological "marriage" with the savior. Finally in Ephesians 6 he shows both psychics and pneumatics how their present life is to reflect this eschatological vision.

Eph 1:1-6: Paul, apostle of Christ Jesus through the will of God, to the holy ones who are (*tois hagiois tois ousin*)   in Ephesus and to the faithful in Christ Jesus. Grace to you and peace from God our Father and from the Lord (of) Jesus Christ. Blessed be the God and Father of our Lord Jesus Christ, who has blessed us in every pneumatic blessing in the heavenly places in Christ, as he elected us in him before the foundation of the cosmos that we might be holy and blameless before him, in love having foreordained us into the adoption through Jesus Christ in him, according to the purpose of his will, in praise of the glory of his grace, in which he graced us in the beloved.

According to Valentinian exegesis, Paul began his letters to the Roman and Corinthian communities by identifying himself in both psychic and pneumatic terms. Here, by contrast (according to the Valentinians), he identifies himself exclusively in pneumatic terms, as an apostle sent "through the will of God."[6] He addresses first the elect—"the holy, those who are," who participate in the God who alone truly "is,"[7] and then the "faithful in Christ Jesus," that is, apparently, the believing psychics.

Paul offers "grace and peace" from "God our Father" (1:3), praising him as "the one who has blessed us in Christ with every pneumatic blessing." Valentinian exegetes insist that Paul intends here to distinguish clearly between "God our Father" and the demiurge. The Father offers "every *pneumatic* blessing," but, they say, the demiurge bestows only "somatic blessings" to those who obey his law.[8] What is that "pneumatic blessing"? That "he has elected us in him before the foundation of the cosmos" (1:4). The apostle refers to the pneumatic ecclesia, "elected before the foundation of the cosmos, accounted together and manifested in the beginning."[9] The writer of the Gospel of Truth explains that the names of the "little children, to whom belongs the gnosis of the Father," were manifested in the "living Book of the living," even "before the foundation of the All."[10] For the elect were "preordained to be his sons . . . according to the purpose of his will, to the praise of the glory of his grace" (1:5-6); in the words of Rheginos' teacher, "We were elected . . . having been destined from the beginning" for redemption.[11]

Origen objects that the term "adoption" (*huiothesia*) cannot refer "to those preordained by nature to be the sons of God": he charges that this exegesis is inconsistent with the Valentinian doctrine of the "adoption" of psychics.[12] Theodotus contends, however, that since Christ serves as the prototype for *both* the psychic and the pneumatic relation to God, he became an "adopted son" to signify the psychics' adoption, as well as the "elect" to signify the pneumatic sonship.[13]

Eph 1:7-11: . . . in which (*en hō*) we have redemption (*apolytrosis*) through his blood, the forgiveness of transgressions, according to the wealth of his grace, which he made to abound in us in all wisdom and understanding (*en pasē sophia kai phronēsei*), having made known to us the mystery of his will, according to his purpose, which he foreordained in him in the economy of the pleroma of times, to sum up all things in Christ, the things in heaven and those in earth. In him, according to the purpose of the one who energizes all things according to the counsel of his will. . . .

The two distinct modes of relationship to the Father work through different means. Paul says that the elect (1:4-6) are redeemed "according to the wealth of his grace" through "blood" (1:7). The Marcosians celebrate the pneumatic redemption (*apolytrōsis*) as a sacrament that echoes the language and imagery of this passage (1:3-10). The celebrant offers wine as the "blood of grace" (*charis*) invoking her (*charis*; the divine aion) to fill the one who partakes of the cup.[14] He prays for the participant that "grace may fill you in the inner man, and multiply in you the gnosis of her," as Paul here praises the "wealth of his grace, which he makes to abound unto us," which has conveyed "all wisdom (*sophia*) and understanding," and has "made known to us the mystery of his will," that is, apparently, the mystery of the pneumatic election, which the gnostic sacrament celebrates.[15] For God preordained the elect "in him," in the savior whom he sent from the pleroma (cf. 1:10).[16] The savior, who is called "the angel of counsel" (cf. Is 9:6; Eph 1:11), recapitulates and unites "all things," the pleroma[17] as well as the elements of cosmic creation ("things in heaven and those on earth").[18]

Eph 1:11-19: In whom we have been made heirs, having been predestined according to the purpose of the one who energizes all things according to the counsel of his will, for the praise of his glory, we who first hoped in Christ. In whom you also, having heard the word of truth, the gospel of your salvation, in which you also have believed, have been sealed with the holy spirit of promise, the guarantee of our inheritance. . . . therefore I, having heard of your faith in the Lord Jesus and your love for all those who are holy, continue in my prayers, that the God of our Lord Jesus Christ, the Father of glory, may give to you a spirit of wisdom and redemption in the knowledge of him (*pneuma sophias kai apokalypseōs en epignōsei autou*), the eyes of your hearts having been enlightened so that you may know what is the hope of his calling, and what is the wealth of the glory of his inheritance among the holy ones, and what is the surpassing greatness (*megethos*) of his power in us who believe. . . .

The initiated reader could note how Paul contrasts the elect ("we," 1:11-12) with the psychics ("you," 1:13-14). For the elect, "having been predestinated according to the purpose of his will" *already* have inherited what belongs to the Father (1:11); but the rest receive only the promise that guarantees their future inheritance (1:13).[19] Those who were "predestined" are those who "first hoped in Christ" (1:12b), and have been graced to receive wisdom (*sophia*, 1:8). To them God has revealed "the mystery of his will" (1:9) through their redemption (*apolytrōsis*, 1:7). Through the elect, others then are led to hear the "word of truth" (1:13), as Heracleon explains: "through the spirit and by the spirit the soul is led to the savior."[20] These others have not yet received wisdom, revelation or gnosis (1:17); they are still foolish, ignorant, and blind (1:18). They perceive the "word of truth" only, it seems, in psychic terms,[21] as "the gospel of (their) *salvation*" (1:13). Paul, as one of the elect who has already received redemption, wisdom, and gnosis, expresses his concern for those who have received only salvation (1:13). He assures them that they have been sealed by "the holy spirit of promise" as a guarantee of their future inheritance (1:14).[22] He prays that the "spirit of wisdom" may dispel their foolishness and ignorance,[23] and that the gnosis of the "Father of glory" (1:7) may enlighten the blind, darkened "eyes of (their) heart." What gnosis do they lack? First, they must come to know the hope that underlies their "calling" (1:18); second, the "immeasureable greatness" of the Father (1:19). Although the demiurge himself, according to Heracleon, confesses that he can understand neither the Father's "greatness" nor the mystery of the pneumatic economy,[24] the psychics here are promised that they shall come to understand these things.

Eph 1:20-23: . . . which he accomplished in Christ when he raised him from the dead and made him sit at the right hand of him in the heavenly places, far above every rule and authority and power and dominion, and above every one that is praised, not only in this aion, but in that which is to come: and he subjected all things under his feet, and gave him as head above the entire ecclesia, which is his body, the pleroma of the one who fills all things in all.

Paul anticipates that the psychics too will come to recognize how the Father raised Christ "from the dead," that is, from among the psychics and from cosmic existence, so that now the psychic Christ sits at the right hand of the demiurge ("him in the heavenly places," 1:20 . . . until "the end of the age."[25] Only then shall he be seen not only "far above every rule, authority, and power" (1:21) of the cosmic creation, but even above the demiurge himself. When the believer now subjected to the demiurge comes to recognize this, then he too will be "raised" to heights "beyond the threats of every other power."[26] Basilides, like Theodotus, interprets Eph 1:21 to mean that the psychic shall be "raised beyond the very one he now worships" as god.[27] Becoming "higher than all the other powers," he, like the resurrected Christ, shall reign "not only over the elements, but over the powers and evil rulers."[29] Then "the entire ecclesia" shall recognize the pneumatic Christ as its "head"[30] as he fills "all things," the entire pleroma (1:23).[31]

Eph 2:1-8: And you being dead in transgressions and in your sins, in which you once walked according to the aion of this cosmos, according to the archon of the power of the air, the spirit that now works in the sons of disobedience—in which even we all lived once in the desires of our flesh, doing the things willed by the flesh and the imagination, and we were also children by nature of wrath, as are the rest. But God, being rich in mercy, through the great love with which he loved us, even when we were dead in transgressions, made us alive together with Christ—for "by grace you have been saved"—and raised us and put us in the heavenly places in Christ Jesus, that the surpassing wealth of his grace toward us in Christ Jesus might be demonstrated among the aions to come. For you have been saved in grace, through faith: this is not from yourselves, it is the gift of God, not from works, lest anyone should boast.

Again Paul speaks to the psychics as "you" who are (or "have been") "dead in transgression and in your sins." Heracleon and Theodotus both use this metaphor: the psychics are dead "in sins,"[32] "deadened in this existence."[33] For, the apostle continues, "you have walked according to the aion of this cosmos," the demiurge, whom Paul also calls "the god of this cosmos" (2 Cor 4:4),[34] and according to "the archon of the power of the air" (2:2b). To whom does Paul refer? The Valentinians say that the demiurge created the devil from the passion of grief (*lupē*) which was transformed into the cosmic element of air.[35] The "power of the air," then, is the devil, the "spirit that now works in the sons of disobedience." Theodotus explains (citing Eph 6:12) that the devil and his angels are spirits, the "spiritual beings of evil with whom is our struggle."[36] The demiurge, apparently, is the "*archon* of the power of the air," the ruler and creator of the "evil spirit" which now works in those whom Heracleon calls "sons of the devil," who fulfill what is "willed by the flesh" (cf. Eph 2:3).[37]

Paul admits that "even we," the pneumatic elect, once fulfilled "the desires of the flesh," and were virtually "by nature children of wrath, like the rest."[38] Although the elect were, in effect, "dead in transgressions" (2:5, *paraptōmasin*; apparently, the transgressions of Sophia, for Paul does *not* say, as he does of psychics, that they were "dead in *sins*" *hamartiais*, 2:1) God "has made us alive together with Christ and has raised us up with him." So, according to the teacher of Rheginos, "as the apostle says, we suffered with him; and we arose with him, and we went to heaven with him."[39] The elect, then, celebrate the resurrection-life (which they received in baptism) as their present experience.

Paul reminds the elect that they have been redeemed "by grace, through faith" (2:8), completely apart from works. They have no grounds for "boasting," since once they were merely "Gentiles in the flesh" (2:11a), pneumatics living sarkically. They were even despised by the psychics, the "circumcision" ("you were called uncircumcision by what is called circumcision, which is made in the flesh by hands" 2:11b).[40]

Eph 2:12-18: For (*hoti*) at that time you were without Christ, having been alienated from the community of Israel, and strangers to the covenants of promise, having no hope, and godless (*atheoi*) in the cosmos. But now in Christ Jesus you, who once were far off, have been made near in the blood of Christ. For he is our peace, who has made the two one, and has broken down the partition separating us, the enmity: having abolished in his flesh the law of commandments and ordinances in order to create the two in himself into one new mankind, making peace, and restoring both in one body to God through the cross, having destroyed the enmity. And coming he preached peace to us, both to those afar off and to those who were near: for through him we both have access in one spirit to the Father.

What does Paul mean? Taken literally, this passage describes the reconciliation of Jews and Gentiles. Interpreted symbolically, it discloses the future reconciliation of the psychic "Jews" with the pneumatic "Gentiles"![41] For the elect, who "for a time" were alienated from the psychic "community of Israel," who refused to worship the "god of this cosmos," and seemed "godless in the cosmos," were actually, secretly, "near" to the Father, while the psychics were "far" from him. But Christ has come to break down the partition that separates the psychic from the pneumatic region, as Theodotus indicates. [42] The writer of the Gospel of Truth may be alluding to this passage as he describes how the "cold fragrances," the "psychic plasma," were the result of separation"; yet "because of this, faith came. It destroyed the separation and brought the warm fullness (*plerōma*) of love," uniting the psychics with the elect (the "warm fragrance") who are the Father's "aroma."[43] The savior, reconciling the two, abolishes the "law of commandments and ordinances" instituted through the demiurge.[44] Christ accomplishes this "through the cross" (2:16), which (Heracleon explains) symbolizes the power of the spirit to separate what is hylic, and to purify what is pneumatic.[45]

Christ then creates "the two in himself as one new mankind" (2:15; *hena kainon anthrōpon*) in which all are reunited. When there is no longer any distinction between psychic and pneumatic (cf. Gal 3:28; "neither Jew nor Greek, neither male or female, neither slave nor free"), all shall be joined together, "the elect and the called," in "one body"—in the one ecclesia.[46] Then Christ shall offer to both together "access in one spirit to the Father" (2:18).

Eph 2:19-22: So you are no longer aliens and transients, but fellow citizens with the holy, members of the house of God, built upon the foundation of the apostles and the prophets, Jesus Christ himself being the chief cornerstone, in whom the whole building grows into a holy temple in the Lord, in whom you also are built into it for a dwelling place of God in the spirit.

Heracleon says that the ecclesia *is* "the house of God."[47] He explains that at present, however, the temple is divided: psychics dwell in the "outer court" separated by a "veil" (i.e., the "partition separating us," 2:14) from the "holy of holies," where the pneumatics dwell with Christ.[48] Using this symbology, the initiated reader could see from 2:19-22 that the apostle anticipates that the division between the two will be abolished so that the psychics may join with the elect in the "holy of holies," becoming part of "God's house," in pneumatic worship of the Father.[49]

Eph 3:1-7: By means of this grace I Paul, a prisoner of Christ Jesus for the sake of the Gentiles—if, indeed, you have heard of the economy of the grace of God given to me for your sake, that by revelation the mystery was made known to me, as I wrote before in brief, from which you can, in reading, recognize my insight onto the mystery of Christ. In other generations it was not made known to the sons of men, as it now has been revealed to his holy apostles and prophets in the spirit, that the Gentiles are fellow-heirs and members of the same body, participants in the promise of Jesus Christ through the gospel, of which I became a servant according to the gift of grace of God given me, according to the energy of his power.

Previously Paul has characterized himself as a slave who voluntarily accepted his servitude to the demiurge for the sake of the psychic Jews (Rom 1:1; 1 Cor 9:20; Gal 1:10). Here, by contrast, he acknowledges himself as a prisoner through grace for the sake of the pneumatic Gentiles (1:1).[50] Before, he preached the economy of the demiurge: now he proclaims "the economy of the grace of God" the Father.[51] Ptolemy says that in this Paul reveals his superiority to the psychic apostles, for "he alone knew the truth, since to him 'the mystery was made known by revelation.' "[52] For while psychics participate in grace only "provisionally," the elect receive it as "their own," a gift which "descends upon them from above by means of an ineffable and indescribable syzygy."[53] Paul says he only alluded to this briefly in writing (3:3): the gnostic would know that only those who have "*heard* of the economy of the grace of God" (3:2) through secret, oral teaching would be able to recognize his insight onto "the mystery of Christ" (3:4).[54] So, according to the Gospel of Truth, "that, then, is the mystery of Him whom they seek, which he revealed to the perfect (*teleioi;* to the initiates) . . . as a hidden mystery; He, Jesus the Christ."[55] That the mystery of Christ was not made known "in other generations" means to the Valentinians that it was not known to the psychics, through the demiurge, as now it is known to "the sons of God," the elect.[56] Basilides agrees that the psychics remain ignorant of God the Father, and of what he reveals to the "sons of God."[57] The mystery is revealed only through initiation into the (pneumatic) gospel which Paul received by revelation.

Eph 3:8-11: To me, the least of all the holy ones, this grace was given: to preach to the Gentiles the unsearchable riches of Christ, and to enlighten the economy of mystery hidden from the aions in the God who has created all things, that the manifold wisdom (*sophia*) of God might be made known to the rulers and powers in heavenly places, through the church, according to the purpose of the aions which he made in Christ Jesus our Lord. . . .

Paul discloses that the "economy of mystery" had remained hidden even from the aions (3:9): it remained "in the God who created *all things,*" that is, the divine pleroma (3:11).[58] For the aions themselves were ignorant of the Father until Christ and the holy spirit were sent to enlighten them and to offer them gnosis of "his greatness."[59] Subsequently, the Valentinians explain, the pneumatic element (*to pneumatikon*)—Christ and the elect—were sent from the pleroma "through the purpose of the aions" (3:11a) into the kenoma and the cosmos to reveal "the manifold wisdom of God," the mystery of Sophia, to the cosmic "rulers and powers."[60]

Eph 3:14-19: Because of this grace I bow my knees before the Father, from whom every paternity in the heavens and on earth is named, that he might give to you, according to the wealth of his glory, to be strengthened through his spirit in the inner man (*ton esō anthrōpon*), that Christ may dwell in your hearts through faith: that you, being rooted and grounded in love, may have power to receive with all the holy ones what is the breadth and length and height and depth, and to know the love of Christ surpassing gnosis, that you may be filled with the whole pleroma of God.

Paul declares that he worships God the Father, through whom alone (according to Valentinus and his disciples) the demiurge is named "father," as "an image of the Father" (3:14) above.[61] Paul's prayer in 3:15-19 may have served as the basis for the Marcosian prayer at the apolytrosis sacrament, where the celebrant prays that "grace, who transcends all knowledge (*gnosis*) and speech, fill you in the inner man"[62] (since it is "the inner man [that] is redeemed through gnosis)."[63]

What is that gnosis? Taking 3:18 as their clue, the Valentinians interpret the secret meaning of Paul's terminology. The initiate comes to know "what is 'the depth,' which is the Father of the all, 'and what is the breadth,' which is Stauros, the limit of the pleroma, and 'what is the length,' that is, the pleroma of the aions."[64] Receiving the gnosis, the initiate is "filled with the whole pleroma of God," when Christ, who "bears within himself the whole pleroma"[65] comes to "dwell in him" (3:17-19).

Eph 4:1-10: I beseech you, then, I, a prisoner in the Lord, that you walk worthy of the calling in which you were called, . . . eager to maintain the oneness of the spirit. . . . there is one body and one spirit, just as you were called to the one hope of your calling: one Lord, one faith, one baptism, one God and Father of all, who is above all things, and through all things, and in all things. To each one of us was given grace according to the measure of Christ's gift. Therefore it says, "ascending on high he led a host of captives, and gave gifts to men." In saying, "he ascended," what does it mean but that he also descended into the lower regions of the earth? He who descended is he who also ascended far above the heavens, that he might fill all things.

Now Paul abruptly changes his tone. As the "prisoner of grace" he has celebrated the pneumatic election; now, as "prisoner of the *Lord*" (4:1), that is, of the demiurge, he addresses the psychic "calling" (4:1).[66] For the "one spirit" (4:3) works in the "one body"—the psychic ecclesia[67]—as it works in the pneumatic ecclesia.[68] For psychics there is "one Lord," the demiurge: "one faith," for they receive only the psychic version of the gospel: and "one baptism," since they remain ignorant of the pneumatic "second baptism."[69] Yet besides this there is the "one God and Father of all," the "incomprehensible, inconceivable One, the perfect Father who brought forth the all, in whom is the all, and whom the all needs" (cf. 1:6).[70] Yet not all recognize him, since "to each one grace is given according to the measure of Christ's gift" (4:7).[71]

Does this mean that the psychics are excluded from redemption? Paul's address suggests that they are not, for now he reveals how the psychics, presently enslaved to the demiurge, are to be released from their captivity and "led on high" (4:8). Theodotus interprets this passage to mean that Christ came to lead the psychics from the "place below," the cosmos, "on high";[72] citing 4:8, he says that the one who ascended into the pleroma had "descended" into the place below, so that he might."lead (the psychics) into the pleroma."[73]

Eph 4: 12b-16: . . . to build up the body of Christ, until we all attain to unity of faith and of the recognition of the son of God, into a perfect man (*andra teleion*) in the measure of the growth of the pleroma of Christ . . . from whom the whole body . . . grows and builds itself up in love.

Paul anticipates here that the pneumatic element (Christ and the elect) shall "unite in faith" (cf. 4:13) "elements that seemed to be divided,"[74] that is, the psychic and the pneumatic. What is now *woman* (the psychic) shall be transformed to become *man* (pneumatic), joined with the man to constitute the "perfect man" who is Christ.[75] The Valentinians explain that both psychics and pneumatics need to "grow," but the process of growth differs in each case. The pneumatic seed, sown in a state of infancy, grows continuously, naturally, to maturity;[76] the psychic must be transformed and changed from his slave status to that of adopted sonship.[77] Both processes effect the growth of the whole ecclesia into "one body" united and headed by Christ.[78]

Eph 4:22-30: Put off from you the old man (*ton palaion anthrōpon*) which belongs to your former way of life, and is being destroyed according to the desires of deceit; be renewed in the spirit of your mind, and put on the new man (*ton kainon anthrōpon*) which was created according to God in righteousness and holiness of truth.

Therefore, putting away the lie, let each one speak truth to his neighbor, for we are members of one another . . . do not give place to the devil. Let him that steals no longer steal, but rather let him labor, working with his own hands at what is good. . . . and do not grieve the holy spirit of God, by whom you were sealed unto the day of redemption.

Paul urges the psychics, who stand midway between what is material and what is spiritual,[79] to put off the "old man" which bears the stamp of the demiurge's creation, which is corruptible, ridden with deceitful desires. Rheginos learns that he is "corruption," so long as he remains identified with the body that grows old and decays.[80] Those regenerated are to "put on the new man," to "wear him" who is the "new creation."[81] They must also "put off the lie," that is, the devil, the principle of falsehood and materiality,[82] and not "yield place (topos)" to the devil. The author of the Gospel of Truth interprets this to mean "do not become (yourselves) a place for the devil, for you have already annihilated him."[83] Theodotus explains that to yield to the devil is to "grieve the holy spirit of God" (4:30), since the devil is the evil spirit made from the element of grief (lupē).[84]

Eph 5:1-5: Become imitators of God, as beloved children, and walk in love as Christ loved us. . . . but fornication and all impurity or greed should not even be named among you, as is fitting to the holy ones, as well as shamefulness and foolish talk or nonsense, which are not appropriate, but rather the celebration of eucharist (eucharistia). For know this: no fornicator, and no one marked by impurity or greed, which is idolatry, has an inheritance in the kingdom of Christ and God.

Read literally, Ephesians 5 teaches how Christians are to conduct their social relationships: read esoterically, it discloses the secret of enlightenment, and the "great mystery" of the divine marriage. Paul speaks first to the elect as the "beloved children of God." The gnostics, having rejected the sexual moralism of the law, interpret Paul's warning against "fornication" symbolically: it signifies the involvement with materiality that prevents the pneumatic from realizing spiritual enlightenment.[85] Paul also warns the elect against the "foolish talk" (5:4a) of the "foolish" psychics,[86] and against "greed, which is idolatry"—that is, greed signifies the idolatry of the psychics, who idolatrously worship the "image," the demiurge, instead of the Father.[87]

Instead of "fornication," the elect are to practice "eucharist" (5:4b). Origen's discussion of the passage suggests that the Valentinians take both terms as sexual metaphors—for opposite conditions. The pneumatic, delivered from "fornication," receives her divine "bridegroom" from the savior,[88] apparently in that spiritual "marriage" ritually enacted in the

Marcosian celebration of the eucharist.[89] The Valentinians caution against taking this symbolism literally. They say that psychics, being literalists, regard sexual intercourse in merely physical terms, as the experience of being overcome with sexual desire. Their sexuality debases them; they should practice abstinence instead. But the elect understand sexuality as a symbol of the "mystery of the syzygy": to practice this mystery is to participate in the divine marriage; it is the very opposite of "fornication."[90]

The Valentinian could note that Paul names six conditions (5:3-4) that render persons involved in them unfit for spiritual inheritance. Six, as Heracleon points out, is the symbolic number that designated "all material evil."[91] What the apostle is saying in 5:5, then, is that no one who involves himself in materiality can "inherit the kingdom of God and Christ" (i.e., in gnostic exegesis, apparently a parallel to 1 Cor 15:50).

Eph 5:6-21: Let no one deceive you with empty words. On account of these the wrath of God comes upon the sons of disobedience. . . . you were once darkness, but now you are light in the Lord. Walk as children of light . . . and try to learn what is pleasing to the Lord. . . . Therefore, it is said, "Awake, o sleeper, and arise from the dead, and Christ shall give you light." . . . Therefore do not be foolish, but understand what the will of the Lord is. . . . being subject to each other in the fear of Christ.

Now, apparently, Paul speaks to the psychics, who are susceptible to deceit and to error.[92] Those who allow themselves to be deceived become the "sons of disobedience," that is, of the devil, and incur "wrath."[93] But those who have renounced the devil, although once they were "darkness," are now "light in the Lord": they have received Jesus as their "light."[94] Through Christ, the Father "enlightened those who were in darkness because of oblivion; he enlightened them, and showed them a way."[95] Paul encourages them to do "what is pleasing to the Lord," since the demiurgic "Lord" has been appointed to rule over them for the present time.[96]

Yet the apostle promises that eschatologically even those who were oblivious to the Father shall be (according to 5:14) "aroused from sleep," and "awakened from the dead." For, according to gnostic exegesis, their sleep signifies "the oblivion of the soul"; but when the savior comes, he shines as light to awaken "the soul" and to resurrect the "dead."[97] Anticipating this resurrection, they are to "watch (their) conduct," and discern "the will of the Lord" (5:17). They are also to "subject themselves" to others "in fear of Christ" (5:21) since their position (*topos*) is still that of "slaves," and (as Theodotus says) "in this place (*topos*) they fear him."[98]

Eph 5:22-32: The women are to be subject to their own men as to the Lord; for the man is the head of the woman, as also Christ is head of the church, he himself being the savior of the body. But as the church is subject to Christ, so also the women are to the men in every respect. Men, love your women, as Christ also loved the church and gave himself for it, so that he might sanctify it, having purified it in the bath of water with the word, that he might present it to himself in glory . . . holy and blameless. So the men should love their own women as their own bodies. Whoever loves his woman loves himself. For no one ever hates his own flesh, but cares for it and nourishes it: as Christ does for the church, for we are members of his body. . . . This is a great mystery: I speak concerning Christ and the church.

What is Paul saying? Is he concerned here with the actual relationships between men and women? Ptolemy notes that Paul himself says he is speaking allegorically; he is using sexual terminology to allude to the "mystery of Christ and the church," to "the mystery of syzygies."[99] The initiate could see, then, that Paul, having urged the psychics to subject themselves to others (5:21), now is rephrasing his counsel in metaphor. As one Valentinian explains, "the males . . . are the elect, but the females the called":[100] so, according to Eph 5:22, the psychics, characterized as "women," "the woman," or "the females," are to subject themselves to the pneumatics, as to "men," to "man," or to "the males."[101] Paul draws the same contrast in 5:23; for Christ is the head of the ecclesia (the pneumatic ecclesia)[102] but "the savior (is head) of the body" (that is, of the psychics who are saved). Theodotus offers a similar parallel: Christ is the head of the "body of Christ," the elect, as Jesus is the "shoulders" of the "body of Jesus," the totality of psychics.[103] Paul describes the relationship between the two in 5:25, 28, 33) as they, in turn, are to "fear" the elect (5:33) as they fear Christ (5:21), reverently submitting to superior authority.

How are the elect, the "husbands," to express their love? Christ expresses his love for the church by cleansing her "in a bath of water in the word" (5:26) that is, in baptism. How then are the elect to cleanse and purify their psychic "wives"? The Valentinians answer that they do so by means of another baptism—a special proxy baptism they perform for the sake of the psychics! Taking 1 Cor 15:29 ("those baptized on behalf of the dead") as their clue, gnostic initiates, as "males," receive baptism "for the sake of the females." At the laying on of hands, they conclude the baptismal formula with the words, "for the angelic redemption." By this means they purify the one for whom the baptism is performed so that he (or she) may receive the "same divine name" that the elect have received.[104] This, then, is the "bath of water in a word" (5:26) that prepares the psychic "wife" to consummate the divine marriage.[105] In this way the elect "bathe" and care for the psychics as for "their own bodies" (5:28-30 according to a consistent Valentinian metaphor).[106] All their loving concern will receive its consummation in the "great mystery" to which Paul alludes in 5:32.

Here the initiated reader sees Paul's allusion to the pleromic reunion, the "marriage of syzygies."[107] Although often described as the marriage of Sophia with the savior,[108] the "marriage" is conceived in universal terms: the totality of the psychics who are saved, having been purified in the baptism "for the pneumatic redemption," are now joined with the elect: "The females, becoming male, and united with the angels. . . . Thus the woman is said to be changed into a man, and the church on earth into angels."[109]

Ascending into the Ogdoad, psychics celebrate the "marriage feast, which is in common for all who are saved," together with the pneumatics. At that feast, the "rest in the marriage," all become equal; all are united.[110] When this has taken place, there are neither "psychics" nor "pneumatics" any longer. The differences that characterized their cosmic existence apparently have now been obliterated; all are in perfect harmony with each other.[111] Psychics and pneumatics alike had worn "souls" as their "garments" in the cosmos; but now the whole company of the redeemed "puts off their souls," leaving them with the demiurge, who bestowed them, outside the "bridechamber"[112] (since "nothing psychic can enter into the pleroma").[113] The whole company now joins with the divine syzygies to become "noetic aions," and to ascend into "the bridechamber," the pleroma, to the vision of God.[114]

The "great mystery" of Eph 5:32, then, includes the eschatological vision that all who are redeemed shall attain to equality and harmony before God. According to one writer, "when Sophia receives her syzygy . . . then the pleroma will receive Sophia joyfully, and the all will come to be in unity and reconciliation (*apokatastasis*)."[115] The elect, who receive gnosis of this, are to "celebrate continually this mystery of syzygy." Paul instructs each "husband" to "love his own woman" (5:33); the Valentinians say, indeed that "whoever does not love a woman so that he joins with her is not of the truth, nor shall he attain to the truth"[116] since the elect themselves cannot enter into the pleroma except in conjunction with their psychic counterparts.[117]

Eph 6:1-8: Children, obey your parents in the Lord, for this is just (*dikaion*). "Honor your father and mother" (which is the first commandment in promise) "that it might be well with you." . . . Slaves, obey your masters according to the flesh with fear and trembling, in the simplicity of your hearts, as you obey Christ, as slaves of Christ, doing the will of God from the soul, rendering service with good will, as to the

Lord . . . knowing that whatever good one does, he will receive the same from the Lord.

The readers who see only instructions for married persons in Ephesians 5 would see in Ephesians 6 only practical household instruction. But the initiated reader could recognize here again Paul's deeper concern as he defines spiritual relationships. Paul contrasts what is "just"—obedience "in the Lord" (6:1)—with the "promise" given to the elect (6:2). Obedience is required only of psychics (6:1); but the elect are to "honor" their "father and mother"—the good Father of all and the divine Mother, Sophia. For as the author of Philip explains, "when we were Hebrews we were orphans but when we became Christians we obtained a father and a mother."[118] The "slaves" are to obey those who rule them "according to the flesh," the cosmic powers, because (as Heracleon explains from Rom 13:1-7) the Father has instituted these temporal authorities for their own good.[119] The best they can do is to "serve" and "do the will of God from the *soul*," that is, to the extent of psychic capacity, obeying "the Lord" who repays them according to their works (6:5-8).

Eph 6:10-22: For the rest, be strong in the Lord. Put on the whole armor of God, so that you may be able to stand against the wiles (*methodeias*) of the devil. For our struggle is not against the flesh and blood, but against the rulers, against the powers, against the cosmic rulers (*kosmokratoras*) of darkness, against the spiritual forces of evil (*ta pneumatika tēs ponērias*) in the heavens. Therefore, put on the whole armor of God, so that you may stand firm on the evil day. . . . keep awake in all perseverance, and in prayer for all the holy ones, and for me, that the Lord might give to me to open my mouth, to make known the mystery of the gospel in boldness, which now I represent in bonds, that I may become bold in it as I ought to speak it. So that you may know us and how things are with me, what I do, I am sending to you Tychicus, beloved brother and faithful servant in the Lord, who will make known all things to you, so that you may know the things concerning us, and your hearts may be consoled.

Paul warns the psychics that they face a struggle against the "world rulers and powers of darkness," against the agents of the devil, (who is called *cosmocrator*)[120] and against the whole host of demonic spiritual powers, as Theodotus says, interpreting 6:12.[121] He explains that the cosmic powers (including those that motivate the stars and planets) are not all malevolent: some are beneficial to mankind, and ally themselves with mankind against the evil powers. Others are hostile to mankind, and fight on the side of the "evil one" to oppress mankind.[122] Theodotus describes the means of this warfare: the evil powers attack the human soul "through the body," in order to gain power over the soul and enslave it. The soul itself is too weak to resist, "being easily led toward the worse, and captured by those who hate it."[123] Since the beneficent powers themselves were too weak to defend the soul, the savior came into the cosmos, attacked and conquered the powers, and rescued the soul from this tyranny.[124] Yet Theodotus warns that even those who have been rescued remain vulnerable to demonic attack, as "the Lord himself, after baptism, was tried in the desert." Therefore "we must put on the Lord's armor and keep the body and soul invulnerable—armor that is 'able to quench the darts of the devil,' as the apostle says."[125]

Finally, the apostle asks the psychics to pray for him, that he might be able to "open his mouth" (the physical organ that utters psychic speech) to speak "the word" (*logos*).[126] He longs to speak to them freely without the constraint that so far has confined his teaching to the psychics' limited perceptive abilities. He wants to speak boldly, pneumatically, "to make known the mystery of the gospel." Finally he promises to send his "beloved brother and faithful servant in the Lord" (6:21; that is, a pneumatic "brother" who, like Paul, also assumes the psychic role of "servant in the Lord") to "make known all things to you." For what purpose is he sending Tychicus? The initiated reader would take this to mean that he sends Tychicus to offer the secret, oral teaching (which he could not communicate in writing)[127] to those who now are ready to receive it.

NOTES: EPHESIANS

1. See intro., n. 29; on canon lists; cf. W. C. van Unnik, "The Gospel of Truth and the New Testament," in: *The Jung Codex* (London, 1955): 81-129; K. H. Schelkle, "Das Evangelium Veritatis als Kanongeschichtliches Zeugnis," *BZ*, n.f., 5 (1961): 90-91; J. E. Ménard, *L'Évangile de Vérité* (Leiden: Brill, 1972), 3-9; *The Gospel of Philip*, ed. R. M. Wilson (London: Mowbray 1962), 6-7. The discussion that follows adopts the stylistic convention of referring to "Paul" as author.
2. Irenaeus, by contrast, cites them extensively: he even opens his treatise citing 1 Tim 1:4 as the saying of "the apostle"; I. Praef.
3. Irenaeus, conversely, when he discusses the question of the "authenticity" of the Gospels, regards historical witness and verified transmission as a major criterion of their authenticity (AH 3.4.1-11.9): cf. N. Brox, *Offenbarung*, 79-113, 133-167.
4. *JTS* 3 (1902): 223-244, 398-420, 554-576.

5. Manuscript traditions divide over the inclusion of the phrase ἐν Ἐφέσῳ. While later texts include it (A, R, D, G), the second-century text of Marcion (Tert) and the third-century witness of Chester Beatty papyrus p. 46 omit it; *Novum Testamentum Graece*, ed. E. Nestle (Stuttgart: Württ, 1953), 489; see discussion of 1 Cor 1:2.

6. Origen indicates that his Valentinian opponents take the use of the preposition *διά* in 1:1 as indicating the pneumatic relationship, as the preposition ἐκ indicates the psychic; cf. Tertullian, DC 20; *JTS* 3.234-235; see also the similar discussion in Scherer, 170-174; discussion of 1 Cor 1:1.

7. *JTS* 3.235.

8. *JTS* 3.236: Origen, discussing their exegesis, concludes, "so the heterodox show, thinking that they have a basis for dividing the divinity from such an interpretation." Heracleon and Ptolemy agree that the prophetic order and the law, instituted by the demiurge, confer through somatic means merely somatic benefits: CJ 6.20; EF 5.8; 6.4.

9. Exc 41.2; Scherer, 160; AH 1.6.4; ER 46.25-32.

10. EV 19.27-20.2.

11. ER 46.25-32; on Χάρις as the aion through which redemption occurs, AH 1.13.1-3.

12. *JTS* 3.237; for a statement of the doctrine to which he refers, cf. CJ 20.24.

13. Exc 33.1-2.

14. AH 1.13.2.

15. Ref 5.2; 3.14.

16. AH 1.2.5-6.

17. Exc 43.2-3; on τὰ πάντα as a technical term for the pleroma, cf. Sagnard, *Gnose*, 158-159; 274-276; 364.

18. On Eph 1:11; cf. Exc 43.2-3.

19. Cf. EP 100.3-6; 108.1-6.

20. CJ 13.31.

21. CJ 13.60; Exc 23.

22. See *JTS* 3.242-244 for Origen's counter argument.

23. Ref 6.34; CJ 13.19.

24. τὸ μέγεθος: CJ 6.39; Sagnard, *Gnose*, 646.

25. Cf. Exc 62.1-2; 21-22; 61.6-8.

26. Exc 80.3; 61.8.

27. Ref 7.20-25.

28. Exc 76.4.

29. Exc 81.3.

30. On Christ as "head": Exc 42.2; 33.2; 43.2; Ref 7.27.9; CG 11,*1*.18.30-33; 19.33-34; 20.30-40.

31. AH 1.2.6.

32. CJ 13.60.

33. Exc 22.2; cf. ER 44.20-21.

34. Cf. AH 3.7.1; see discussion of 2 Cor 4:4.

35. AH 1.5.4.

36. Exc 48.1-3.

37. Cf. CJ 20.24: some psychics choose to do the will of the devil.

38. For Theodotus' exegesis of the Pauline term flesh (σάρξ), cf. Exc 67.1-68; for Heracleon's description of the pneumatic involved "in the flesh," cf. CJ 13.15. Origen declares that he cannot understand how "those who introduce

natures that are pneumatic from the beginning (οἱ τὰς πνευματικὰς ἀρχῆθεν φύσεις εἰσάγοντες)" can claim that this passage supports their position; nevertheless he indicates that they do make that claim; *JTS* 3.404. For the resurrection as present experience, see discussion of 1 Corinthians 15.

39. ER 45.24-28; see discussion of 1 Corinthians 15. Origen censures this exegesis of 2.6 as "naive"; *JTS* 3.405.
40. Cf. discussion of Rom 3:28-29.
41. *JTS* 3.5.408: The Naassenes also interpret those "afar off" as those immersed in materiality, while those "near" are, they say, the "pneumatic, noetic, perfect *anthrōpoi*"; Ref 5.18.
42. Exc 38.2-3.
43. EV 34.1-36.
44. EF 6.5.
45. CJ 10.33; AH 1.3.5.
46. Exc 63.2-65; CG 11,*1*:13.20-24.
47. CJ 10.33:

   ...τὴν ἐκκλησίαν κατασκευάσῃ ὀυκέτι λῃστῶν καὶ ἐμπόρων σπήλαιον, ᾽αλλὰ οἶκον τοῦ πατρὸς αὐτοῦ.

48. Ibid., CJ 13.25.
49. See discussion of Hebrews 9.
50. *JTS* 3.408.
51. Cf. Exc 23.1-3.
52. AH 3.13.1.
53. AH 1.6.4.
54. AH 3.2.1-3.1.
55. EV 18.12-16.
56. Ref 5.30.
57. Ref 7.13-14.
58. Cf. note 14.
59. AH 1.2.6.
60. AH 1.6.1; 1.7.4.
61. Exc 47.1-3:

   Καὶ πρῶτον πάντων προβάλλεται εἰκόνα τοῦ Πατρὸς Θεόν...Οὗτος ὡς εἰκὼν Πατρὸς πατὴρ γίνεται....

   Strom 4.89.
62. AH 1.13.2.
63. AH 1.21.5; Ref 5.35; cf. AH 3.20.7: on the Valentinian definition of the "inner man," see Tertullian, DR 40; 45.
64. Ref 6.29.
65. AH 1.2.6; Exc 31.1-2.
66. Exc 22.1-2.
67. Exc 42.3.
68. CJ 13.25.
69. AH 1.21.1-5: on the first and second baptism, see CG 11,*2*:40.37-42.39.
70. EV 18.33-35.
71. *JTS* 3.412-413.
72. Exc 37-38.3; CG 11,*2*:33.32-36.
73. Exc 42-43.5.
74. Exc 1.3.
75. Exc 21.3; CJ 2.21; ET 113; EP 103.11-12.

76. AH 1.6.4.
77. Exc 61.2-3.
78. Cf. note 29; on Christ's "body," CG 11.*1*:15.17-19.37.
79. AH 1.6.1.
80. ER 47.17-19; Tertullian explains that the Valentinians identify the "old man" with the "flesh" (*sarx*), DR 40; 45.
81. On "wearing" Christ, ER 45.30; on "new creation," Ref 6.35.
82. CJ 20.38.
83. EV 33.19-21.
84. Exc 48.2:

Καὶ ποιεῖ ἐκ τῶν ὑλικῶν τὸ μὲν ἐκ τῆς λύπης, οὐσιωδῶς κτίζων Πνευματικὰ τῆς πονηρίας, πρὸς ἃ ἡ πάλη ἡμῖν (διὸ καὶ λέγει ὁ Ἀπόστολος· Καὶ μὴ λυπεῖτε τὸ Πνεῦμα τὸ ἅγιον τοῦ Θεοῦ...

On "members (4:25b), see CG 11,*1*:15.18-18.38.
85. CJ 13.11-15. See discussion of 1 Cor 5-7.
86. Ref 5.35.
87. CJ 13.19; cf. EP 110.35-111.4.
88. CJ 13.11-15.
89. AH 1.13.1-5; 1.21.3.
90. AH 1.6.4.
91. CJ 10.38.
92. EV 17.29-35.
93. CJ 20.24.
94. Exc 35.1.
95. EV 18.16-19.
96. AH 1.7.4.
97. Exc 2.1-3.2; ER 45.31-40.
98. Exc 23.3.
99. AH 1.8.4:

Καὶ τὰς συζυγίας δὲ τὰς ἐντὸς πληρώματος τὸν Παῦλον εἰρηκέναι φάσκουσιν ἐπὶ ἑνὸς δείξαντα · περὶ γὰρ τῆς περὶ τὸν βίον συζυγίας γράφων ἔφη. Τὸ μυστήριον τοῦτο μέγα ἐστίν, ἐγὼ δὲ λέγω εἰς Χριστὸν καὶ τὴν Ἐκκλησίαν.

100. Exc 21.1-3.
101. Ibid.
102. Exc 33.2
103. Exc 42.1-3.
104. Exc 22.1-6.
105. Exc 21.3.
106. Irenaeus contests this exegesis: AH 5.7.1.
107. AH 1.8.4.
108. AH 1.7.1; 1.8.4; Exc 17.1-3; 63.1-65.2; CG 11,2:39.10-39.
109. Exc 21.3; 80.1; CJ 2.21; Ev Thom 113; EP 112.29-114.4; 129.21-130.26.
110. Exc 63.2-64.
111. For discussion, see Pagels, "Conflicting Versions of Valentinian Eschatology," *HTR* 67.1 (1974): 35-53.
112. Exc 64.
113. AH 1.7.1.
114. Exc 64; AH 1.2.6.
115. CG 11,2:39.10-39.
116. AH 1.6.4.

117. Exc 35.3-4.
118. *JTS* 3.268; EP 100.21-24; Exc 68.
119. CJ 20,38; AH 1.7.4.
120. AH 1.5.4.
121. Exc 35.3-4.
122. Exc 71.2-72.2.
123. Exc 73.1-3. On this "warfare," CG 11,2:38.27-33; CG 11,1:20.18-36.
124. Exc 69-73.3.
125. Exc 85.1-3.
126. CJ 2.21.
127. AH 3.2.1-3.1.

VI

PHILIPPIANS

Phil 1:21-2:11: For me to live is Christ, to die is gain. If I am to live in flesh, this to me is fruit of labor; yet what I shall choose I cannot discern. I am hard pressed between the two, having the desire for release, to be with Christ, which is far better; but to remain in flesh is more necessary for your sake. . . . To you it has been given for the sake of Christ, not only to believe in him but also to suffer for his sake, having the same agony you have seen in me. . . . Fulfill my joy, being of the same mind, having the same love, united in soul (or: with the psychics: *sympsychoi*). Do nothing in self-seeking or conceit, but in humility consider others better than yourselves. Let each one concern himself not with what is his own, but with what concerns others. Have this mind among you, which you have in Christ Jesus, who, being in the form of God, considered equality with God not something to be grasped, but emptied himself, taking on the form of a slave, coming to be in the likeness of men. And being found in human form, he humbled himself, becoming obedient unto death, the death of the cross. Therefore God exalted him and bestowed on him the name above every name, that in the name of Jesus every knee should bow, of those of earth and in heaven, and every tongue confess that Jesus Christ is Lord to the glory of God the Father.

Their references to Philippians indicate that the Valentinians, like other Christians, were fascinated by the christological passage of 2:6-11. Yet as the gnostics assume the essential identity of the elect with Christ, their exegesis, one suspects, would stress the parallel between the apostle's "agony" (1:30) and that of Christ. Paul himself reminds them of Christ's voluntary humiliation to account for his own (1:21-30). He intends, as he says, to encourage the elect to participate in "the same agony" and willingly to accept humiliation and suffering (1:29-2:5).

The initiate could recognize from 1:21-30 the situation that Paul describes as that of the elect; they suffer conflict between their responsibility for the psychics, on the one hand, and the desire "for release to be with Christ" (1:23). To "remain in flesh" (1:24) means, as Theodotus says, to remain bound to the conditions of "this existence," which for the apostle (as for Theodotus) is "death."[1] Yet Paul admits that "to die is gain" (1:21): that is, to live "in the flesh," pervaded by death, means "gain" for others. The apostle goes on to say that "for me this is the fruit of labor" (1:22); it is "necessary" so that those for whom he labors may "progress in faith" (1:25), and he may gather "fruit." Heracleon says that the elect and the savior labor among the psychics to gather "fruit for eternal life" which is the "salvation and restoration to rest of those that are harvested."[2] So, according to the author of A Valentinian Exposition, a cultivator is sent to "every field," for "this is the will of the Father . . . always produce and bear fruit."[3]

But Paul himself longs "to live" and for him "to live is Christ" (1:21); it is to be "released" from flesh and "to be with Christ, which is far better."[4] Recognizing that his fellow pneumatics share his desire, Paul encourages them instead to engage in "the same agony you see in me" (1:29-30) since they too have received grace "not only to believe, but also to suffer" for the sake of Christ, whose example he himself emulates.

Theodotus explains from 2:7 how "Jesus our light" being an angel of the pleroma "emptied himself" (of light) and came into existence outside the limit of the pleroma (in the place of emptiness; *kenoma*).[5] When he came into the cosmos, "through great humility he appeared not as an angel but as a man."[6] According to the Interpretation of the Gnosis, the savior says, "I became very small, so that through my humility I might bring you up to my great height. . . . if you will believe in me, it is I who will bring you above by means of this form (*schēma*) which you see."[7] For he "put on" the psychic Christ, and finally even the bodily form of Jesus ("taking on the form of a slave, coming to be in the likeness of men," 2:7), in order to become humanly visible.[8] The Valentinians could cite this passage (along with Rom 8:3: "God sent his son in the likeness of sinful flesh") to support the teaching that this form was that of a human likeness.[9] In this form he became "obedient unto death," that is, apparently, to the power that presently rules the cosmos,[10] so that through the cross (2:8) he might manifest the powers above.[11] Therefore "God has highly exalted him" and given him a "name that is above every name," so that all "in heaven and on earth," that is, the totality of cosmic powers, angels, and men, should "confess with the mouth Jesus as Lord" (2:10)[12] that glory might finally be given to "God the Father" (2:11).

The Valentinian exegete who assumes that the elect, like Christ, participate in "the same nature with God"[13] could include the elect with

Christ as those who are "in the form of God," for whom "equality with God" is not "beyond reach" (2:6). Consequently he could read in Philippians Paul's encouragement to the elect to follow Christ's example to humble and empty themselves for the sake of the psychics. Paul himself goes on to relate how he "runs," "labors" (2:16), "slaves," and "pours himself out" for their sake. Throughout their agony, however, they know that their own "citizenship is in heaven" (3:20): for, as one Valentinian exegete explains, this means that they have been generated pneumatically "according to the nature of God."[14]

NOTES: PHILIPPIANS

1. Exc 22.1-2; ER 44.17-21.
2. CJ 13.46-49.
3. CG 11,2:36.28-34; cf, CG 11.1:19.28-30; see discussion of 1 Cor 3:9b.
4. Exc 67.1-4.
5. Exc 35.1-2; cf. EP 102.5-18; 124.4-10; EV 24.22-24; CG 11,2:33.32-34.
6. Exc 4.1-3.
7. CG 11,1:12.29-34.
8. Exc 59.1-4.
9. AH 1.7.2.
10. Exc 58.1.
11. AH 1.3.4; 1.8.2-3.
12. See discussion of Rom 12:10.
13. CJ 13.25.
14. Exc 54.1-3:

  Ἀπὸ δὲ τοῦ Ἀδὰμ τρεῖς φύσεις γεννῶνται · πρώτη μὲν ἡ ἄλογος, ἧς ἦν Κάιν · δευτέρα δὲ ἡ λογικὴ καὶ ἡ δικαία, ἧς ἦν Ἀβελ · τρίτη δὲ ἡ πνευματική, ἧς ἦν Σήθ. Καὶ ὁ μὲν χοϊκός ἐστιν κατ᾽ εἰκόνα · ὁ δὲ ψυχικὸς καθ᾽ ὁμοίωσιν θεοῦ · ὁ δὲ πνευματικὸς κατ᾽ ἰδίαν...Ὅτι δὲ πνευματικὸς ὁ Σήθ...ἄνω βλέποντα, οὗ τὸ πολίτευμα ἐν οὐρανῷ, τοῦτον ὁ κόσμος οὐ χωρεῖ.

VII

COLOSSIANS

Col 1:15-17: (The son of his love, 1:13) is the image of the invisible God, the first born of all creation (*prōtotokos pasēs ktiseōs*), for in him all things were created, in the heavens and on earth, the visible and the invisible, thrones, dominions, rulers, or powers: all things were created through him and in him: he is before all things, and all things are constituted in him.

The Valentinians explain that the unknown Father, "willing to be known to the aions," generated the "only begotten" as his son, in an act of simultaneous self-knowledge and self-disclosure[1] in which the spirit of love mingled with the spirit of gnosis.[2] Yet he who was "only begotten son" in the pleroma then became revealed as "firstborn" (*prōtotokos*) in creation, that is, "in relation to things here."[3] Ptolemy cites 1:6 to explain that "the savior . . . was endowed with all power by the Father, who placed everything under his authority, the aions participating in this, so that 'by him all things were created, visible and invisible, thrones, dominions, rulers and powers.' "[4] The savior, then, became "first universal creator" of the invisible host of cosmic powers even before he created the demiurge and the elements of cosmic creation that were made visible.[5] For "many lordships and deities" came into existence before the cosmic system (*systasis*) was made.[6] Such statements as Col 1:16-17 show (according to Valentinian exegesis) that the savior not only is "from the aions" but contains within himself "all things" (i.e., the pleroma) as he descends from the pleroma into the regions below.[7]

Col 1:18-20: He is the head of the body, the *ecclesia*; he is the beginning, the firstborn from the dead, that in all things he might have pre-eminence. For in him the whole pleroma was pleased to dwell, and through him to reconcile all things in him, whether on earth or in heaven. . . .

137

Now the apostle turns to consider the savior's relation specifically to the ecclesia. As Theodotus says, he is the head of the church that is "his body."[8] The author of Interpretation of the Gnosis describes this relationship: the Head (the Logos) gives freely the "grace" and "gift" of participating in "the body" to each of the members; therefore all are to give thanks and to share their gifts with each other in unity and love.[9] Another Valentinian exegete cites this passage to show that the savior is "the pleasure (*eudokia*) of the whole pleroma," since 'the pleroma was pleased (*eudokein*) to dwell in him, and through him to reconcile all things.' "[10]

Col 1:24-2:10: Now I rejoice in the elements of suffering (*en tois pathemasin*) for your sake, and I fill (*antanaplero*) the deficiencies (*hysteremata*) of the afflictions of Christ in my flesh for the sake of his body, that is the eccelesia, of which I have become a servant according to the economy of God which was given to me, to fulfill (*plerosai*) in you the logos of God—the mystery hidden from the aions and from the generations, but which now has been revealed to his holy ones, in whom God willed to make known what is the wealth of the glory of this mystery among the Gentiles, which is Christ in you, the hope of glory. . . . We teach in all wisdom (*en pase sophia*) so that we might present every man perfect (*teleion*) in Christ. See that no one deceives you . . . according to the elements of the cosmos (*stoicheia tou kosmou*) and not according to Christ. For in him dwells the whole pleroma of divinity somatically, and you in him have been fulfilled, who is the head of every rule and every authority.

Where most Christians read Paul's reference to his own physical afflictions (1:24) the Valentinians read his reference to his participation in the constraining elements (*ta pathemata*) of cosmic existence. Like the savior, Paul "fills the deficiencies" (*hysteremata*) of the deficient members of "Christ's body," the ecclesia.[11] For, according to the Gospel of Truth, "having filled deficiency"—the deficiency of those ignorant of the Father—he establishes "unity," which is "pleroma."[12] The homilist of Interpretation urges each pneumatic member of that "body" to share his pneumatic gifts with the psychics in order to "fill" their "deficiencies."[13]

Gnostic exegetes explain from 1:26 that although the "mystery" of the election ("Christ in you," 1:27) was hidden even from the aions, as well as from previous generations (the demiurge, the archons, and those they generated) now God has willed to reveal it to his "holy ones," to the "Gentiles," the pneumatic elect "in whom" Christ dwells.[14] The apostle warns the elect not to be deceived (as psychics are) into worshiping "according to the elements of the cosmos."[15] Theodotus interprets 2:9 to show how "the whole pleroma" participated when the savior revealed in his passion that of Sophia, "since 'in him was the whole pleroma somatically.' "[16] The author of Interpretation offers a similar exegesis of 2:9: Sophia's restoration can only occur through the Father's "own son, in whom alone is 'the fulness (*plēroma*) of divinity' (2:9). He willed within himself bodily (*sōmatikos*) to leave the powers and he descended."[17]

Col 2:13-15: And you who were dead in transgressions and the uncircumcision of your flesh he made alive with him, having given grace for all transgressions, having canceled the handwritten bond (*cheirographon*) of ordinances that was against us: this he set aside, having nailed it to the cross. He stripped the rulers and powers, having exhibited them openly, and triumphed over them in him.

Why did the savior come into the cosmos? Valentinian exegetes agree in interpreting 2:14 as a metaphor for revelation. The author of the Gospel of Truth says that he came to reveal the Father's will: "he was nailed to a tree; he fastened the edict (*diatagma*) of the Father to the cross."[18] While this author reverses the image of 2:14, the author of Interpretation offers an exegesis more faithful to the text.[19] He agrees that the Son came in search of his own brothers "to publish the edict (*diatagma*) of the Father," adding that "he proclaimed it, giving to some (i.e., to the elect) the whole of it." But he goes on to say (following 2:14) that the savior "took (down) the old handwritten bond (*cheirographon*), that of condemnation (*katadikē*). And this is the edict that was in existence: 'Those who have been made slaves have been condemned in Adam.' " The old edict, then, condemned the psychics ("those who have been made slaves") to death "in Adam," in the demiurge's somatic and psychic creation. But now that Christ has "stripped the rulers and powers" and has triumphed over them (2:15)[20] "they (the psychics) have been acquitted from death: they have received pardon from their sins."[21] Christ delivers the psychics from "the law of sin and death," offering forgiveness, and then leads them "above" as he ascends into the pleroma.[22]

NOTES: COLOSSIANS

1. AH 1.1.1; Exc 7.1-3.
2. Exc 7.2-3; 8.1-2.
3. Exc 33.1:

Ὑιόθετος μέντοι γέγονεν ὁ Χριστός, ὡς πρὸς τὰ πληρώματα Ἐκλεκτὸς γενόμενος καὶ Πρωτότοκος τῶν ἐνθάδε πραγμάτων.

4. AH 1.3.4; see note 7.
5. Exc 47.1; CG.11,2:35.10-37; AH 1.4.5.
6. ER 44.36-38.
7. AH 1.3.3-4:

Τὸ δὲ Σωτῆρα τὸν ἐκ πάντων ὄντα τὸ πᾶν εἶναι...Καὶ ὑπὸ τοῦ Παύλου δὲ φανερῶς διὰ τοῦτο εἰρῆσθαι λέγουσι · καὶ αὐτός ἐστι τὰ πάντα · καὶ πάλιν, πάντα εἰς αὐτον, καὶ ἐξ αὐτοῦ τὰ πάντα. καὶ πάλιν, ἐν αὐτῷ κατοικεῖ πᾶν τὸ πλήρωμα τῆς θεότητος. καὶ τό, ἀνακεφαλαιώσασθαι δὲ τὰ πάντα ἐν τῷ Χριστῷ διὰ τοῦ Θεοῦ, ἑρμηνεύουσιν εἰρῆσθαι...

CG 11,2:33.30-34; EV 18.29-38; 19.7-10.

8. Exc 33.2; 42.2.
9. CG 11,1:15.35-38; 18.30-20.40.
10. Exc 31.1:

Ἀλλὰ καὶ εἰ ὁ κατελθὼν εὐδοκία τοῦ Ὅλου ἦν (ἐν αὐτῷ γὰρ πᾶν τὸ Πλήρωμα ἦν σωματικῶς) ἔπαθεν δὲ οὗτος, δῆλον ὅτι καὶ τὰ ἐν αὐτῷ σπέρματα συνέπαθεν, δι' ὃν τὸ Ὅλον καὶ τὸ Πᾶν εὑρίσκεται πάσχον.

EV 17.4-7, CG 11,2:26.21-22; 33.30-34.

11. Exc 26.1-3.
12. EV 24.20-32.
13. See note 9.
14. Ref 6.25; Ev 18.15; CJ 2.21.
15. CJ 13.17-19; EP 102.18-103.5; 110.35-111.4.
16. Exc 31.1; see note 10.
17. CG 11.2:33.30-34.
18. EV 20.23-27.
19. As Grobel points out, the author has reversed the image of Col 3.14:

> In Colossians the writing is "against us," and is "expunged" by Christ, while here it is (implicitly) "for us," and is validated by being fastened to the cross. There can be little doubt but that the Colossians passage inspired this one, but did so in an author who desired to vary images. The Gospel of Truth (Nashville: Abington, 1960), 67. n. 116.

20. Exc 69-74.1.
21. CG 11,1:16.130-40.
22. Ibid., 12.28-35; Exc 42.1-2; 61.1-6.

VIII

HEBREWS

Valentinian theologians give close attention to the treatise they know as Paul's letter to the Hebrews; apparently they find its special terminology and its schema of exegetical typology[1] compatible with their own. They read its theme—the superiority of the covenant Christ gives over Israel's covenant—as a clear exposition of the contrast between the pneumatic and the psychic relationship to God.

Heb 1:1-6: In many parts (*polumeros*) and in many ways (*polutropos*) in former times God spoke to the fathers in the prophets; but in the last of these days he spoke to us in the son, whom he appointed heir of all things, through whom also he made the aions; who is the radiance of his glory, the character of his hypostasis, bearing all things (the all; *ta panta*) in the word of his power. Having made purification for sins, he sat down at the right hand of the greatness (*tes megalosynes*) on high, having become much greater than the angels, as he had obtained a name superior to theirs. For to which of the angels did he ever say, "You are my son" . . . or "I shall be a Father to him, and he shall be my son"? And again, when he brings the first born (*prototokos*) into the cosmos, he says, "Let all the angels of God worship him."

Paul begins his letter explaining that God spoke through the prophets "in many parts (*polumeros*) and in many ways" (1:1). Ptolemy, accordingly, divides the prophecies into three distinct "parts" (*meroi*).[2] The first part, he says, originated from the pleroma and was transmitted through the elect seed; the second part from the intermediate region, through Sophia; and a third and large part derived from the cosmos through the demiurge.[3] Basilides, like other gnostic teachers, finds evidence for such division in the diverse epithets that prophetic writers use (Elohim, Adonai, Sabaoth, the Lord of powers, God almighty, the Most High God, the demiurge, etc.)[4]

141

Valentinian exegetes say that the demiurge, amazed by the prophecies that originated "from above," and were revealed "in the prophets" (1:1) failed to comprehend their source; he generally attributed them either to the prophets' own subjective excitement, or to deceit.[5] For how could the demiurge understand those prophecies that came from the pleroma, which set forth in symbolic terms the pleromic mysteries, and above all "the mystery of Christ"?[6]

But "in the last of these days" (1:2), "in the last times of the cosmos,"[7] Ptolemy explains, God sent his son to reveal these mysteries. This "son" is the one "through whom also God made the aions" (1:2b), that is, the pleromic aions.[8] The son "bears the all" (*ta panta,* 1:3) in that he bears within himself the whole pleroma.[9]

That he has "made purification for sins" and has "sat down at the right hand of the greatness on high" (1:3b) means for the Valentinians that Christ, having offered to the psychics forgiveness of sins,[10] "sat down with "the Topos," the demiurge,[11] to reign at his "right hand" for the duration of this age. For Christ has "become much greater than the angels" (1:4), much greater even than the demiurge,[12] whom the Valentinians include among the merely angelic powers.[13] His "name," Theodotus explains, is "only begotten son"[14] as the apostle reveals in 1:5-7. According to the Gospel of Truth, "the name of the Father is the son. It is He who, in the beginning, gave a name to him who came forth from Him and was Himself, whom He engendered as a son. He gave him His name which belonged to Him—He, the Father, of whom are all things . . . this name does not belong to . . . appellations, but . . . He gave the name to Him alone."[15] The Father himself has generated the son;[16] "which of the angels" can claim such generation? Since the Father did not *generate* the demiurge, but only caused him to be *created,*[17] the Valentinians include him among the "angels" called to worship Christ (1:6).[18] If Christ so far surpasses the demiurge and his angels, what is their role and function? This question Paul takes up next.

Heb 1:7-14: Of the angels he says: "He makes his angels spirits, and his servants flames of fire". But of the son; 'Your throne, O God, is among the aions of aions' . . . and 'You, O Lord, founded the earth in the beginning; the heavens are the works of your hands; they will be destroyed, but you shall remain; they will all grow old like a garment; like a mantle you shall roll them up, and they shall be changed. . . . are they not ministering spirits, sent forth for service for the sake of those who were to inherit salvation?

The demiurge, created from the psychic substance of fire,[19] himself "appears as fire."[20] The space (*ho topos*) he rules is "fire," burning with flames that portend the destruction of the cosmos. When this occurs, the demiurge's reign shall end,[21] but the son's throne shall remain "in the aion of the aion" (1:8).

The next citation addresses the demiurge as "the Lord" who founded the earth and shaped the heavens,[22] promising that when his material creation is destroyed, he himself shall remain.[23] Theodotus describes how the psychic substance, from which the demiurge made bodies and souls as "garments" for mankind, shall be discarded like old clothes; and those who wore them shall be "changed" (1:12; cf. 1 Cor 15:51-52) so that they may enter into the pleroma.[24] The demiurge, then, serves God in forming the cosmic elements, supervising the psychic church,[25] and finally in receiving back the souls of mankind. In all these tasks he was "sent forth in service for the sake of those who were to inherit salvation" (1:14) as the prophets themselves were sent.[26]

Heb 2:2-10: For if the word spoken through angels became sure, and every transgression and disobedience received just retribution, how shall we escape if we neglect such a great salvation, which in the beginning was spoken through the Lord . . . while God also bore witness by signs and wonders and many powers which the holy spirit distributed according to his own will?

For it was not to angels that he subjected the cosmos to come. . . . for having subjected all things to him, he left nothing that was not subjected to him. Now we do not yet see all things subjected. But we see Jesus, who for a short time was made lower than the angels, crowned with glory and honor through the suffering (*pathēma*) of death, as by the grace of God he tasted death for everyone. For it was fitting that he, through whom and by whom all things are, bringing many sons to glory, should perfect the leader (*archēgon*) of their salvation through sufferings (*pathēmatōn*).

The initiated reader could discern here three distinct stages of revelation. First the law, transmitted "through angels," exacted and requited strict justice (2:2); then "the Lord," the demiurge, converted through the savior, "spoke" in witness to the coming salvation (2:3);[27] finally "God" (2:4) the Father himself, also attested it "by signs and wonders" that convey the revelation to psychics,[28] and by distributing the "holy spirit" to the elect.

But Christ's superiority to the demiurge is, for the present, *invisible.*[29] The psychics, dependent upon sense-perception alone,[30] "see Jesus" (2:9), that is, they see only the *son of the demiurge,* the visible manifestation of the psychic Christ.[31] For he "in great humility" appeared "as a man"[32] to those who otherwise could not have perceived him. As one Valentinian teacher explains, the savior appears to the psychics wearing "the flesh," the "garment of condemnation," promising that "if you now believe in me, it is I who shall bear you above through this shape (*schēma*) that you see."[33] What they *cannot* see (2:8) is the pneumatic Christ, to whom the Father has subjected "all things."[34]

For he descended from the pleroma "because of the suffering (*pathēma*) of death," that is, because of the passions (*pathēmata,* 2:10) of Sophia that became the elements of creation[35] and now constitute the present "reign of death."[36] He came "to taste death for all" (2:9), that is, not actually to *die* ("then death would have overcome the savior himself, which is absurd")[37] but to destroy the power of death through his coming. For Valentinian teachers cite 1 Cor 15:54 to show that when he "tasted death" the enemy was "swallowed up in victory."[38] Thereby he became a "guide" (*hodēgos,* cf. 2:10) to "lead the soul which is invisibly being saved" into the pleroma.[39]

Heb 2:14-18: Since the children share in flesh and blood, he himself virtually (*paraplēsiōs*) partook of them, so that through death he might destroy him who has the power of death, that is, the devil, and release those who, by fear of death were, throughout their lives, in slavery. . . . for he cared for (or: took on, *epilambanetai*) the seed of Abraham (*spermatos Abraam*). Therefore he had to be made like his brethren in every way (*kata panta*) so that he might become a merciful and faithful high priest in the service of God. . . . Because he suffered and has been tested, he can help those who are being tested.

Theodotus explains that "it was necessary (for Christ) when he came into the cosmos that he be made visible, tangible, to become a dweller here, and to be associated with a perceptible body."[40] Could the initiated reader assume from 2:14b that the pneumatic Christ actually *died*? Theodotus rejects this idea as absurd,[41] and interprets the terms symbolically: through his coming the savior offered to those enslaved "to death" a means of release from its power:

Therefore baptism is called "death," and an "end of the old life," when we take leave of the evil rulers, but it is "life according to Christ" . . . but the power of transformation in baptism is not that of the body, but of the soul . . . they "die to the cosmos," but "live to God" that death may be released by "death," and corruption by resurrection. Whoever has been sealed by the Father, son, and holy spirit, has been released from the triad of corruption. [42]

The savior, then, was "made like" his brethren (2:17) although, Theodotus insists, not actually identical with them.[43] Rheginos' teacher apparently refers to this passage when he says that "he rose again from the dead; this is he of whom we say that he became the destruction of death."[44] The author of the Gospel of Truth cites 2:17 to describe how "Jesus, the 'merciful and faithful,' patiently accepted the endurance of suffering . . . since he knew that his death meant life for man."[45] Of Jesus' "testing" Theodotus says that "even the Lord after his baptism was troubled as we are," having been tested (*peirastheis*) in the desert (cf. 2:18); his victory over temptation encourages others to fight against demonic temptation.[46]

Heb 3:1-6: Therefore, holy brethren, who partake of a heavenly calling, consider Jesus, the apostle and high priest of our confession, faithful to the one who appointed him, just as Moses was faithful in the house of God. Yet Jesus has been considered worthy of much more glory than Moses, as the builder of a house has more honor than the house. For every house was built by someone, but God has prepared all things. And Moses was faithful in his whole house as a servant, for a witness to the things that were to be spoken later. But Christ is as a son in his own house.

Paul calls upon those "who share a heavenly calling"—the psychics—to acknowledge the superiority of *Jesus,* the son of the Father, to *Moses,* his servant.[47] For as the high priest enters the holy of holies, so "Jesus enters into the pleroma," opening the way of access there to the psychic as well.[48] But Moses, the demiurge, remained only an administrator,[49] a witness,[50] and a servant,[51] however "faithful" he has proven himself in administering the cosmic "household." Christ surpasses him as the architect surpasses the house he builds; for, according to the Valentinians, Christ himself is "first universal creator"; second after him, Sophia "built a house for herself and hewed out seven pillars," that is, she created the demiurge, and through him the cosmic creation of the hebdomad.[52] Beyond the three agents of creation—Jesus, Sophia, the demiurge— "God" the Father effects the whole process (3:4).

Heb 4:1-4: Let us fear lest while the promise of entering his rest remains, any one of you should seem to be wanting. We who believe have come into his rest, as it is said, "as I said in my wrath, they shall not come into my rest," although his works were finished from the foundation of the cosmos. For he has somewhere spoken of the seventh day in this way: "And God rested on the seventh day from all his works."

Since psychics receive only a "potential for salvation," as Heracleon says, they are to "fear" lest they fail to attain to the final "rest."[53] It is the demiurge who promises this "entrance into rest"; he himself, despite his "natural tendency for work (*philergos on physei*) blesses the sabbath day as the rest from his labors.[54] By contrast with the demiurge, "the Father does not keep the Sabbath, but works for the son and through the son."[55] So the elect who belong to the Father are, like the savior, to continue "the work of redemption" even on the Sabbath.[56] The initiate would be likely to discern the demiurge's tone in 4:3 and 4:5 where he "swears" in "wrath" to deny his "rest" to some.

Heb 4:6-10: Since therefore it remains for some to enter into it, and those previously evangelized did not enter in on account of disobedience, again he sets a certain day—"today"—saying in David concerning this time, . . . 'today if you hear his voice, do not harden your hearts." For if Jesus gave them rest, he would not have spoken after that concerning another day. So then there remains a sabbath rest for the people of God; for whoever enters the rest of God ceases from his labors as God has from his.

Why does the apostle insist that "today" is the decisive time? The Valentinian could learn from secret tradition that the three different "days" signify three distinct stages in the process of spiritual development. The "first day" signifies the hylic stage of immersion in materiality; the second day represents the psychic stage of conversion; the "third day, the pneumatic day," signifies enlightenment or resurrection. [57] For psychics the first day denotes the *past*, the second the *present*, and the third the eschatological *future*. The apostle, then, here insists that the psychic must choose salvation "today," that is, in the present cosmic age.

Nevertheless, the Valentinians explain, the message of salvation is communicated on each of these three "days" in a different way. During the past, hylic day, it "sounded" like a meaningless tone (*ēchos*); on the present psychic day it is "heard" as a "voice" (*phōnē*); and on the future pneumatic day, it is understood as *logos*. During the present age, "today," it comes as the "voice" (4:7) of the demiurge who cries "as a voice in the wilderness," calling men to repent and believe in the savior. [58] Throughout the psychic "day" the savior appears only in psychic form, not yet as the pneumatic Christ: for this reason the author adds mysteriously, "if *Jesus* had given them rest, he would not have spoken of *another day* beyond these: therefore there remains the Sabbath of the people of *God*" (4:8-9). The initiated reader would grasp what he means: that beyond the "rest" promised by the demiurge through faith in Jesus, there is another rest—the "rest in the marriage" [59] given through the pneumatic Christ from God the Father! The author of the Gospel of Truth speaks of the Father's "Sabbath" as "that day from on high, which has no night"; its light "does not fail, since it is perfect." He goes on to explain that "you (the elect) *are* this perfect day." [60]

Heb 4:11-13: Let us hasten, then, to enter into that rest . . . . for the *logos* of God is living and active and sharper than any two-edged sword, piercing even to divide the soul from the spirit, the joint from the marrow, discerning the thoughts and intentions of the heart. Before him no creature is invisible, but all things are naked and open before the eyes of him, of whom is our *logos*.

What does this mean? Having previously mentioned the *voice* that proclaims the psychic message of salvation, the apostle now mentions the *logos* that (according to Heracleon) reveals the pneumatic gospel of redemption. Theodotus, interpreting 4:12, takes the sword as an image of the pneumatic power of discrimination. Psychics have, in effect, only a "single-edged sword": they can only "pierce the appearance" of the savior, dividing the "flesh" from the "bone," what is *hylic* from what is *psychic.*[61] They do not have the logos—the double-edged sword that "pierces to divide the *soul* from the *spirit* (*diiknoumenos achri merismou psyches kai pneumatos*), the *bone* from the *marrow*" (4:12). Theodotus explains from 4:12 that "the bone" signifies the "rational and heavenly soul" and the "marrow" the spirit (*pneuma*) hidden with the bone.[62] As the piercing of flesh from bone signifies the dividing of the *hylic* from the *psychic*, so the logos divides the *psychic* from the *pneumatic*. For, according to the Gospel of Truth, "such is the judgment which has come from on high, which has judged each one, a drawn sword with a double blade which cuts on one side and on the other," the "Logos."[63] At present, the psychics lack that second power of discrimination; but the pneumatic Christ perceives "all things" in the total clarity of spiritual vision (4:13).

Heb 4:14-16: Having then a great high priest who has passed through the heavens, Jesus the son of God, let us hold to our confession. For we do not have a high priest who cannot sympathize with our weaknesses, since he has been tried in every way in our likeness, yet without sin. Let us come then with boldness to the throne of grace. . . .

Valentinian theologians describe Jesus' role as the "great high priest"[64] who has passed from the divine pleroma "through the heavens" of the hebdomad, in order to enter into the cosmic region and share "in human likeness" the "weakness"[65] of the human condition. Through his mediation the psychics too may hope to receive "mercy and grace" and finally to approach "the throne of grace with boldness" as do the elect.

Heb 5:1-4: For every high priest chosen from men is appointed for men in relation to God, that he may offer gifts and sacrifices for sins. He can deal gently with those who are ignorant and erring, for he himself is beset with weakness, since he needs to offer sacrifice for his own sins as well as for the sins of the people. . . . he is called by God, as Aaron was.

What does this mean? Is the reader to take Paul's words "literally" as an account of the Levitical priests of ancient Israel? Ptolemy cites Paul as his authority to show that the whole ritual section of the law is to be interpreted symbolically in terms of the *present* Christian community.[66] Heracleon identifies the Levitical priests specifically: they are "a symbol of the psychics who are saved" who remain at present outside the pleroma.[67] These "human priests" are able to deal with other psychics in their "error and ignorance" (5:2)[68] since they themselves are beset with "weakness" (the condition of material creation).[69]

Heb 5:5-10: So also Christ did not glorify himself to become a high priest, but he who spoke to him said, . . . "You are a priest forever, according to the order of Melchizedek." In the days of his flesh, Jesus offered up prayers and supplications with loud cries and tears, to him who was able to save him from death. . . . although he was a son, he learned obedience from what he suffered, and having been perfected, he became to all who are obedient the source of eternal salvation, appointed by God a high priest according to the order of Melchizedek.

Heracleon, having explained that the psychics are "priests and Levites," goes on to say that the savior himself is "high priest," who alone had access into the "holy of holies."[70] Yet "in the days of his flesh" (5:7), "when he was in flesh"[71] during the hylic and psychic "days" of his manifestation, he cried out and wept. What does this mean? The Valentinians say that through this means he demonstrated the cries and tears of Sophia's passion.[72] Through his revelation he has offered "to those who were obedient," apparently to the psychics who were saved, access into the "holy of holies," into the pleroma.[73]

Heb 5:11-14: Concerning this we have much teaching (*polus logos*) which is hard to interpret, since you have become deaf in your hearing. For indeed, you should be teachers by now, but again you need someone to teach you the elementary things (*ta stoicheia*) of the beginning of the words of God: you need milk, not meat. Everyone who takes milk is inexperienced in the word of righteousness; he is still immature (*nēpios*). Meat is for the mature (*teleiōn*) who have disciplined their perceptive powers to discriminate good from evil.

The gnostic would understand at once the apostle's frustration. The majority of his hearers remain on the mere psychic level, and still need the basic elements of instruction; they are too immature to receive the pneumatic doctrine (*logos*) that he would offer to the mature (the initiate: *teleios*).[74] What does the apostle consider to be the "elementary things"? He goes on to enumerate them.

Heb 6:1-6: Therefore let us leave behind the elementary doctrine of Christ and go on to the level of maturity (*tēn teleiotēta*: initiation), not laying again a foundation of repentance from dead works and of faith toward God, with teaching of baptisms, of laying on of hands, of the resurrection of the dead, and of eternal judgment. . . .
For it is impossible for those who have been enlightened, who have tasted the heavenly gift, and have become partakers of the holy spirit, and have tasted the goodness of God's word and the powers of the age to come, to have fallen back to renew repentance again. They recrucify for themselves the son of God. . . .

As the gnostic reader could anticipate, these "elementary doctrines" include the very doctrines considered essential by the majority of his Christian contemporaries—doctrines which came to be incorporated into the forms of confession of the *regula fidei.* These include repentance, faith, baptism, laying on of hands, the resurrection of the dead, eternal judgment. The author urges that they proceed from these to the level of maturity which is received in the gnostic initiation.[75] For he says it is impossible for those who have received this "enlightenment" and the "heavenly gift" (the holy spirit), to regress to the beginning of psychic teaching ("to fall back to renew *repentance* again"). To do so would be equivalent to "recrucifying the sons of God"—reversing the process symbolized in the crucifixion, which separates the psychic from the pneumatic elements.[76]

Heb 6:7-8: For earth that has drunk the rain that has come upon it, and brings forth plants good for those for whom it was cultivated, receives blessing from God. But if it bears thistles and thorns, it is worthless, and is about to be burned.

The initiated reader could recognize that this passage contains a parable concerning the pneumatic seed. For every gnostic teacher hopes (as Ptolemy writes to Flora) that his words come as rain upon "good ground" in which the pneumatic seed may grow and "bear fruit."[77] But those who "bring forth thorns" (according to Valentinian exegesis of the parable of the sower in Matthew 13) are those in whom the seed cannot grow: these are cast out and burned in the final conflagration of the cosmos.[78] Yet the apostle goes on to encourage psychics with hope that offers "a sure and steadfast anchor for the soul" (6:19; that is, for the *psychic*), a hope that "enters into the inner place beyond the curtain, where Jesus has gone before for our sake, having become a high priest according to the order of Melchizedek, having come into the aion" (6:20). This suggests that when the "veil" concealing the holy of holies is "rent,"[79] some of the psychic "Levites" "in the tribe of the priesthood" will be able to go within the veil with the high priest."[80] The apostle goes on in Hebrews 7-9 to show how Christ offers the psychics hope that they themselves may pass into the pleroma.

Heb 7:1-26: This Melchizedek, King of Salem, priest of the Most High God, met Abraham . . . and blessed him. . . . see how great he is! Abraham the patriarch gave him a tenth part of the spoils. The descendants of Levi . . . are descended from Abraham; but he who is not descended from Abraham . . . blessed him who had received the promises. . . . If perfection (*teleiōsis*) then, were through the Levitical priesthood, under which the people received the law, what need would there have been for another priest to arise. . . . having become a priest, not according to the law of a sarkic commandment, but according to the power of an indestructible life? . . . The former commandment was set aside because of its weakness and uselessness. For the law perfected nothing; a greater hope is introduced, through which we draw near to God. . . . The former priests were many; on account of death they were prevented from remaining: but he remains in the aion. . . . for it was fitting that we have such a high priest, holy, blameless, unstained, separated from sinners, and become exalted above the heavens.

Paul now reveals the pneumatic meaning of the ancient patriarchy, of the law, and of the priesthood. First he notes Abraham's obeisance to Melchizedek (7:1-10) which the initiate could see as an allegory of the demiurge's obeisance to the savior.[81] The "Levites," as the "descendants of Abraham," the demiurge, are psychic believers,[82] but the savior, being pneumatic, is "not descended from Abraham" (7:7); instead, as Heracleon says, he "descends from the greatness" beyond (cf. 7).[83]

Psychics, worshiping the demiurge, obeying the law, cannot thereby attain perfection (teleiōsis, 7:11, 19) for "the law perfected nothing," being a law of "sarkic commandment" (7:16), finally "weak" and "useless" (7:18). Those who served under law, the "Levites," are the "many" (that is, psychics)[84] who were bound under death (7:23). But the pneumatic Christ, through the power of divine life, offers a "greater hope" since he remains "in the aion" (7:21, 24). After his appearance to the psychics, he is "separated from them," as Heracleon says (cf. 7:26)[85] and has "become exalted above the heavens" (7:26).

Heb 8:1-5: The primary point of what has been said is this: we have such a high priest, who is seated at the right hand of the greatness in the heavens, minister of the holy of holies and the true tent. . . .There are priests who offer gifts according to the law; they serve as a paradigm and shadow of the heavenly things, as, when Moses was about to build the tent, he was instructed, "see that you make all things according to the type shown to you in the mountain."

Paul now reveals the main point of his discussion (8:1); the priesthood of Christ, who sits enthroned beside "the greatness on high," the demiurge,[86] surpasses the psychic priesthood as truth (alētheia) surpasses its representation (typos). So Heracleon says of the psychics that "the Jews worship in flesh and error the one who is not the Father," since the elements of their worship are only "images of the things in the pleroma" and not the realities themselves.[87] The demiurge, whom they mistakenly worship as creator, did not originate the elements of the creation. Like Moses preparing to build the temple (8:5), the demiurge was shown the pleromic prototypes of all creation from above, from the savior and from Sophia;[88] what he created consists only of "images and shadows" of the things in the pleroma.[89]

Heb 9:1-10: Now the first covenant had regulations for worship and a cosmic sanctuary, in which was prepared the first tent . . . which is called "holy." Behind the second curtain was a tent called "holy of holies". . . . of these things it is not now the time to speak in detail. These things having been thus prepared, the priests go continually into the first tent, performing the duties of worship; but into the second tent only the high priest goes alone, once a year. . . . The holy spirit shows this to reveal that the way into the holy of holies is not accessible while the outer tent remains standing—*which is a parable for the present age*—in which gifts and sacrifices are offered that cannot perfect the conscience of the worshiper, but concern only food and drink and diverse ablutions, regulations of the flesh, until the time of rectification (*diorthōseōs*) comes.

The apostle himself interprets his parable: the outer tent, the "cosmic sanctuary" (9:1) is "a parable of the present age" (9:9). Heracleon, interpreting this passage, explains that the "outer tent" symbolizes the *psychic topos,* where psychics worship the demiurge. But the "holy of holies" symbolizes the *pneumatic topos,* where the elect "who are of the same nature of the Father, being spirit, and who worship in truth and not error," worship the Father. Only the savior may enter as "high priest" there to cleanse and purify the elect, who themselves are the "house of the Father."[90] The psychics receive baptism, but only the elect receive the "bridechamber, concealed from the rest by the veil."[91] For the present time, the cosmic region (the *topos*) where psychics dwell is separated from the pleroma by the partitioning "second curtain" (9:3), the "second universal curtain of the all."[92] Because of this barrier "the way into the holy of holies is not accessible" while the "present age" (9:9) remains. But at the close of this age, the savior will open and lead the way for psychics to follow him from the cosmos into the pleroma.[93] The "priest" (psychic) who "enters within the second veil" must lay aside the hylic body and the psychic body, in order to pass "naked" into the pneumatic region, becoming in the process "truly rational and high priestly" (like the "high priest" himself) so that he too may partake in the "vision of God."[94]

Heb 12:18-24: You have not come to what may be touched, a burning fire, darkness and obscurity, and a storm and the sound (*echōs*) of a trumpet, and a voice (*phonē*) whose words made the hearers plead that no word (*logon*) should be added, for they could not bear the commandment, "if even a beast touches the mountain, it shall be stoned." Indeed, so terifying was the sight that Moses said, "I tremble with fear."

But you have come to Mt. Zion, to the city of the living God, the heavenly Jerusalem, and to innumerable angels gathered in celebration, and to the assembly of the firstborn who are enrolled in heaven, and to a judge who is the God of all, to spirits of the just who have been perfected, and to Jesus, the mediator of a new covenant, and to the sprinkled blood, which speaks better than Abel's blood.

Through this powerfully drawn image, the apostle contrasts the old covenant with the new. The Valentinian sees in 12:18-21 Paul's characterization of the old, obsolete covenant which is passing away (8:13) the psychic covenant with the demiurge.[95] There, in the "firey space" of the cosmos, psychics "feel the fire,"[96] perceiving their god as a "burning and consuming fire."[97] There, "in the place (*topos*) created for darkness,"[98] they hear the "sound" (echos, 12:19), that is, the hylic utterances of "the whole prophetic order."[99] They also hear the "voice" (phone) (12:19), the psychic speech of the demiurge himself; but, having heard it in terror, they plead that they may be spared the third stage of revelation, which is logos. For they could not endure what they had heard already—the sentence of death for any "beast," that is, for any of the passions.[100] What appeared to their senses was so terrifying that even "Moses" (the demiurge) trembled with fear (12:21).

Yet as one Valentinian exegete explains, Paul reveals in this passage another possibility for the psychic besides impending destruction. If they choose to become like "the image of those above," they may become pneumatic, and ascend toward the "heavenly Jerusalem."[101] The psychics who are saved, having been delivered from "Egypt," that is, from the hylic region, have advanced toward "Mt. Zion," the psychic region. From there, where they worship the demiurge, they are to advance further, to the "city of the living God," the "heavenly Jerusalem," the pneumatic region.[102] Ascending there, they join the "angels," the elect,[103] the "ecclesia of the firstborn;"[104] which is the pneumatic ecclesia. They approach the demiurgic "judge," and finally the "God of all," the Father himself. Finally they join the "spirits of the just who have been perfected," those formerly psychics ("the just") who have now become "spirit," as they themselves through Jesus receive perfection which they could never attain through Abel (who symbolizes "the just," the psychic).[105]

Heb 13:20-21: May the God of peace, who brought back from the dead our Lord Jesus, the great shepherd of the sheep . . . supply you with every good thing that you may do his will . . . through Jesus Christ, to whom be glory among the aion of aions.

Paul's final blessing commends the "Hebrews" to the "God of peace," the Father, who raised "from the dead" the savior. For he is, as Theodotus agrees, the "good shepherd" who protects the psychics as his "sheep"; he rescues them from the dangerous attacks of the evil powers.[106] As shepherd, he sought out the lost sheep, the ecclesia (as the Valentinians interpret the parable of Mt 18:12-14), until he recovered it, and transformed it to lead all who believe "into the pleroma."[107]

NOTES: HEBREWS

1. See L. Goppelt, *Typos: Die typologische Deutung des Alten Testaments im Neuen* (Gütersloh: Bertelsmann, 1939), 193-212; cf. R. Bultmann, *Theology of the New Testament*, II, 332.
2. AH 1.7.3.
3. AH 4.35.1. Ptolemy uses the same principle of threefold division to analyze the law (EF 4-5) and the words of the savior (AH 1.7.3).
4. AH 2.35.3.
5. AH 1.7.4.
6. .AH 4.35.2-4.
7. AH 1.8.2; Ref 5.2.
8. AH 1.1.1; 1.3.1; 1.8.5; Exc 6.1-3; CG 11, 2:23.19-36.
9. AH 1.2.6; 1.8.5; Exc 6.3; EV 23.33-24.8.
10. CJ 13.60.
11. Exc 62.1-2:

Κάθηται μὲν οὖν ὁ ψυχικὸς Χριστὸς ἐν δεξιᾷ τοῦ Δημιουργοῦ, καθὸ καὶ ὁ Δαβὶδ ιέγει · Κάθου ἐκ δεξιῶν μου καὶ τὰ ἑξῆς. Κάθηται δὲ μέχρι συντελείας...

12. According to Heracleon, the demiurge himself confesses this, saying (CJ 6.23):

Οὐπ ἐγώ εἰμι ἱπανὸς, ἵνα διεμέ κατέλθῃ ἀπὸ μεγέθους καὶ σάρκα λάβῃ ὡς ὑπόδημα, περὶ ἧς ἐγὼ λόγον ἀποδοῦναι οὐ δύναμαι οὐδὲ διήγησασθαι ἢ ἐπιλῦσαι τὴν περὶ αὐτῆς οἰκονομίαν.

13. AH 1.5.2:

Ἀγγέλους δὲ αὐτοὺς ὑποτίθενται, καὶ τὸν δημιουργὸν δὲ καὶ αὐτὸν ἄγγελον Θεῷ ἐοικότα.

14. Exc 26.1.
15. EV 38.6-40.26.
16. Ibid., AH 1.1.1.-2.1.
17. *Strom* 4.89.6-90; AH 1.5.1-2; Exc 47.1-2.
18. CJ 6.39.
19. AH 1.5.4; Exc 48.3-49.1.
20. Ref 6.32.7: So the Naassenes describe the "demiurge of this creation" as a "firey god," Ref 5.7.30; AH 1.31.1; 5.10.1.
21. Exc 58.1-80.3.
22. Exc 47.1-49.2; 65.1-2.
23. AH 1.7.1; Exc 65.1-2.
24. Exc 63.1-65.
25. AH 1.7.4.
26. Exc 24.1:

Λέγουσιν οἱ Οὐαλεντινιανοὶ ὅτι ὃ κατὰ εἷς τῶν Προφητῶν ἔσχεν Πνεῦμα ἐξαίρετον εἰς διακονίαν, τοῦτο ἐπὶ πάντας τοὺς τῆς Ἐκκλησίας ἐξεχύθη.

27. CJ 2.21-6.39.
28. CJ 13.60; AH 1.30.12.
29. Exc 26.1; 59.1-4; EV 38.14-19; ER 45.20-21.
30. CJ 13.60.
31. Exc 59.1-60; CJ 6.60.
32. Exc 4.1.
33. CG 11, 1:10.27-33; 11.27.
34. Exc 62.1-3.
35. Exc 67.4.
36. Exc 51.8; 80.1-3.

37. Exc 61.6-7.
38. CJ 13.60; cf. Exc 80.3; ER 45.14-23; 48.38-5.
39. Exc 61.5:

Καὶ Προάξω ὑμᾶς, λέγει, τῇ τρίτῃ τῶν ἡμερῶν εἰς τὴν Γαλιλαίαν. αὐτὸς γὰρ προάγει πάντα · καὶ τὴν ἀφανῶς σῳζομένην ψυχὴν ἀναστήσειν ἠνίσσετο, καὶ ἀποκαταστήσειν οὗ νῦν προάγει.

26.2-3; 35.3; 42.2; compare EV 19.17; CG 11,*I*:10.27-33.

40. Exc 59.3; cf. CG 11,*I*:12.18-19: "He . . . appeared as flesh and blood"; 12.37-38.
41. Exc 61.5.
42. Exc 77.1-80.2.
43. Exc 7.3-5.
44. ER 46.16-19.
45. EV 20.10-14.
46. Exc 85.1-3.
47. CJ 20.38.
48. Exc 38.2.
49. AH 1.7.4.
50. CJ 6.39.
51. CJ 20.38.
52. Exc 47.1-3; AH 1.5.1-5; CG 11,2:35.10-33; CJ 13.19; see discussion of 1 Cor 3.10.
53. CJ 13.60; Exc 23.1-3.
54. Exc 49.2.
55. CG 11, *I*:11.18-19; 32-34.
56. EV 32.18-25.
57. CJ 10.37; Exc 61.5.
58. CJ 2.20.
59. CJ 10.19; EP 119.3-15.
60. EV 32.23-32.
61. Exc 62.2.
62. Exc 53.5.
63. EV 25.35-26.4.
64. Ref 6.32:

Ἰάντες οὖν ηὐδόκησαν οἱ τριάκοντα αἰῶνες ἕνα προβαλεῖν αἰῶνα, κοινὸν τοῦ πληρώματος καρπόν...καὶ προβέβλητο ὁ κοινὸς τοῦ πληρώματος καρπός, ὁ Ἰησοῦς τοῦτο γὰρ ὄνομα αὐτῷ) ὁ ἀρχιερεὺς ὁ μέγας.

CJ 10.33; Exc 38.2.

65. Exc 67.1-4.
66. EF 5.8-15:

..τὰ ἐν προσφοραῖς λέγω καὶ περιτομῇ καὶ σαββάτῳ καὶ νηστείᾳ καὶ πάσχα καὶ ἀζύμοις...πάντα γὰρ ταῦτα, εἰκόνες καὶ σύμβολα ὄντα, τῆς ἀληθείας φανερωθείσης ἀετετέθη...καὶ τὸ πάσχα δὲ ὁμοίως καὶ τὰ ἄζυμα, ὅτι εἰκόνες ἦσαν, δηλοῖ καὶ Ἰαῦλος ὁ ἀπόστολος   [1 Cor 5.7]

67. CJ 10.33:

ἁ δὲ τοῦ προνάου, ὅπου καὶ οἱ Λευῖται, σύμβολον εἶναι τῶν ἔξω τοῦ πληρώματος ψυχικῶν εὑρισκομένων ἐν σωτηρίᾳ.

68. CJ 13.19.
69. Exc 67.1.
70. CJ 10.33; Exc 38.2.
71. ER 44.14-15.

72. AH 1.8.2; CJ 10.19.
73. Exc 67.1-4.
74. Cf. discussion of 1 Cor 2:6.
75. AH 1.21.2.

> Τὸ μὲν γὰρ βάπτισμα τοῦ φαινομένου Ἰησοῦ, ἀφέσεως ἁμαρτιῶν, τὴν δὲ ἀπολύτρωσιν τοῦ ἐν αὐτῷ Χριστοῦ κατελθόντος, εἰς τελείωσιν · καὶ τὸ μὲν ψυχικὸν, τὴν δὲ πνευματικὴν εἶναι ὑφίστανται.

76. AH 1.3.5.
77. EF 7.10; AH 1.13.2; see also CJ 13.50.
78. CJ 13.60.
79. See discussion of Eph 2:14.
80. EP 132.25-29. R.M. Wilson, acknowledging that EP 132.21-35 "deal . . . with the destiny of the psychic," claims that "133.1-5 turn to the spiritual" (*The Gospel of Philip*, 192), apparently reasoning that the psychic could *not* enter the pleroma. Comparison with Heracleon's use of the Levite priesthood as a "symbol of the psychics found in salvation" (CJ 10.33) and the *Excerpts from Theodotus* (cf. Pagels, "Conflicting Versions of Valentinian Eschatology," *HTR* 67.1 [1974]: 35-53) suggests that 133.1-5ff, describes the *psychics* whom the savior purifies (132.31-133.1) and brings with him into the "holy of holies" where the elect *already* are. Only on this reading does the rest of the saying prove consistent; the author of the Gospel of Philip explains that the veil was not rent "only at the top, since it would be open only for those above" but was rent "from top to bottom," which means that "those above (the elect) opened to us who are below" (133.10-11), so that the psychic "slaves will be free, and the captives delivered" (133.28-29).
81. CJ 6.39.
82. CJ 10.33.
83. CJ 6.39; CG 11,*1*:12.33-36.
84. CJ 13.25.
85. CJ 13.52.
86. Exc 62.1.
87. CJ 13.19.
88. AH 1.5.1; 2.6.3-7.6.
89. AH 1.7.7-8.1.
90. CJ 10.33.
91. EP 117.14-118.4; 132.21-133.29.
92. Exc 38.2; EP 132.21-133.29.
93. Exc 26.2-3; 38.2-3.
94. Exc 27.1-5; cf. note 80.
95. Ref 6.27: The Valentinian exegete cites passages used in Hebrews 12 (Deut 9:3, Ps 50:3), to show that "the soul" can either be destroyed by the "fire" of the Hebdomad, or "become immortal" and proceed to the "heavenly Jerusalem"; cf. CG 11.*1*: 14.33-36.
96. Exc 37-38.2.
97. Ref 6.27.
98. Exc 37.
99. CJ 2.21.
100. CJ 13.16; *Strom* 2.114; Exc 85.1.
101. Ref 6.27.
102. CJ 10.33; Exc 54.

103. Exc 21.1-3.
104. Exc 33.1.
105. Exc 54.1; AH 1.7.5; Ref 5.6.6-7.
106. Exc 73.1-3.
107. AH 1.8.4; EV 31.36-32.20; ET 107.

Conclusion:

GNOSTIC EXEGESIS
OF THE
PAULINE LETTERS

Investigation of gnostic exegesis discloses traces of the process whereby Paul became known in the second century as the "apostle of the heretics." Irenaeus, Tertullian, Hippolytus, and Origen, through the energy they devote to its refutation, pay unwilling tribute to the power and appeal of such Valentinian appropriation of Paul. Irenaeus deplores the fact that many bishops and deacons themselves have become convinced by Valentinian propaganda;[1] Tertullian admits that some of the most faithful and outstanding members of his community ("even bishops, deacons, widows, and martyrs") have sought initiation into the Valentinian circle.[2] Both consider the Valentinians far more insidious than the Marcionites or any others who openly criticize the church. For, as Irenaeus says, "outwardly such persons seem to be sheep, for they appear to be like us, from what they say in public, repeating the same words (of confession) as we do; but inwardly, they are wolves."[3] While insisting that they accept and agree with the whole of church confession and doctrine, privately they offer to remedy the "deficiencies" of that faith through their own "apostolic tradition." Irenaeus expresses outrage that they claim Paul's own authority for their violations and contradictions of church doctrine and proceed to defend their views through arguments from scripture![4]

Analysis of gnostic exegesis indicates, indeed, how "wiley and deceptive" Irenaeus must have found these heretics who reply to ecclesiastical critics with exegeses that even Irenaeus admits sound plausible, and who defend their practices by citing Paul's example. The heresiologists recognize, for example, the obvious allure that the promise of hearing "hidden mysteries" exerts over the curious. Tertullian compares the Valentinian initiation to the Eleusinian: both, he says, prolong the process in order to arouse the candidate to a state of suspenseful anticipation for what follows; both flatter and fascinate the naive with their invitation to join the inner circle of those "in the know."[5] Nevertheless, what Irenaeus and Tertullian denounce as a manipulative technique undoubtedly appears quite different to the Valentinians themselves. They can claim both the Lord himself (cf. Mark 4) and the apostle Paul as examples of those who recognize that only a few select members of their audience were ready to receive the "wisdom of God hidden in a mystery."[6]

The Valentinians also invoke Paul's example to defend a second element of their teaching that Irenaeus condemns: the gnostic offer of liberation from specific restrictions on their conduct. Irenaeus complains that Valentinian Christians ignore what he himself, as bishop of the Lyons community, considers to be minimal standards of practice incumbent upon all believers: namely, to abstain from eating meat offered to idols, to avoid public feasts and entertainments, and to abhor deviation from monogamy in matters of sexual behavior.[7] These Valentinians (and other gnostic Christians) interpret their own freedom not as libertine but as libertarian, exemplifying the liberty of those who "have gnosis," who are "strong"; the liberty of the pneumatics who, like Paul, celebrate their release from the curse of the law.[8]

When Irenaeus and Tertullian charge that the Valentinians resist church discipline, the latter could reply that they, like Paul, acknowledge only the authority of "the pneumatics" among them.[9] Accused of undermining church sacraments by offering in addition the sacrament of apolytrosis, they could reply that the apostle himself not only endorses their practice, but has himself taught the sacrament that echoes liturgically his own words.[10] Even the psychic Christians, they say, acknowledge unwittingly the aions above as they recite the eucharistic liturgy.[11]

Heresiologists and gnostics both acknowledge that the Valentinians' greatest appeal (or greatest deception, depending on one's viewpoint) lies in their theological teaching. Heracleon describes how the person gifted with pneumatic nature finds ecclesiastical teaching to be "unnourishing, stagnant" water, inadequate to satisfy spirtual thirst; the pneumatic must discover through gnosis the "living water" Christ offers to the elect.[12] Ptolemy apparently considers Flora to be such a person, a believer frustrated by seeming contradictions in scripture: he offers her a new hermeneutical framework to resolve these contradictions, and encourages her to seek further theological enlightenment from esoteric "apostolic tradition."[13] Origen realizes that his friend and student Ambrose became a Valentinian initiate out of genuine concern to understand the "deeper mysteries" of scripture.[14]

The Valentinians offer such seekers of enlightenment an explanation for their condition. Such persons, they say, need to recognize that they are among the elect, of pneumatic nature, and thus are impelled by the spirit to seek the "deep things of God."[15] Those so gifted could not be satisfied with the teaching Jesus offers "to those outside"[16] or with the doctrine that Paul admits he directs to those who are "still sarkic," and who remain incapable of receiving the "wisdom hidden in a mystery" that he would prefer to offer them.[17] This "hidden wisdom," which apparently relates the myth of Sophia,[18] reveals the secret of their election through grace, and teaches the "deeper interpretation" of the scriptures.

So, while the author of 2 Peter warns that "the ignorant and unstable" distort Paul's wisdom, teaching as they do the "other scriptures" (3:16), Valentinian exegetes read in Galatians Paul's proclamation of his independence of Peter. They infer that, since Paul declares that he received his gospel neither "from men nor through man" (Gal 1:1; 1:12), certainly he did not receive it from Peter or the Jerusalem apostles, who remained "under the influence of Jewish opinions."[19] Instead he received it from Jesus Christ and from God the Father (1:1) "through revelation" (1:12) that liberates the elect from the demiurgic law binding upon "the Jews." In Romans the Valentinians read how God's elect are justified "by faith, apart from words" (3:28). Nevertheless, they claim to recognize in chapter 9 his concern for kerygma" that he offers to psychic believers (2:6-3:4). In 1 Corinthians 7 For although the Father elects only "a remnant" from Israel, he has not rejected the rest of the Jews: the apostle discloses that their present "hardness," their blindness to his purpose, contains a mystery to be resolved only when "all Israel" (the totality of the psychics who are saved) shall be raised and joined with the "Gentiles" (11:5-26).

The Valentinian reader sees in 1 Corinthians how Paul contrasts the secret wisdom teaching he discloses "to the initiates" with the "foolishness of the kerygma" that he offers to psychic believers (2:6-3:4). In 1 Corinthians 7 Valentinian exegetes see Paul's "veiled" discussion of human conjunction in marriage. This, they claim, suggests a double signification: first, the conjunction of Christ with his elect, celebrated in the apolytrosis sacrament; second, the relation of the elect with psychic believers, the "marriage in the cosmos," which the elect enact in the baptism they perform "for the dead" (psychics). Finally, they continue, Paul reveals in 1 Corinthians 15 the "mystery of the resurrection," disclosing that those who are "dead" shall be raised, the psychic transformed and changed, so that "God shall be all in all."[20]

For the duration of the present age, however, they consider that Paul counsels those who, like himself, have gnosis, to modify their expression of pneumatic freedom for the sake of "the weak" (Romans 14-15; 1 Cor 2:15, 8, 9). In Philippians he urges the elect to "become as I am" (Phil 3:17), indeed, to become like Christ, who voluntarily yielded up his divine prerogatives in order to "take on the form of a slave," the "likeness of human form" (2:6-8). In Ephesians and Colossians the Valentinians see Paul's praise for the pneumatic Christ, who heads the whole body of his ecclesia: this is the "mystery revealed among the Gentiles," which the elect recognize as "Christ in us" (1:27). Finally, the Valentinians claim to discern in Hebrews Paul's contrast between Moses, the demiurgic "servant" and Levitical priests who worship him "in the outer tent, which is a parable of the present age," that is, the psychics, and the pneumatic elect who worship God "spiritually" in the holy of holies. In this epistle "the apostle" urges those who are enlightened to leave behind them the "elementary doctrines" and to go on to attain the initiation (*teleiōsis*) offered to those who are pneumatic (Heb 6:1-6).

As we learn to recognize basic patterns and themes of Valentinian exegesis, simultaneously we can appreciate more clearly the danger they presented to those in the church who were attempting to unite the Christian communities and to consolidate them against the threat of political persecution. Certainly Irenaeus considers them as men whom Satan inspired to divide the church internally.[21] He condemns their teaching on election as one that effectively splits the church into factions, encouraging arrogance and contempt among the initiates, and evoking envy, resentment, or false admiration from those excluded from their circle.[22] So long as their presence is tolerated, Irenaeus warns, they incite confusion and controversy; they call into question the authority of church leaders, and disturb the faith of simple believers. They raise doubts, for example, concerning the efficacy of the sacraments, causing many to wonder whether the baptism they received is, after all, genuinely efficacious, or whether it is only a preparation for the "higher" sacrament of apolytrosis.[23]

It is no wonder that ecclesiastical Christians, confronted with such an exegesis of Pauline thought, tended to avoid discussion of Paul's theology. H. Schneemelcher observes that Paul's influence on ecclesiastical theology before Irenaeus remains astonishingly slight.[24] While Ignatius, for example, reveres Paul as an apostle and martyr, his letters betray little or no influence of Paul's theology: Schneemelcher suggests that he may not even have read or known Paul's letters.[25] Similarly Polycarp and the apologists, Hegesippus, Justin, and Athanagoras, mention Paul (if at all) as an apostolic leader; concerning his theology they remain virtually silent (possibly, Schneemelcher says, even ignorant).[26] Ecclesiastical sources that do refer to Paul often express hostility; the Pseudo-Clementines suggest that he, like Simon Magus, is a satanically inspired divider of the Roman community that is properly headed by Peter.[27] Schneemelcher suggests that ecclesiastical Christians might have preferred to exclude Paul's letters from the canon entirely, "but it was too late: he was already a chief apostle, and, next to Peter, the martyr of Rome: despite the unfamiliarity of his theology, he already stood in high regard."[28]

Irenaeus, however, convinced that the Valentinians teach only a false and distorted view of Paul, takes up the counteroffensive against the Valentinians. He declares that

> . . . it is necessary to examine [Paul's] opinion, and to expound the apostle, and to explain whatever passages have received other interpretations from the heretics, who totally have misunderstood what Paul has said. Further [it is necessary] to point out the madness of their misperceptions, and to demonstrate from that same Paul, from whose [writings] they raise questions for us, that they are indeed liars, but the apostle was a preacher of truth, and that he taught all things consonant with the preaching of truth.[29]

Drawing upon resources already available to him (which the gnostics had either not known or had ignored), Irenaeus opens his treatise quoting the Pastoral Letters to show that "the apostle" stands on his side against gnostic heretics.[30] He cites Acts 15 to prove that Paul worked in perfect agreement with the other apostles;[31] he insists that Luke, Paul's "constant companion," attests beyond doubt that Paul withheld nothing from the other apostles, and in no way differs from them.[32] He cites the Pastorals along with 1 Corinthians 15 to show that Paul does teach bodily resurrection;[33] he assumes, with Tertullian, that the "same Paul" who wrote Romans and Corinthians condemned all heretics in his letters to Timothy and Titus.[34] Irenaeus, like Origen after him, offers what some scholars have characterized as a "one-sided" exegesis of Paul's theology, stressing that the apostle clearly taught the freedom of the will.[35] Analysis of gnostic exegesis may help account for his notable neglect of Paul's teaching on grace and election: this doctrine, apparently, had served the gnostics too well in their account of "pneumatic natures." From such elements of earlier tradition which the Valentinians ignored, Irenaeus and his followers construct the "antignostic Paul," reinterpreting his letters in an "orthodox" direction: by the late second century he becomes the church's champion, the challenger of "the gnostic Paul."

What perspectives can such analysis offer—if any—on the question of Paul's own relation to gnostics? Much of the discussion, as B. Pearson notes,[36] has focused on alledgedly "gnostic terminology" in Paul's letters. How are we to account for this?

R. Reitzenstein, observing parallels between Paul's terminology and that of the second-century gnostics, has argued that Paul himself was a gnostic.[37] Such scholars as U. Wilckens and W. Schmithals object to this theory: they insist instead that where such parallels occur, the apostle is adopting the language of "gnostic" opponents in order to refute them.[38] Both theories, however, share a methodological premise: both attempt to read first-century Pauline material primarily in terms of second-century gnostic evidence. H. Koester has pointed out that such investigation applies criteria for distinguishing between true and false belief which emerge from the works of the second-century heresiologists—criteria which may not at all apply to the theological situations and problems of the first generations of Christians:

> The question is not whether we should characterize Paul's opponents as gnostic heretics. . . . The danger of this way of setting the question is clear: one falls into the error of equating theological questions of the Pauline era with cliches of the second and third century controversies.[39]

Certainly it is not impossible, as proponents on both sides of the argument assume, that extant written materials which date from the second century may represent tradition known to the apostle himself some sixty to eighty years earlier (whether one argues that Paul endorsed or condemned it). Nevertheless, this remains largely an argument from silence, or, at any rate, from later sources. What the sources can document, however, is that the opposing positions more recently debated between Reitzenstein, Lügert, and others, each found defenders in the second-century hermeneutical debate— the gnostics themselves contending that Paul was a gnostic, and the heresiologists taking the opposite stand, arguing that if Paul seems to use gnostic language, he only does so in order to controvert what "he himself" calls "falsely so-called gnostics." Nevertheless, H. Conzelmann, assessing the latter theory, has declared (and indeed, in his own commentary, has demonstrated) that "one does not need this hypothesis in order to explicate the text."[40]

The present study of gnostic exegesis lends support to Conzelmann's view. It seems that we can account for allegedly "gnostic terminology" in Paul's letters if we assume that Paul's theological language subsequently is appropriated and developed by the Valentinians (and other gnostics) into a technical theological vocabulary. (Wilckens, Pearson, and others agree that Paul seems to have adapted his theological language from Jewish and other religious traditions available to him in the first century.)

A survey of the historical evidence reminds us that after Paul's death (c. 60 A.D.) traditions concerning the apostle (like those concerning Jesus) developed in several different directions. The author of Acts (c. 80-90 A.D.) describes Paul as an "apostle" and teacher who was involved in controversy, but agreed to compromise and to work with the Jerusalem Christians in fraternal accord, and who subsequently was sent as a prisoner to Rome. The Pastoral Letters (c. 100-110 A.D.) stress Paul's role as an organizer of ecclesiastical congregations, a mainstay of church discipline, and unswerving antagonist of all heretics. Ephesians, Colossians, and Hebrews (c. 70-95 A.D.), on the other hand, virtually ignore Paul's organizational activity, in order to elaborate and extend the theological conceptions expressed in his letters.[41] These various deutero-Pauline materials—the Pastorals, on the one hand, and Ephesians, Colossians, and Hebrews on the other—although divergent in theological and ecclesiological conception, later are accepted into the canonical collection as basically non-contradictory.

Nevertheless, the tensions in Pauline interpretation which they evince apparently broke into open conflict during the generations following their composition. While Marcion sought to exclude elements of the texts he considered inauthentic, Valentinus tended instead to accept the full texts available to him, interpreting them esoterically. Valentinus' followers accepted, apparently, the full texts of Paul's own letters; and while they virtually ignored the Pastorals,[42] they willingly included (and, indeed, highly revered) Ephesians, Colossians, and Hebrews as sources of Pauline tradition. Often, in fact, they used the latter epistles to interpret the former: the followers of Ptolomy, for example, refer to Eph 5:32 to interpret Paul's teaching on sexuality and marriage (cf. 1 Corinthians 7) as symbolic references to the "ineffable marriages of syzygies" and the marriage of the pneumatic Christ with Sophia, his bride.[43] Similarly, the author of The Interpretation of Knowledge (CG II, 1) interprets Paul's image of the "body of Christ" (cf. Romans 12, 1 Corinthians 12) in the direction indicated in Ephesians and Colossians.[44] Other Valentinians apply the language of Colossians, which describes the believer's ascent with Christ, to the baptismal teaching of Romans.[45]

Some of what has been described as "gnostic terminology" in the Pauline letters may be explained more plausibly instead as Pauline (and deutero-Pauline) terminology in the *gnostic* writings.[46] This reconstruction not only fits the chronological evidence without distortion, but also accords with the Valentinians' own witness: their reverence for Paul as their great teacher, and their claim that his letters have served as a primary source for their own theology. Tertullian notes that Valentinus, unlike Marcion, developed his theology independently of the ecclesiastical community by means of "different emendations and expositions" of the scriptural texts.[47] His followers, convinced that his hermeneutical method derives directly from Paul's own wisdom tradition, insist that far from contradicting church tradition, such exegesis complements and completes it.

By studying gnostic exegesis, the NT scholar may recognize how ecclesiastical tradition since Irenaeus has directed the course of Pauline interpretation: even today the "antignostic Paul" predominates in the contemporary debate. Yet for the historical theologian to attempt to decide between gnostic and orthodox exegesis would be to accept a false alternative. Each of these opposing images of Paul (and each of the hermeneutical systems they imply) to some extent distorts the reading of the texts. To read Paul either way—as hypergnostic or hyperorthodox—is to read unhistorically, attempting to interpret the apostle's theology in terms of categories formulated in second-century debate. On the other hand, whoever takes account of the total evidence may learn from the debate to approach Pauline exegesis with renewed openness to the texts.

NOTES: CONCLUSION

1. AH Praef; 4.26.3; 4.41.3-4; 5.31; Frag 51.
2. DP 3.
3. AH 3.15.8; cf. 3.15.6.
4. AH 4.41.3-4; for example, that Paul authorizes the doctrine of aions, 1.3.1; 4; doctrine of Logos/Stauros, 1.3.5; of Sophia, 1.8.2-3; 3.2.1; 3.3.1; the tripartite anthropology, 1.8.3; 2.22.2; doctrine of *apolytrōsis*, 1.21.1-2; Exc 22.1-6; cf. also Tertullian, DP 4-6, 33, 38. Hippolytus testifies that the Valentinians cite Paul's words as "scripture," Ref. 6.34. For discussion see: H. Langerbeck, *Aufsätze zur Gnosis* (Göttingen: Vandenhoeck, 1967), H. F. von Campenhausen, *Die Entstehung der Christlichen Bibel* (Tübingen: Mohr, 1968), 171-172; T. Zahn,

Geschichte des neutestamentlichen Kanons, (Erlangen/Leipzig: A. Deichert, 1889, I), 755-56.

Wie von Johannes, so auch von Paulus haben sie nicht die leitenden Gedanken, die religiösen Anschauungen, so gut es eben ging, sich anzueignen bemüht, sondern Worte und Wortverbindungen haben sie den apostolischen Schriften entlehnt . . . Dabei ist der Ton, in welchem sie die paulinschen Briefe zitieren, ein ebenso ehrerbietiger wie die, welchen wir bei den Kirchenlehrern . . . antreffen. "Der Apostel spricht," "Paulus zeigt": das steht überall ebenbürtig neben dem "der Heiland lehrt."

5. AV 1; DP 24; cf. AH Praef; 2.14.8; 3.2.1; 3.15.2.
6. AH 3.2.1-3.3.1; DP 24-26.
7. AH 1.6.1-4.
8. See discussion of 1 Corinthians 6.
9. AV 4; cf. discussion of Romans 15; 1 Cor 2:14-16.
10. Cf. discussion of Eph 3.14-19; AH 1.21.1-2:

...καὶ τὸν Παῦλον ῥητῶς φάσκουσι τὴν 'εν Χριστῷ 'Ιησοῦ 'απολύτρωσιν πολλάκις μεμηνυκέναι • καὶ εἶναι ταύτην τὴν ὑπ' αὐτῶν ποκίλως καὶ 'ασυμφώρως παραδιδομένην.

Exc 22.1-6; DP 24, Zahn, *Geschichte,* I, 752.

11. AH 1.3.1:

Καὶ τὸν Παῦλον φανερώτατα λέγουσι τούσδε Αἰῶνας 'ονομάξειν πολλάκις...'αλλὰ καὶ ἡμᾶς 'επὶ τῆς 'ευχαριστίας λέγοντας, εἰς τοὺς αἰῶνας τῶν αἰώνων, 'εκείνους τοὺς αἰῶνας σημαίνειν.

12. CJ 13.10; for discussion, see Pagels, *Johannine Gospel,* 86-92.
13. EF 3.1; 7.10.
14. *CJ 5.1-8 (Philocalia c.5).
15. AH 1.6.1-2; 7.3; 3.15.2.
16. DP 22, 26; AH 3.5.1-3.
17. DP 24-26; AH 3.
18. AH 3.2.1; 1.8.4.
19. AH 3.12.12.
20. AH 1.8.4; 1.6.4; Exc 22.1-6.
21. AH 4.41.1-3; 5.26.2.
22. Cf. AH 1.6.1-7.5; 10.1-3; for discussion, see Pagels, "Conflicting Versions of Valentinian Eschatology," *HTR* 67.1 (1974): 35-53.
23. AH 1.21.1-2.
24. H. Schneemelcher, "Paulus in der griechischen Kirche des zweiten Jahrhunderts," in *Zeitschrift für Kirchengeschichte,* 4.13: #75 (1964): 1-20.
25. Ibid., 4-6. Schneemelcher concludes. *"Es ist nicht beweisbar, ja es ist unwahrscheinlich, dass Ignatius eine solche Briefsammlung der paulinischen Briefe gekannt hat."*
26. Ibid., 6-7.
27. G. Strecker, "The Kerygmata Petrou," in Hennecke-Schneemelcher, *New Testament Apocrypha,* E.T. ed. R. McL. Wilson (Philadelphia: Westminster, 1965), II. 102-111 (also for references).
28. "Paulus in der griechischen Kirche," 11.
29. AH 4.41.3-4.
30. AH Praef; cf. DP 25-26.
31. AH 3.13.3.
32. AH 3.14.1-4.
33. AH 5.3.1-14.4.
34. AH Praef; DP 4-6.

35. AH 4.14-17; 37-41.
36. B. Pearson, *The Pneumatikos-Psychikos Terminology in I Corinthians*, SBL dissertation series 12, University of Montana (1973), 1.
37. R. Reitzenstein, *Die hellenistischen Mysterienreligionen* (3d ed. Stuttgart: Teubner, 1956), chap. 16: "Paulus als Pneumatiker," 333-393.
38. U. Wilckens, *Weisheit und Torheit* (Tübingen: Mohr. 1959). Wilckens concludes that 1 Corinthians evinces Paul's struggle *"zwischen christlichen und gnostischen theologischen Denken . . . Paulus hier gegen eine ganz bestimmt Ausprägung der Gnosis argumentiert"* (221). W. Schmithals, *Die Gnosis in Corinth* (Göttingen: Vandenhoeck & Ruprecht, 1965); translated by J. Steely as *gnosticism in Corinth* (Nashville: Abingdon, 1971).
39. H. Koester, "Häretiker im Urchistentum als theologisches Problem," in *Zeit und Geschichte* (Tubingen: Mohr, 1964), 62.
40. H. Conzelmann, *Der erste Brief an die Korinther* (Göttingen: Vandenhoeck & Ruprecht, 1969), 29. Elsewhere ("Paulus und die Weisheit," NT Stud. 12, 231-244), Conzelmann declares that the teaching Paul mentions in 1 Cor 2.6 corresponds to the form of a revelation scheme, although not a pre-Christian gnostic scheme: *"Vielmehr sehen wir es in 1 Cor 2.6 ff. in statu nascendi."*
41. Tertullian hints that "heretics" considered the Pastoral Letters to be inauthentic (DP 6); Clement says that "the heretics reject the letters to Timothy" (*Strom* 2.52). Nevertheless it is possible that this characterization does not apply to the Valentinians: Clement himself cites Heracleon's apparent reference to 1 Tim 2:13 (*Strom* 2.13). T. Zahn (*Geschichte*, I, 753-754) sees no certain evidence that the Valentinians had the Pastorals included in their collection of Pauline epistles; however, if they were, Zahn suggests that the Valentinians would tend to either ignore or reinterpret them rather than to reject them outright; cf. Tertullian's account of Valentinus' own method of exegetical procedure (DP 38).
42. Cf. note 41 above: *Strom* 2.13 offers the only evidence known to me of a Valentinian teacher citing any of the Pastoral epistles.
43. AH 1.8.4; 1.7.1.
44. For references, see discussion of these passages.
45. For references, see discussion of Romans 6.
46. H. Conzelmann, *Der erste Brief*, 29-30:

> *Es ist methodisch zu unterscheiden zwischen Gedanken und Begriffen, die an sich gnostisch sind, und solchen, die von der Gnosis aufgenommen werden können, aber schon vorher in einem ganz anderen weltanschaulichen Zusammenhang entworfen sind. Das Begriffs- und Motiv-material im I Kor gehört ohne Ausnahme zur zweiten Gruppe . . . Jüdische, griechische (popularphilosophische) Gedanken, wie sie auf der Strasse aufzulesen waren, traditionelle Anschauungen der griechischen Religion, Mysterienwirkungen (Weihen, Ekstasen)—alles ist da und ist gar nicht reinlich zu sondern. Einzelne Spuren weisen auch darauf, dass sich das zu formieren beginnt, was sich später als "Gnosis" präsentiert, also Gnosis in statu nascendi. Man mag die Korinther als Proto-Gnostiker charakterisieren.*

In distinction from Conzelmann, however, I would suggest that such elements may occur not only in the theology of the Corinthians, but in that of the apostle as well.
47. DP 30; 38.

SELECT
BIBLIOGRAPHY

(Textual sources are listed in the list of Abbreviations on pp. xi-xii).

Barth, Carola. *Die Interpretation des Neuen Testaments in der Valentinianischen Gnosis.* (TU 37.3.) Leipzig: Hinrichs, 1911.

Bauer, Walter. *Orthodoxy and Heresy in Earliest Christianity.* English translation ed. R.A. Kraft, G. Krodel. Philadelphia: Fortress, 1971.

Bianchi, Ugo. "Gnosticismus und Anthropologie." *Kairos* II (1969):6-13.

——. *Le origini dello Gnosticismo: Colloquio di messina 13-18 Aprile 1966.* (Supplements to *Numen,* XII.) Leiden: Brill, 1967.

Bornkamm, Günther. *Paul.* English translation, D. G. M. Stalker. New York: Harper & Row, 1971.

Brox, Norbert. *Offenbarung, Gnosis und gnostischer Mythos bei Irenäus von Lyon: Zur Charakteristik der Systeme.* (Salzburger Patristische Studien, I.) Salzburg/München: Anton Pustet, 1966.

Bultmann, Rudolph. *Theology of the New Testament.* English translation K. Grobel, 2 vols. New York: Scribner, 1951-55.

Campenhausen, Hans F. von. *Die Entstehung der Christlichen Bibel.* Tübingen: Mohr, 1968.

Conzelmann, Hans. *Der erste Brief an die Korinther.* (Meyer, 11th ed.) Göttingen: Vandenhoeck und Ruprecht, 1969.

——— "Paulus und die Weisheit." *NTS* 12 (1965/66):231-244.

Cross, F. M. L. *The Jung Codex: A Newly Recovered Gnostic Papyrus. Three Studies by H. Ch. Puech, G. Quispel, and W. C. van Unnik.* London: Mowbray, 1955.

Dahl, Nils. "Paul and the Church at Corinth according to I Corinthians 1-4." In

Christian History and Interpretation: Studies Presented to John Knox, 313-335. Cambridge: University Press, 1967.

De Faye, Eugène. *Gnostiques et Gnosticisme.* Paris: Leroux, 1913.

Dupont, Jacques. *Gnosis: La Connaissance Religieuse dans les épitres de saint Paul.* (Universitas Catholica Lovaniensis, Diss. ser. II. 40.) Louvain: Nauwelaerts/Paris: Gabalda, 1949.

Eltester, Walther. *Christentum und Gnosis.* Berlin: Töpelmann, 1969.

Georgi, Dieter. *Die Gegner des Paulus im 2 Korintherbrief.* (WMANT 11.) Neukirchen: Neukirchener, 1964.

————, "Der vorpaulinische Hymnus Phil 2.6-11." In *Zeit und Geschichte,* edited by E. Dinkler, 263-293. Tübingen: Mohr, 1964.

Goppelt, Leonhard. *Typos: Die typologische Deutung des Alten Testaments in Neuen.* Gütersloh: Bertelsmann, 1939.

Grant, Robert M. *Gnosticism and Early Christianity.* New York: Columbia University, 2d ed., 1966.

————, "The Wisdom of the Corinthians." In *The Joy of Study,* edited by Sherman Johnson, 51-55. New York: Macmillan, 1951.

Gregg, J. A. F., ed. "The Commentary of Origen upon the Epistle to the Ephesians." Text corr. C. H. Turner, *JTS* 3 (1902):233-244; 398-420; 554-576.

Grobel, K. *The Gospel of Truth: A Valentinian Meditation on the Gospel.* Nashville/ New York: Abingdon; London: Black, 1960.

Henrici, Georges. *Die valentinianische Gnosis und die heilige Schrift.* Berlin: Akademie-Verlag, 1871.

Jonas Hans. "Delimitation of the Gnostic Phenomenon—Typological and Historical." In *Le origini dello Gnosticismo,* edited by U. Bianchi (Leiden: Brill, 1967), 90-104.

————. *Gnosis und spätantiker Geist,* I (FRLANT 51). Göttingen: Vandenhoeck und Ruprecht, 1934 (1st ed.); 1954 (2d ed.); 1964 (3d ed.).

————. "Origenes' Peri Archon—ein System patristischer Gnosis" *ThZ* 4 (1948):101-119.

Koester, Helmut. "Gnosis." Lexikon der Alten Welt, 1100-02. Zürich: Artemis, 1965.

————. "ΓΝΩΜΑΙ ΔΙΑΦΟΡΟΙ : The Origin and Nature of Diversification in the History of Early Christianity." *HTR* 58 (1965):279-318.

————. "Häretiker im Urchristentum als theologisches Problem." In *Zeit und Geschichte,* edited by E. Dinkler, 61-76. Tübingen: Mohr, 1964.

————. "Paul and Hellenism." In *The Bible in Modern Scholarship,* edited by J. P. Hyatt, 187-195. Nashville: Abingdon, 1965.

————. "Valentinus von Alexandria." Lexikon der Alten Welt, 3176-77. Zürich: Artemis, 1965.

MacRae, George W. "Anti-Dualist Polemic in 2 Cor. 4,6." *Studia Evangelica,* IV (TU 102):420-31. Berlin: Akademie-Verlag, 1968.

———. "The Jewish Background of the Gnostic Sophia Myth." *Novum Testamentum* XII (1970):86-101.

———. "Sleep and Awakening in Gnostic Texts." In *Le origini dello Gnosticismo,* edited by U. Bianchi, 496-507.

———. "Valentinus." New Catholic Encyclopedia (14), 518-19. New York: McGraw-Hill, 1967.

Menard, J. E. *L'Évangile de Vérité: Rétroversion grecque et commentaire.* Paris: Letouzey et Ane, 1962.

Pagels, Elaine. "Conflicting Versions of Valentinian Eschatology: Irenaeus' Treatise vs. the Excerpts from Theodotus." *HTR* 67.1 (1974):35-53.

———. *The Johannine Gospel in Gnostic Exegesis.* Nashville: Abingdon, 1973.

———. "The Mystery of the Resurrection: A Gnostic Reading of I Corinthians 15," *JBL* 93.2 (1974):276-288.

———. "The Valentinian Claim to Esoteric Exegesis of Romans as Basis for Anthropological Theory." *Vig Chr* 26 (1972):241-258.

———. "A Valentinian Interpretation of Baptism and Eucharist and Its Critique of 'Orthodox' Sacramental Theology and Practice." *HTR* 65.2 (1972):153-169.

Pearson, Birger A. "Jewish Haggadic Traditions in *the Testimony of Truth* from Nag Hammadi (CG IX, 3)." In *Ex Orbe Religionum. Studia Geo. Widengren,* I (Suppl. to *Numen* 21), 457-470. Leiden: Brill, 1972.

———. "I Thessalonians 2:13-16: A Deutero-Pauline Interpolation." *HTR* 64 (1971):79-94.

———. *The Pneumatikos-Psychikos Terminology in I Corinthians.* (SBL Diss. ser. 12.) Missoula: University of Montana Press, 1973.

Peel, Malcolm L. *The Epistle to Rheginos: A Valentinian Letter on the Resurrection: Introduction, Translation, Analysis and Exposition.* (New Testament Library.) London: SCM; Philadelphia: Westminster; 1969.

——— "Gnostic Eschatology and the New Testament." *Novum Testamentum* XII (1970):141-165.

Puech, H. Ch.; Guillaumont, A.; Quispel, G.; Till, W. C.; 'Abd al Masīh, Y. *The Gospel According to Thomas: Coptic Text Established and Translated.* Leiden: Brill; London: Collins; New York: Harper; 1959.

Puech, H. Ch.; Malinine, M.; Quispel, G.; Till, W.; Kasser, R.; Wilson, R. McL.; Zandee, J. *Epistula Iacobi Apocrypha: Codex Jung F.I-VIII.* Zürich and Stuttgart: Rascher, 1968.

Puech, H. Ch.; Quispel, G. "Les écrits gnostiques du Codex Jung." *Vig. Chr.* 8 (1954):1-51.

———. "Le quatrième écrit gnostique du Codex Jung." *Vig. Chr. 9* (1955):65-102.

Quispel, G. "La conception de l'homme dans la gnose valentinienne." *Eranos Jahrbuch* 15 (1947; published 1948):249-86.

―――. "The Gospel of Thomas and the New Testament." *Vig Chr.* 19 (1957):189-207.

―――. *Makarius, Das Thomasevangelium, und das Lied von der Perle.* Leiden: Brill, 1967.

―――. "Note sur 'De Resurrectione.' " *Vig Chr.* 22 (1968):14-15.

―――. "The Original Doctrine of Valentine." *Vig Chr.* 1 (1947):43-73.

Quispel, G.; Guillaumont, A.; Puech, H. Ch.; Till, W.C.; 'Abd al Masih, Y. *The Gospel According to Thomas: Coptic Text Established and Translated.* Leiden: Brill; London: Collins; New York: Harper; 1959.

Quispel, G.; Malinine, M.; Puech, H. Ch.; Till, W.; Kasser, R.; Wilson, R. McL.; Zandee, J. *Epistula Iacobi Apocrypha: Codex Jung F. I-VIII.* Zürich/Stuttgart: Rascher, 1968.

Quispel, G.; Puech, H. Ch. "Les écrits gnostiques du Codex Jung." *Vig Chr* 8 (1954):1-51.

Reitzenstein, Richard. *Die Hellenistischen Mysterienreligionen.* Stuttgart: Teubner, 3d ed., 1956.

Richardson, Cyril C. "The Gospel of Thomas: Gnostic or Encratite?" Orient. Christ. Analecta 195.

Sagnard, F. *La Gnose valentinienne.* Paris: Vrin, 1947.

Schenke, H. M. *Die Herkunft des sogennanten Evangelium Veritatis.* Berlin: Evangelischen Verlag, 1958; Göttingen: Vandenhoeck und Ruprecht, 1959.

Schmithals, Walter. *Gnosticism in Corinth.* English translation by J. Steely. Nashville: Abingdon, 1971.

―――. *Paul and the Gnostics.* English translation by J. Steely. Nashville: Abingdon, 1972.

Schneemelcher, H. "Paulus in der griechischen Kirche des zweiten Jahrhunderts." *Zeitschrift für Kirchengeschichte* 13, v. 75 (1964):1-20.

Segelberg, Eric. "The Coptic-Gnostic Gospel According to Philip and Its Sacramental System." *Numen* 7 (1960):189-200.

Simonetti, Manlio. ΨΥΧΗ e ΨΥΧΙΚΟΣ nella gnosi valentiniana." *Revista di Storia e Letteratura Religiosa* 2 (1966):1-47.

Tröger, Karl-Wolfgang. *Gnosis und Neues Testament.* Berlin: Gütersloher, 1973.

Unnik, C. van. "The Newly Discovered Gnostic 'Epistle to Rheginos' on the Resurrection." *JEH* 15 (1964):141-52; 153-67.

Wilckens, Ulrich. *Weisheit und Torheit* (BHT 26). Tübingen: Mohr, 1959.

Zahn, Theodor. *Geschichte des Neutestamentlichen Kanons,* I. Erlangen/Leipzig: Deichert, 1889.

INDEXES

INDEX OF SCRIPTURAL REFERENCES

OLD TESTAMENT

Genesis
1:26 — 17, 75

Deuteronomy
9:3 — 151 n. 95

Psalms.
50:3 — 151 n. 95

Isaiah
9:6 — 117

NEW TESTAMENT

Matthew
10:28 — 86
13 — 149
18:12-14 — 151
22:9 — 56 n. 16

Mark
4 — 158
4:11 — 7

John
1:3 — 17
3:5-6 — 53 n. 1
4 — 64, 68
4:18 — 64 n. 65
4:24 — 42

4:48 — 55
8:32-36 — 36 n. 141
8:44 — 17 n. 24

Acts
15 — 101, 104, 161

Romans
1 — 17, 18
1-4 — 84 n. 185
1:1 — 13, 103 n. 14, 121
1:3 — 5, 99 n. 28
1:3-4 — 13, 14
1:5 — 7, 14
1:5-7 — 14
1:7 — 53 n. 2
1:8 — 15
1:9 — 15
1:9-14 — 15
1:11 — 7, 14, 15
1:13 — 10
1:14 — 7, 14, 15, 18
1:19-20 — 16
1:20 — 16
1:20-25 — 18
1:20-27 — 17 n. 29
1:21 — 17
1:21-22 — 16
1:21-25 — 16, 17
1:23 — 16 n. 18
1:25 — 16, 18, 55 n. 15
1:26-27 — 17, 18
1:27 — 18

2 — 18
2:1-10 — 18
2:2 — 19
2:4 — 19
2:6-9 — 97 n. 12
2:9 — 19
2:9-10 — 19
2:12 — 9
2:12-16 — 19
2:14 — 7, 19
2:14-15 — 96 n. 6,
    34 n. 130
2:15 — 19
2:16 — 19
2:17-20 — 20
2:17-25 — 20
2:26 — 19
2:26-29 — 19
2:27 — 20
2:28 — 6-7, 20
3:1 — 24
3:1-2 — 20
3:5-6 — 21
3:9 — 21, 22
3:9-20 — 21
3:10 — 21
3:12-18 — 21, 22
3:19 — 21, 22, 23
3:21-24 — 22
3:23 — 22
3:25 — 22, 23
3:25-28 — 22-23
3:27 — 23

171

3:28 — 23, 24, 159
3:28-29 — 119 n. 40
3:29 — 7, 23-24
3:29-31 — 23, 105 n. 30
3:30 — 23, 24, 53 n. 1
4 — 57, 62 n. 51,
    106 n.42
4:1 — 35
4:1-3 — 24
4:2 — 24
4:3 — 24
4:4-8 — 24
4:5 — 24-25
4:9-12 — 25
4:13-15 — 25
4:15 — 22, 25, 28
4:16-17 — 25, 26
4:18-22 — 26
4:23-24 — 26
4:24 — 22 n. 133
5:1 — 32 n. 116
5:6-9 — 26
5:7 — 27
5:8-9 — 27
5:12-14 — 27
5:13 — 22, 25
5:14 — 28
5:15 — 28
5:15-21 — 28
5:23 — 27
6 — 164 n. 46
6:3-11 — 28
6:6 — 30
6:12 — 30
6:12-19 — 30
7:4 — 31
7:4-14 — 31
7:5 — 31
7:8-11 — 33
7:9 — 32
7:14b-25 — 32, 17 n. 71
7:19 — 32
7:21 — 106
7:23 — 19, 33
8 — 33
8:1-4 — 33
8:3 — 33 n. 129, 135
8:8-11 — 34 n. 133
8:10 — 36 n. 147,
    42 n. 183

8:10-11 — 34
8:11 — 30, 34
8:12-15 — 34-35
8:14 — 109 n. 61
8:16 — 35, 37
8:18-23 — 35
8:20 — 36 n. 141
8:23 — 36, 42 n. 183
8:28-39 — 36-37
8:36 — 33
9 — 159
9:1-5 — 37
9:6-8 — 37
9:10-18 — 34 n. 138, 38
9:14 — 38
9:19-26 — 38
9:23 — 39
9:27-32 — 39
10:1-13 — 39
10:10 — 39-40
10:14-18 — 40
10:15-20 — 40
11:1-10 — 40
11:5-26 — 159
11:8 — 82
11:11-16 — 41
11:15 — 41-42
11:16 — 36 n. 145, 41,
    65, 65 n. 73, 82 n. 173
11:17-24 — 42
11:17-26 — 41-42
11:25 — 42
11:33 — 42
11:36 — 42
12 — 3, 42, 164
12:1 — 13, 42
12:1-2 — 42-43
12:3-6 — 43
12:4-5 — 79
12:5 — 43-44
12:10 — 71 n. 12
12:16 — 43
13:1 — 19, 43
13:1-7 — 27 n. 78, 68
13:3-5 — 19
13:4 — 19, 43
13:6 — 44
13:7 — 44
13:8-10 — 44
13:11-13 — 44

14-15 — 160
14:1 — 45
14:1-15:1 — 44-45
14:3 — 45
14:3-21 — 45
14:12 — 45
14:14 — 45
14:22 — 45
15 — 158 n. 9
15:1 — 45
15:6 — 29
15:9-13 — 45
15:14 — 45
15:16 — 45
15:29 — 46
16:27 — 46

1 Corinthians
1 — 83
1:1 — 53, 53 n. 6
1:1-3 — 53
1:2 — 53
1:4-9 — 53-54
1:10 — 40 n. 164, 54, 62
1:14-17 — 54
1:18-20 — 55
1:21-24 — 55
1:26-27 — 26 n. 66
1:26-28 — 56
1:29 — 56-57
1:29-31 — 56
2 — 9
2:1-5 — 57
2:2 — 1, 5, 57
2:4 — 54, 54 n. 9
2:6 — 4, 5, 6, 15,
    15 n. 10, 57, 62,
    78 n. 74, 85 n. 40
2:6-8 — 57
2:6-9 — 97
2:6-3:4 — 159
2:8 — 58
2:9 — 58, 58 n. 28
2:10-13 — 58
2:11 -- 59 n. 30
2:13-15 — 61
2:14 — 8, 20 n. 42,
    55 n. 18
2:14-16 — 59, 158 n. 9
2:15 — 20, 66, 160

3:1-3 — 59
3:4-9 — 60
3:9b-11 — 60
3:12-15 — 61
3:16-17 — 61
3:18-23 — 61
4:1-5 — 62
4:6 — 62
4:7 — 62
4:7-8 — 62-63
4:9-13 — 63
4:14-21 — 63
4:17 — 64
4:19 — 64
5-7 — 66 n. 85
5:1-2 — 64, 68
5:3-5 — 64-65
5:6-8 — 65
5·9-13 — 65
6 — 158 n. 8
6:1-6 — 65-66
6:2-3 — 67
6:7-9 — 66
6:11 — 66
6:12 — 66-67
6:13 — 67
6:14-20 — 67
6:17 — 68, 73
6:20 — 68, 74
7 — 68, 159, 163
7:1-2 — 68
7:2-3 — 69
7:3 — 96
7:4-5 — 69
7:7 — 69
7:10-14 — 70
7:14-16 — 70
7:17 — 70
7:17-31 — 70
7:21-22 — 70
8 — 160
8:1-8 — 70-71
8:7 — 71
8:9-13 — 71
9 — 63 n. 60, 63, 160
9:1-23 — 71-72
9:20 — 121
10:1-6 — 72
10:5 — 72
10:11-15 — 73

10:16-19 — 73
10:23 — 17 n. 27
10:23-29 — 73
10:29b-33 — 74
11:1-12 — 74-75
11:3 — 75
11:9 — 75-76
11:10 — 75-76, 81 n. 158
11:11-15 — 76
11:12 — 75-76
11:17-21 — 76-77
11:19 — 4
11:23-32 — 77
11:27-34 — 77
12 — 3, 43, 164
12:1-7 — 77
12:4 — 78
12:5 — 78
12:8-11 — 78
12:12-27 — 78
12:28-31 — 78-79
13:1-2 — 79
13:7-10 — 79
13:11-13 — 80
14:33-34 — 76
15 — 9, 21 n. 46,
    34 n. 137, 81 n. 165,
    160
15:1 — 80
15:1-7 — 80
15:1-11 — 80
15:3 — 102
15:3-4 — 80
15:4 — 82
15:5-7 — 80
15:8 — 81 n. 158
15:8-10 — 80-81
15:10 — 81 n. 162
15:12 — 81
15:13-19 — 81-82
15:20-23 — 81
15:22 — 82
15:23 — 84
15:24-28 — 82
15:29 — 83, 126
15:30-34 — 83
15:35-40 — 84
15:42-43 — 84
15:42-49 — 84
15:43-47 — 84

15:46 — 103
15:46-48 — 85
15:50 — 85, 125
15:50-52 — 85
15:50-57 — 82 n. 178
15:51 — 42, 80, 84
15:51-52 — 86 n. 205,
    143
15:54 — 86, 144
15:54-56 — 86
15:57-58 — 86

2 Corinthians
2:14-17 — 95
2:17 — 95
3:1-6 — 96
3:7 — 97
3:7-15 — 96
3:14-15 — 96
3:17-18 — 96-97
4:1-6 — 97
4:4 — 101, 119,
    119 n. 34
4:6 — 97-98
4:7-16 — 97-98
4:10 — 98
4:10-16 — 98
5:1-8 — 98
5:3-4 — 99
5:11-18 — 99
5:14-16 — 99
8:9 — 63 n. 58
11:13 — 1

Galatians
1:1 — 101, 110, 159
1:1-5 — 101
1:3 — 110
1:6-8 — 102
1:7 — 54 n. 12
1:10 — 121
1:11-17 — 102-103
1:12 — 102, 159
1:15 — 13
2:1-5 — 103-104
2:5 — 81 n. 163, 104
2:6-10 — 104-105
2:7 — 7
2:11-16 — 105

2:19-21 — 105-106
3:1-5 — 106
3:6-11 — 106-107
3:13-14 — 107
3:15-18 — 107
3:19 — 107
3:19-20 — 107
3:23-28 — 108
3:28 — 105 n. 30, 108,
    120
4 — 108
4:1-7 — 108-109
4:8-11 — 109
4:21-26 — 110
4:24f — 27 n. 67
4:27 — 110
5:1-24 — 110-111
5:14 — 60
5:16-17 — 110
6:1-5 — 111
6:2 — 111
6:7-9 — 111
6:14 — 106
6:14-16 — 111-112
6:15 — 112
6:18 — 112

Ephesians
1 — 115
1:1 — 121
1:1-6 — 115-116
1:3-10 — 117
1:6 — 123
1:7 — 116, 117, 118
1:7-11 — 116-117
1:8 — 116, 117
1:9 — 116, 117
1:11 — 117
1:11-19 — 117
1:13 — 117, 118
1:18 — 117-118
1:20-23 — 118
1:21 — 118
2 — 115
2:1-8 — 118-119
2:11a — 119
2:11b — 119
2:12-18 — 119-120
2:14 — 120, 147 n. 79
2:19-22 — 120-121

3 — 115
3:1-7 — 121
3:8-11 — 121-122
3:14-19 — 122, 158 n.10
3:21 — 16 n. 20
4-5:30 — 115
4:1 — 123
4:1-10 — 122
4:8 — 123
4:12b-16 — 123
4:22-30 — 123-124
5 — 124, 128
5:1-5 — 124-125
5:6-21 — 125-126
5:14 — 44 n. 188
5:21 — 125, 126
5:22 — 127
5:22-32 — 126-127
5:31 — 83 n. 183, 115
5:32 — 127, 163
5:33 — 126, 127
6 — 115, 128
6:1-8 — 127-128
6:10-22 — 128-129
6:12 — 119, 128

Philippians
1:21 — 135
1:21-30 — 134-135
1:21-2:11 — 134
1:29-2:5 — 134
2:6-8 — 160
2:6-11 — 134
2:7 — 135
2:7-9 — 63 n. 59
2:16 — 136
3:17 — 136, 160
3:20 — 136

Colossians
1:6 — 137
1:13 — 137
1:15-17 — 136
1:18-20 — 137-138
1:24-2:10 — 138
1:27 — 138
2:9 — 138-139
2:13-15 — 139
2:14 —139
3:4 — 29
3:9-10 — 103

3:14 — 73 n. 19

1 Thessalonians
5:21 — 4

1 Timothy
1:4 — 5, 61 n. 2
2:13 — 163 n. 41

Titus
3:9 — 5

Hebrews
1:1 — 141, 142
1:1-6 — 141-142
1:5-7 — 142
1:7-14 — 142-143
1:12 — 143
2:2-10 — 143-144
2:10 — 144
2:14-18 — 144
2:17 — 144
3:1-6 — 145
4:1-4 — 145
4:5 — 145
4:6-10 — 145-146
4:11-13 — 146-147
4:12 — 147
5:1-4 — 147
5:5-10 — 148
5:11-14 — 148
6:1-6 — 148-149
6:7-8 — 149
6:19 — 149
6:20 — 149
7-9 — 149
7:1-26 — 149-150
7:10 — 150
7:26 — 150
8:1 — 150
8:1-5 — 150
8:13 — 151
9 — 121 n. 49
9:1-10 — 150-151
9:9 — 151
12 — 151 n. 95
12:18-24 — 151-152
13:20-21 — 152

2 Peter
3:16 — 159
3:16-17 — 4

INDEX OF PATRISTIC SOURCES

CLEMENT OF ALEXANDRIA

Stromata
2.114 — 30 n. 105,
32 n. 118
4.89f — 16 n. 17,
27 n. 80, 28 n. 91,
122 n. 61, 142 n. 17
7.17 — 2 n. 7, 5 n. 31,
54 n. 7

Excerpta ex Theodoto
1.3f — 84 n.187,
123 n. 74, 125 n. 97
2.1f — 38 n. 159,
44 n. 188
4.1f — 135 n. 6,
143 n. 32
7.1f — 137 nn. 1, 2;
144 n. 43
17:2 — 70 n. 104,
127 n. 108
21-22 — 2 n. 10,
10 n. 42, 13 n. 2,
18 nn. 30, 32;
26 n. 66, 28 n. 88,
69 n. 102, 70 n. 106,
75 n. 132, 81 n. 167,
82 n. 172, 83 n. 183,
84 n. 188, 98 n. 20,
119 n. 33, 126 n. 100,
126 n. 104,
127 n. 109, 135 n. 1,
152 n. 103
23.1f — 21 n. 49,
27 n. 77, 28 n. 87,
82 n. 171, 98 n. 16,
99 n. 27, 121 n. 51
123 n. 75
23.3-4 — 2 n. 10,
5 n. 30, 7 n. 38,
14 n. 8, 125 n. 98
24.1 — 143 n. 26
26.1 — 53 n. 4,
138 n. 11, 142 n. 14,
151 n. 98
30.1f — 36 n. 147,
82 n. 170

31.1f — 109 n. 63,
122 n. 65, 138 n. 10
33.1f — 75 n. 134,
116 n. 13, 126 n. 102,
137 n. 3, 138 n. 8,
152 n. 104
35.1 — 2 n. 10,
125 n. 94, 135 n. 5
35.3-4 — 36 n. 148,
79 n. 147, 127 n. 117,
128 n. 121
36.1f — 28 n. 89,
68 n. 94, 69 n. 102
36.2 — 25 n. 61, 95 n. 3
37 — 61 n. 47,
123 n. 72, 151 n. 98
38 — 61 n. 42,
120 n. 42, 145 n. 48,
151 nn. 92, 96
39 — 13 n. 2, 84 n. 187,
84 n. 191
41.2 — 116 n. 9
42.1 — 73 n. 126,
75 n. 134, 78 n. 144,
123 n. 73, 126 n. 103,
138 n. 8, 139 n. 22
43.2 — 117 nn. 17, 18
44.1f — 76 n. 137
46.1f — 109 n. 62
47.1 — 27 n. 81,
60 n. 44, 76 n. 135,
122 n. 61, 137 n. 5,
143 n. 22, 145 n. 52
47.2 — 16 nn. 18, 21;
142 n. 17
48.2 — 2 n. 10,
119 n. 36, 124 n. 84
49.1f — 2 n. 10,
35 n. 140, 36 nn. 141,
142; 145 n. 54
50.1f — 84 nn. 191, 192
51.1f — 65 n. 71,
110 n. 77, 144 n. 36
52 — 33 n. 121, 67 n. 86
53 — 85 n. 193,
107 n. 53, 147 n. 62
54 — 136 n. 14,
152 nn. 102, 105

56 — 13 n. 1, 20 n. 41,
110 n. 70, 111 nn. 80,
84
57 — 65 n. 75,
70 n. 105, 97 n. 11,
110 n. 70
58.1-5 — 13 n. 2,
27 n. 82, 28 n. 84,
36 n. 145, 41 n. 172,
63 n. 61, 65 n. 73,
82 n. 175, 83 n. 181,
86 n. 207, 96 n. 8,
98 n. 18, 135 n. 10,
143 n. 21
59 — 27 n. 77,
82 n. 170, 98 n. 19,
109 n. 64, 135 n. 8,
143 n. 31
61.1-3 — 123 n. 77
61.5 — 44 n. 189,
82 n. 178, 118 n. 25,
144 nn. 37, 41;
146 n. 57
62.1f — 14 n. 6,
37 n. 151,
83 n. 181, 118 n. 25
142 n. 11, 143 n. 34,
147 n. 62, 150 n. 86
63.1f — 65 n. 75,
70 n. 106, 120 n. 46,
127 n. 110, 143 n. 24
64 — 127 nn. 112, 114
65.1f — 143 nn. 22, 23
67.1f — 2 n. 10,
22 n. 52, 26 nn. 70,
72; 31 n. 112,
65 n. 69, 71 n. 113,
110 nn. 73, 74;
119 n. 38, 135 n. 4,
144 n. 35, 147 nn. 65,
69; 155 n. 73
68 — 26 n. 67,
80 n. 160, 109 n. 60
69.1f — 26 n. 69,
139 n. 20
71.1f — 128 n. 122
72.1f — 26 n. 71,
28 n. 83, 109 n. 68

73.1-3 — 26 n. 71
28 n. 83, 109 n. 68,
129 nn. 123, 124,
152 n. 106
74.1 — 87 n. 6
76.1f — 30 n. 99,
108 n. 54, 118 n. 28
77.1f — 29 n. 97,
105 n. 33, 144 n. 42
79-80 — 26 n. 67,
109 n. 60
80.1f — 10 n. 42,
28 n. 88, 29 n. 98,
30 n. 100, 84 n. 189,
85 n. 196, 98 n. 18,
110 n. 74, 114 n. 36,
144 n. 38
81.1f — 118 n. 29
85.1-3 — 129 n. 125,
144 n. 46

ORIGEN

Comm. in Joh.

2.20 — 13 n. 3, 146 n. 58
2.21 — 21 n. 45,
28 n. 90, 32 n. 124,
60 n. 35, 123 n. 75,
138 n. 14
6.10 — 97 n. 11
6.20 — 13 n. 1,
55 n. 12, 79 n. 150,
116 n. 8
6.23 — 142 n. 12
6.30 — 107 n. 46
6.39 — 79 n. 151,
142 n. 18, 145 n. 50,
150 n. 81
6.60 — 98 n. 15,
107 n. 47
10.19 — 22 n. 54,
27 n. 74, 65 nn. 74-75;
73 n. 129, 146 n. 59
10.33 — 30 n. 101,
37 n. 154, 55 n. 13,
60 n. 45, 61 n. 50,
72 n. 118, 95 n. 4,
103 n. 16, 112 n. 82,
120 n. 45, 120 n. 47,
147 n. 67, 148 n. 70,

150 n. 82, 150 n. 90,
152 n. 102
10.37 — 146 n. 57
10.38 — 125 n. 91
13.10f — 33 n. 120,
63 n. 55, 64 n. 64,
124 nn. 85, 88
13.13f — 13 n. 2,
106 n. 35
13.15 — 119 n. 38
13.16 — 35 n. 139,
63 n. 56, 67 n. 85,
73 n. 123, 110 n. 71
13.17 — 39 n. 163,
44 n. 191, 138 n. 15
13.19 — 17 n. 22,
17 n. 25, 31 n. 110,
35 n. 140, 37 n. 153,
40 n. 166, 41 n. 169,
71 n, 112, 72 n. 122,
102 n. 12, 103 n. 15,
110 n. 71, 118 n. 23,
125 n. 87, 145 n. 52,
147 n. 68, 150 n. 87
13.20 — 19 n. 35,
37 n. 152
13.25 — 2 n. 10,
15 n. 13, 28 n. 90,
32 n. 125, 34 n. 132,
42 n. 180, 71 n. 110,
120 n. 48, 123 n. 68,
135 n. 13, 150 n. 84
13.27 — 103 n. 14
13.31 — 107 n. 48,
117 n. 20
13.38 — 34 n. 138,
42 n. 181
13.46 — 72 n. 117,
135 n. 2
13.49 — 111 n. 81
13.50 — 107 n. 52
13.51 — 17 n. 25,
25 n. 61, 28 n. 90,
82 n. 176, 95 n. 3,
107 n. 50
13.60 — 14 n. 6,
25 n. 63, 33 n. 122,
33 n. 128, 55 n. 14,
66 n. 78, 85 n. 197,
86 n. 203, 98 n. 18,
103 n. 18,

107 n. 42, 108 n. 45,
110 n. 71, 117 n. 21,
119 n. 32, 142 n. 10,
143 n. 30, 144 n. 38,
145 n. 53, 149 n. 78
20.24 — 30 n. 105,
31 n. 109, 109 n. 61,
119 n. 32, 125 n. 93
20.28 — 17 n. 24,
43 n. 187, 109 n. 66
20.38 — 19 n. 34,
27 n. 78, 33 n. 127,
37 n. 150, 39 n. 162,
72 n. 119, 96 n. 8,
106 n. 36, 124 n. 82,
128 n. 119, 146 n. 47,
145 n. 50

Comm. in Rom.

7 n. 36, 13 n. 3,
21 n. 47, 22 n. 51,
22 n. 53, 23 n. 57,
24 nn. 58, 60, 25 n. 64,
26 nn. 66, 68,
32 n. 116, 34 n. 133,
98 n. 16, 101 n. 2,
116 n. 9

HIPPOLYTUS OF
ROME

Ref. Omn. Haer.

Praef: 15:11
5.2 — 106 n. 39,
117 n. 15, 142 n. 7
5.3 — 73 n. 125
5.6 — 59 n. 29,
152 n. 105
5.7 — 1 n. 5, 17 n. 29,
40 n. 166, 64 n. 63,
68 n. 89, 142 n. 20
5.8 — 59 n. 32
5.18 — 120 n. 41
5.20 — 27 n. 73
5.21 — 72 n. 120
5.24 — 58 n. 27,
59 n. 33
5.30 — 121 n. 56

6.14 — 77 n. 142
6.25 — 138 n. 14
6.27 — 151 n. 95
6.29 — 122 n. 64
6.30 — 41 n. 173
6.32 — 142 n. 20,
    147 n. 64
6.34f — 14 n. 7,
    15 n. 2, 24 n. 59,
    37 n. 155, 59 n. 32,
    68 n. 89, 68 n. 91,
    72 n. 121, 76 n. 138,
    110 n. 72, 118 n. 23
6.34-35 — 10 n. 42,
    16 n. 16, 20 n. 44,
    40 nn. 166, 168,
    55 n. 15, 76 n. 136,
    106 nn. 37, 41,
    124 n. 81
7.13f — 121 n. 57
7.20, 25 — 118 n. 27,
    60 n. 43, 27 n. 79,
    35 n. 140, 36 n. 143
7.26 — 57 nn. 23-24
7.27 — 19 n. 37,
    36 n. 144

TERTULLIAN

De Praesci — 7 n. 37
De Carne Christi —
    33 n. 129, 34 n. 133,
    53 n. 1, 116 n. 6
Adv. Marc. —
    104 n. 23, 105 n. 29
Adv. Val. — 15 n. 11,
    54 n. 7, 58 nn. 22, 26
De Res. — 19 n. 37,
    29 n. 94, 30 n. 101,
    30 n. 104,
    34 nn. 134, 137,
    68 n. 89, 81 n. 169,
    84 nn. 192, 190,
    85 nn. 198, 200,
    86 nn. 203, 206,
    98 n. 15f, 106 n. 33

IRENAEUS

Adversus haereses

Praef — 5 n. 28,
    157 n. 1, 158 n. 5,
    161 n. 30, 161 n. 34
1. Praef. 2 — 59 n. 29
1.1.1 — 41 n. 173,
    137 n. 1, 142 n. 8
1.1.1-2.1 — 142 n. 16
1.2.1 — 41 n. 173
1.2.1-3.1 — 97 n. 12
1.2.2 — 21 n. 50,
    59 n. 29
1.2.5-6 — 117 n. 16
1.2.6 — 118 n. 31,
    122 n. 59, 122 n. 65,
    127 n. 114, 142 n. 9
1.3.1 — 16 n. 20,
    101 n. 4, 142 n. 8,
    157 n. 4, 158 n. 11
1.3.3-4 — 137 n. 7
1.3.4 — 30 n. 101,
    42 n. 179, 63 n. 62;
    71 n. 109, 107 n. 47,
    135 n. 11, 137 n. 4
1.3.5 — 37 n. 153,
    55 n. 13, 58 n. 25,
    106 n. 34, 111 n. 78,
    112 n. 82, 120 n. 45,
    149 n. 76, 157 n. 4
1.4.1-5 — 110 n. 73
1.4.3 — 109 n. 62
1.4.5 — 16 n. 21,
    17 n. 22, 76 n. 135,
    84 n. 187, 137 n. 5
1.5.1 — 16 n. 18,
    150 n. 88
1.5.1-2 — 16 n. 21,
    142 n. 17
1.5.1-5 — 145 n. 52
1.5.1-6 — 14 n. 7
1.5.2 — 102 n. 9,
    142 n. 13
1.5.3-6 — 60 n. 37
1.5.4 — 119 n. 35,
    142 n. 19
1.5.6 — 17 n. 26,
    25 n. 65, 27 n. 76,
    28 n. 92, 31 n. 108,
    68 n. 92, 71 n. 116,
    82 n. 170, 85 n. 195
1.6.1 — 122 n. 60,
    124 n. 79

1.6.1-2 — 159 n. 15
1.6.1-3 — 33 n. 127
1.6.1-4 — 84 n. 185,
    158 n. 7
1.6.1-7.5 — 160 n. 22
1.6.2 — 38 n. 159,
    66 n. 78
1.6.2-4 — 64 n. 68
1.6.3 — 45 n. 192,
1.6.3-4 — 64 n. 67
1.6.4 — 17 n. 27,
    22 n. 52, 60 n. 36,
    63 n. 55, 63 n. 56,
    80 n. 153, 84 n. 187,
    116 n. 9, 122 n. 53,
    123 n. 76, 124 n. 90,
    127 n. 116
1.7.1 — 20 n. 160,
    61 n. 46, 86 n. 202,
    127 n. 108, 127 n. 113,
    143 n. 23, 163 n. 43
1.7.2 — 53 n. 1,
    76 n. 136, 135 n. 9
1.7.3 — 40 n. 167,
    141 n. 2, 141 n. 3
1.7.3-4 — 20 n. 44
1.7.4 — 106 n. 42,
    122 n. 54, 125 n. 96,
    142 n. 5, 143 n. 25,
    144 n. 49
1.7.5 — 27 n. 73,
    152 n. 105
1.7.7-8.1 — 150 n. 89
1.8.1 — 4 n. 22
    6 n. 33, 13 n. 3
1.8.2 — 16 n. 16,
    23 n. 55, 27 n. 75,
    76 n. 137, 76 n. 138,
    81 n. 158, 96 n. 9,
    142 n. 7, 148 n. 72
1.8.2-3 — 1 n. 5,
    135 n. 11, 157 n. 4
1.8.3 — 10 n. 42,
    15 n. 12, 20 n. 42,
    36 n. 145, 41 n. 171,
    55 n. 13, 58 n. 25,
    59 n. 31, 60 n. 34,
    63 n. 62, 65 n. 73,
    82 n. 173, 82 n. 179,
    157 n. 4
1.8.4 — 58 n. 22,

58 n. 23, 68 n. 90,
68 n. 94, 75 n. 132,
126 n. 99, 127 n. 107,
127 n. 108, 152 n. 107,
159 n. 18, 160 n. 20,
163 n. 43
1.8.5 — 17 n. 23,
142 n. 8, 142 n. 9
1.9.1 — 4 n. 23, 4 n. 25
1.10.1-3 — 160 n. 22
1.13.1-3 — 73 n. 127,
74 n. 130, 116 n. 11
1.13.1-5 — 125 n. 89
1.13.1-6 — 68 n. 94
1.13.2 — 60 n. 42,
117 n. 14, 122 n. 62,
149 n. 77
1.13.2-3 — 53 n. 5,
81 n. 161
1.13.3 — 69 n. 99
1.13.6 — 33 n. 126,
63 n. 57, 67 n. 80
1.14.1-2 — 62 n. 54
1.14.21 — 41 n. 173
1.16.2-3 — 41 n. 170
1.17.1-2 — 16 n. 19
1.19.1 — 21 n. 48
1.21.1-2 — 55 n. 12,
157 n. 4, 158 n. 10,
160 n. 23
1.21.1-5 — 123 n. 69
1.21.2 — 149 n. 75
1.21.3 — 95 n. 1,
125 n. 89
1.21.4 — 30 n. 102,
41 n. 170, 107 n. 47
1.21.5 — 19 n. 36,
41 n. 173, 67 n. 81,
122 n. 63
1.23.3 — 45 n. 193,
67 n. 82
1.23.4 — 106 n. 38
1.24.4 — 57 n. 21,
58 n. 24
1.24.4-5 — 67 n. 83
1.25.1-4 — 64 n. 67
1.25.2 — 63 n. 57
1.25.4-5 — 67 n. 84
1.25.5 — 45 n. 194
1.30.12 — 143 n. 28
1.30.13 — 106 n. 40

1.31.1 — 142 n. 20
2.1.2 — 41 n. 170
2.3.2 — 41 n. 170
2.6.3-7.6 — 150 n. 88
2.14.8 — 158 n. 5
2.19.1-6 — 80 n. 153
2.19.1-9 — 85 n. 195
2.19.2-7 — 60 n. 34
2.19.4 — 60 n. 36,
60 n. 37
2.22.2 — 157 n. 4
2.26.1 — 79 n. 152,
80 n. 154
2.28.4 — 41 n. 170
2.31.2 — 29 n. 94,
81 n. 169
2.35.3 — 141 n. 4
3.1-15.2 — 7 n. 37
3.2.1 — 4 n. 24, 6 n. 32,
6 n. 33, 14 n. 9,
15 n. 14, 58 n. 22,
157 n. 4, 158 n. 5,
159 n. 18
3.2.1-3.1 — 104 n. 20,
122 n. 54
3.2.1-3.3.1 — 1 n. 6,
158 n. 6
3.3.1 — 4 n. 24,
15 n. 15, 58 n. 22,
58 n. 23, 85 n. 201,
157 n. 4
3.3.1-2 — 10 n. 45,
58 n. 26
3.4.1-11.9 — 115 n. 3
3.5.1-3 — 159 n. 16
3.5.1-10.5 — 15 n. 10
3.7.1 — 101 n. 5,
119 n. 34
3.7.1-2 — 97 n. 12
3.12.1-14.1 — 54 n. 8
3.12.6-7 — 14 n. 9,
23 n. 57, 101 n. 2,
102 n. 7, 105 n. 27
3.12.6-8 — 102 n. 12
3.12.7 — 23 n. 56,
81 n. 164, 105 n. 25,
105 n. 30
3.12.8 — 101 n. 2
3.12.12 — 102 n. 8,
102 n. 10, 102 n. 12,
159 n. 19

3.12.12-15 — 102 n. 6,
105 n. 32
3.13.1 — 13 n. 3,
81 n. 163, 101 n. 1,
102 n. 11, 105 n. 26,
105 n. 29, 122 n. 52
3.13.1-14.4 — 97 n. 14
3.13.2-5 — 81 n. 164
3.13.3 — 104 n. 21,
104 n. 22, 104 n. 23,
161 n. 31
3.14.1-2 — 18 n. 31,
57 n. 21, 58 n. 22
3.15.2 — 10 n. 45,
15 n. 11, 15 n. 15,
18 n. 31, 57 n. 21,
58 n. 23, 58 n. 26,
62 n. 54, 63 n. 56,
74 n. 131, 158 n. 5,
159 n. 15
3.15.6 — 157 n. 3
3.15.8 — 157 n. 3
3.16.1 — 40 n. 165,
53 n. 1, 54 n. 11,
105 n. 28
3.16.6 — 40 n. 165,
54 n. 11
3.16.8 — 40 n. 165,
54 n. 10, 62 n. 53
4.8.1-3 — 25 n. 62
4.14.17 — 162 n. 35
4.18.4-5 — 73 n. 128,
74 n. 131
4.26.3 — 157 n. 1
4.26.3-4 — 18 n. 31
4.30.3 — 14 n. 9
4.33.3 — 40 n. 165,
54 n. 11, 62 n. 53
4.35.1 — 141 n. 3
4.37.41 — 162 n. 35
4.41.1-3 — 21 n. 160
4.41.3-4 — 29 n. 161,
157 n. 1, 157 n. 4
5.1-8.1 — 67 n. 88
5.2-7 — 81 n. 165
5.3.1-13.5 — 85 n. 201
5.3.1-14.4 — 161 n. 33
5.3.3 — 34 n. 134
5.7.1 — 34 n. 135,
68 n. 89, 68 n. 91,
127 n. 106

5.7.1-2 — 34 n. 134,
   84 n. 190
5.9.1 — 10 n. 46
5.9.1-4 — 85 n. 199
5.10.1 — 142 n. 20

5.10.2-13.5 — 34 n. 133
5.12.1-5 — 103 n. 13
5.12.5 — 103 n. 14
5.13.1-2 — 85 n. 199
5.24.1 — 43 n. 186

5.26.2 — 18 n. 31,
   160 n. 21
5.31 — 157 n. 1
5.35.2 — 110 n. 72

INDEX OF NAMES

Alexander, 33
Baer, R. A., 69 n. 101
Barth, C., 3, 4, 7
Basilides, 19, 27, 32, 36, 58, 59, 67, 81, 106, 118, 121, 141
Bornkamm, G., 1
Brox, N., 3, 4, 11, 54
Bultmann, R., 1, 9, 74 n. 1
Campenhausen, H. F. von, 157 n. 4
Carpocrates, 45, 67
Clement, 1-2, 8
Conzelmann, H., 162-163
Goppelt, L., 74 n. 1
Grant, R. M., 3
Henrici, G., 3, 4, 7
Heracleon, 2, 8, 15, 17, 19, 31, 33, 37, 40, 42, 43, 55, 60, 61, 63, 68, 71, 72, 79, 86, 103, 106-107, 109, 111, 117, 119, 120, 125, 128, 135, 148, 150, 158
Hippolytus (b. of Rome), 4, 8, 106, 157
Ignatius, 162
Irenaeus, 2, 4, 5, 6, 8, 18, 40, 43, 45, 62, 85, 101, 104, 154, 158, 160-162
Jonas, H., 3, 77 n. 141
Koester, H., 162
Langerbeck, H., 158 n. 4
MacRae, G., 77 n. 141
Marcion, 163-164
Ménard, J., 2, 53 n. 5, 71 n. 115, 85 n. 196
Origen, 8-9, 13, 21, 23 n. 116, 38, 53 n. 3, 61 n. 49, 66 n. 77, 67 n. 88, 78, 81 n. 162, 81 n. 165, 81 n. 168, 95, 116, 124, 157, 159 n. 14, 160, 161
Pagels, E., 7 n. 37, 13 n. 1, 14 n. 6, 16 n. 21, 18 n. 29, 21 n. 45, 22 n. 56, 22 n. 65, 34 n. 135, 35 n. 139, 38 n. 158, 55 n. 12, 55 n. 31, 65 n. 76, 68 n. 96, 68 n. 111, 70 n. 106, 84 n. 188, 149 n. 80, 159 n. 12, 160 n. 22

Pearson, B., 163
Peel, M., 56 n. 20, 80 n. 157, 84 n. 186, 85 n. 190
Philo, 69
Ptolemy, 2, 8, 15, 16, 32, 34, 37, 41, 60, 73, 76, 83 n. 13, 95, 121, 126, 141, 142, 147, 159
Quispel, G., 2, 4, 8, 17 n. 30, 38 n. 159, 81 n. 168, 84 n. 186, 85 n. 196, 86 n. 205
Reitzenstein, R., 162
Sagnard, F., 2 n. 10, 13 n. 1, 16 n. 21, 38 n. 159, 41 n. 173, 59 n. 29, 60 n. 40, 63 n. 17, 63 n. 24, 70 n. 109
Scherer, J., 7 n. 36, 20 n. 40, 21 n. 47, 21 n. 51, 22 n. 53, 23 n. 57, 24 n. 58, 24 n. 60, 26 n. 66, 26 n. 68, 34 n. 133, 51 n. 5, 51 n. 7, 53 n. 1, 53 n. 2, 54 n. 2, 54 n. 8, 56 n. 19, 61 n. 6, 76 n. 136, 81 n. 167
Schmithals, W., 1, 162
Schneemelcher, H., 161
Segelberg, E., 55 n. 12, 68 n. 96
Simon, 45
Tertullian, 2, 4, 5, 8, 9, 13 n. 37, 30, 30 n. 2, 30 n. 8, 33 n. 129, 34 nn. 134-137; 38 n. 89, 53, 53 n. 1, 54, 55, 77 n. 140, 81 n. 165, 83 n. 174, 84, 85, 86, 86 n. 206, 98, 104, 157, 158, 161, 164
Theodotus, 2, 5, 7, 13, 14, 16, 17, 20, 33, 35-36, 41, 42, 69, 81, 84-85, 86, 105, 109, 110, 111, 116, 118, 119, 120, 123, 124, 125, 126, 128-129, 135, 138, 142, 143, 144, 146-147
Theudas, 4, 5, 54, 58
Valentinus, 2, 5, 8, 16, 33, 67, 98, 164
Wilckens, U., 9, 162-163
Wilson, R. McL., 2, 56 n. 18, 149 n. 80, 161 n. 27
Zahn, T., 157 n. 4, 158 n. 10, 163 n. 41

DATE DUE

MAY 30 '77			
AUG 25 '77			
SEP 8 '77			
SEP 22 '77			
NOV 14 '77			
NOV 29 '77			
FEB 24 '82			
MAY 17 '85			
OCT 30 '85			
NOV 20 '85			
DEC 18 '86			
APR 8 '87			
SEP 14 '88			
MAR 28 '89			